STICKY RICE

In the series *Asian American History and Culture*, edited by Cathy Schlund-Vials, Shelley Sang-Hee Lee, and Rick Bonus. Founding editor, Sucheng Chan; editors emeriti, David Palumbo-Liu, Michael Omi, K. Scott Wong, and Linda Trinh Võ.

ALSO IN THIS SERIES:

Marguerite Nguyen, *America's Vietnam: The* Longue Durée *of U.S. Literature and Empire*

Vanita Reddy, *Fashioning Diaspora: Beauty, Femininity, and South Asian American Culture*

Audrey Wu Clark, *The Asian American Avant-Garde: Universalist Aspirations in Modernist Literature and Art*

Eric Tang, *Unsettled: Cambodian Refugees in the New York City Hyperghetto*

Jeffrey Santa Ana, *Racial Feelings: Asian America in a Capitalist Culture of Emotion*

Jiemin Bao, *Creating a Buddhist Community: A Thai Temple in Silicon Valley*

Elda E. Tsou, *Unquiet Tropes: Form, Race, and Asian American Literature*

Tarry Hum, *Making a Global Immigrant Neighborhood: Brooklyn's Sunset Park*

Ruth Mayer, *Serial Fu Manchu: The Chinese Supervillain and the Spread of Yellow Peril Ideology*

Karen Kuo, *East Is West and West Is East: Gender, Culture, and Interwar Encounters between Asia and America*

Kieu-Linh Caroline Valverde, *Transnationalizing Viet Nam: Community, Culture, and Politics in the Diaspora*

Lan P. Duong, *Treacherous Subjects: Gender, Culture, and Trans-Vietnamese Feminism*

Kristi Brian, *Reframing Transracial Adoption: Adopted Koreans, White Parents, and the Politics of Kinship*

Belinda Kong, *Tiananmen Fictions outside the Square: The Chinese Literary Diaspora and the Politics of Global Culture*

Bindi V. Shah, *Laotian Daughters: Working toward Community, Belonging, and Environmental Justice*

Cherstin M. Lyon, *Prisons and Patriots: Japanese American Wartime Citizenship, Civil Disobedience, and Historical Memory*

Shelley Sang-Hee Lee, *Claiming the Oriental Gateway: Prewar Seattle and Japanese America*

Isabelle Thuy Pelaud, *This Is All I Choose to Tell: History and Hybridity in Vietnamese American Literature*

Christian Collet and Pei-te Lien, eds., *The Transnational Politics of Asian Americans*

Min Zhou, *Contemporary Chinese America: Immigration, Ethnicity, and Community Transformation*

Kathleen S. Yep, *Outside the Paint: When Basketball Ruled at the Chinese Playground*

Benito M. Vergara Jr., *Pinoy Capital: The Filipino Nation in Daly City*

Jonathan Y. Okamura, *Ethnicity and Inequality in Hawai'i*

Sucheng Chan and Madeline Y. Hsu, eds., *Chinese Americans and the Politics of Race and Culture*

K. Scott Wong, *Americans First: Chinese Americans and the Second World War*

Lisa Yun, *The Coolie Speaks: Chinese Indentured Laborers and African Slaves in Cuba*

Estella Habal, *San Francisco's International Hotel: Mobilizing the Filipino American Community in the Anti-eviction Movement*

A list of additional titles in this series appears at the back of this book.

STICKY RICE

A POLITICS OF INTRARACIAL DESIRE

CYNTHIA WU

TEMPLE UNIVERSITY PRESS
Philadelphia • *Rome* • *Tokyo*

TEMPLE UNIVERSITY PRESS
Philadelphia, Pennsylvania 19122
tupress.temple.edu

BOOK COVER DESCRIPTION (FOR ACCESSIBILITY IN COMPLIANCE WITH THE AMERICANS WITH DISABILITIES ACT): The image on the front is of two cylindrical sticky rice dumplings wrapped in banana leaves. One lies horizontally, and the other stands vertically to the left, propped against it. The book's title, *Sticky Rice: A Politics of Intraracial Desire*, appears at the top. The author's name, Cynthia Wu, appears at the bottom. The image is set on a white background with borders on the left and right sides that form a top-to-bottom color gradient from maize to olive green.

Library of Congress Cataloging-in-Publication Data

Names: Wu, Cynthia, 1973– author.
Title: Sticky rice : a politics of intraracial desire / Cynthia Wu.
Description: Philadelphia : Temple University Press, [2018] | Series: Asian
    American history and culture | Includes bibliographical references and index. |
Identifiers: LCCN 2018006357 (print) | LCCN 2018008559 (ebook) |
    ISBN 9781439915837 (E-book) | ISBN 9781439915813 (cloth : alk. paper) |
    ISBN 9781439915820 (pbk. : alk. paper)
Subjects: LCSH: American literature—20th century—History and criticism. |
    American literature—21st century—History and criticism. | Asian Americans
    in literature. | Race relations in literature. | Sex in literature. | Desire in literature. |
    Asian Americans—History. | United States—Race relations.
Classification: LCC PS228.R32 (ebook) | LCC PS228.R32 W82 2018 (print) |
    DDC 810.9/353808995—dc23
LC record available at https://lccn.loc.gov/2018006357

Printed in the United States of America

9 8 7 6 5 4 3 2 1

CONTENTS

ACKNOWLEDGMENTS

The idea for *Sticky Rice* came to me entirely by accident. After assembling the manuscript in bits and pieces from unrelated articles, talks, and thought fragments that spanned seven years, I expanded it with new material. The finished product appears so deliberate and planned that I wonder whether the book was always in me, clamoring to get out. The experience of writing this book differed from my experience with the first, which was fraught with the emotional baggage of the longer-than-ideal time spent completing the dissertation, followed by the longer-than-ideal revision period over one contingent and two tenure-track positions. In contrast, the bulk of *Sticky Rice* emerged easily and joyfully during a year's sabbatical. My former department's then chair, Keith Griffler, fought hard to procure that time for me on the heels of my promotion to associate professor at the University of Buffalo.

I benefited greatly from the critical eye of colleagues who read this manuscript in part or in full over the years. Jang Huh, Nguyen Tan Hoang, and Akemi Nishida were generous and honest with their feedback. I initially hired Paul McCutcheon as a proofreader but quickly upgraded his services. His line-by-line edits and expertise in Asian American studies and queer theory proved crucial. He read and commented in such incisive ways that he all but co-authored sections of the book. While some colleagues waded knee deep into my prose, others contributed to my thinking: Carrie Bramen, Tim Dean, Aureliano DeSoto, Kale Fajardo, Cathy Hannabach, Jonathan Katz, Robert McRuer, Julie Minich, Scott Morgensen, Margaret Price,

Jasmina Tumbas, and Christine Varnado. Ellen Samuels was an especially fierce interlocutor. She and Jonathan Zarov provided a place for me to stay in Madison while I was conducting research for Chapter 3.

Audience members at the Association for Asian American Studies conference, Bryn Mawr College, the Graduate Center of the City University of New York, the Modern Language Association convention, the University of North Carolina at Greensboro, and Yale University provided spirited and insightful discussion. I thank Saveena Dhall, Christopher Eng, Jennifer Ho, LiLi Johnson, James Lee, Mary Lui, Nguyen Tan Hoang, Therí Pickens, Mark Rifkin, and Jess Waggoner for the opportunity to speak.

Other companions on the never-lonely road of writing include Ellis Avery, Leslie Bow, Susan Cahn, María Elena Cepeda, Mel Chen, Anne Choi, Elizabeth Donaldson, Nirmala Erevelles, Ann Fox, Elizabeth Freeman, Rosemarie Garland-Thomson, Michael Gill, Lynn Hudson, Douglas Ishii, Jennifer James, Joseph Jeon, Dredge Kang, Stephanie Kerschbaum, Daniel Kim, Eunjung Kim, Jina Kim, Sue Kim, Joshua Kupetz, Paul Lai, Nhi Lieu, Jeehyun Lim, Maren Linett, Martin Manalansan, Anita Mannur, Nicole Markotić, Theresa McCarthy, Uri McMillan, Victor Mendoza, Alyssa Mt. Pleasant, Karen Nakamura, Michael Needham, Tamiko Nimura, Margaret Rhee, Jane Rhodes, Riché Richardson, Theresa Runstedtler, Sami Schalk, Cathy Schlund-Vials, Susan Schweik, Nitasha Sharma, LaKisha Simmons, Min Song, Jordan Stein, Bethany Stevens, Julie Sze, Gwynn Thomas, Kyla Tompkins, Christopher Vials, Amy Vidali, Victoria Walcott, Grace Wang, Hershini Bhana Young, and Timothy Yu. Two of my graduate mentors passed away while this book was in progress. Tobin Siebers and Patricia Yaeger continue to influence me from beyond—in terms of how I write, teach, and take part in the world.

A big show of gratitude goes to my editor, Sara Jo Cohen, for believing in this project. She and her staff, especially Nikki Miller, were invaluable in ushering it to completion. Anonymous readers for Temple University Press posed tough questions, made good suggestions, and trusted me to my own devices. I am thankful in equal measure for their enthusiasm and well-intentioned skepticism.

An earlier version of Chapter 1 was published as "'Give Me the Stump Which Gives You the Right to Hold Your Head High': A Homoerotics of Disability in Asian Americanist Critique," *Amerasia Journal* 39.1 (2013): 3–16. An earlier version of Chapter 5 was published as "Revisiting *Blu's Hanging*: A Critique of Queer Transgression in the Lois-Ann Yamanaka Controversy," *Meridians: feminism, race, transnationalism* 10.1 (2009): 32–53 (copyright © Smith College). Both chapters are heavily revised and expanded adaptations. I thank the University of California Press and Indiana University Press, respectively, for permission to reprint.

STICKY RICE

INTRODUCTION

"Sticky rice," a term affectionately embraced by gay Asian American men who prefer emotional and sexual relationships with other Asian-raced men, refers to the varieties of rice whose grains stick together when cooked. The rice that accompanies many Asian cuisines has a texture different from the rice to which most North American palates are attuned. It has a glutinous consistency meant to be lifted with chopsticks to the mouth in bite-size morsels. It can also be pressed or rolled into forms that hold their shape in sushi, kimbap, musubi, and similar food items. Conversely, most commercially available rice in North America is favored for its very inability to clump. Those who eat it prefer the separation among grains. According to the logic of the metaphor, Asian American men who engage in intraracial sexual socialities, who stick to themselves rather than pursue white men, reverse the terms on which North American tastes stand. "Sticky rice" implies that the sexual practices of gay Asian American men who bond with their own initiate a world making that contests the primacy of whiteness and the valences of power coalescing around it.

In *Sticky Rice: A Politics of Intraracial Desire*, I mobilize a term from gay Asian American cultures to analyze intraracial intimacies in Asian American literature. I argue that the trope of male same-sex desire accompanies a range of literary polemics that grapple with how Asian America's internal divides can be resolved to facilitate coalition building. The embrace of "sticky" politics suggests that forming connectivities within one's racial group intervenes in assimilationist tendencies. It conveys a rejection of entrenched standards of value, desirability, and legitimacy. A common thread passing through many intraracial conflicts in Asian America is the friction between the ascription to Anglo-American ideals and the motivation to challenge them. The disparities between those who capitulate to the former versus those who pursue the latter deepen fractures within Asian America. The literary texts I examine attempt to resolve such conflicts by invoking queer desire between men. These narratives matchmake dyads of characters, each half representing a contingent at odds with the other, in a plea for resolving disputes that stand in the way of coalitional action in Asian America. The characters come into social, erotic, and sexual intimacy with each other as an injunction to vanquish desires for whiteness that prevent intraracial peace. Taken collectively, the chapters that follow show that the configuration of two Asian-raced men paired together is pliable and suits multiple contexts and agendas. At the same time, not all of them are liberating or even innocuous.

Intraracial conflict in Asian America needs to be understood in the context of relational formations *across* racial categories. In other words, it cannot be disarticulated from the conflicts that U.S. capitalism engenders *among* racial groups. These *interracial* dynamics have a history as old as North American expansion itself. The pitting of Asian immigrant laborers against African Americans (as well as against working-class whites) in the nineteenth century sowed the seeds for twentieth-century and present-day conditions of inequality. When aggrieved populations occupy differential positions in their relationships to the state and their places in the economy, resentment follows. This resentment discourages collective revolts against the exploitative conditions that subjugate all. The myth of the model minority, which emerged most saliently in the 1960s (even if its primordial traces appeared much earlier), upholds the perceived industriousness and docility of Asian Americans to demonize African Americans and Latinxs for falling short. It champions a facile multiculturalism without attention to structural inequity. The cultural and economic leverage that Asian Americans glean from the model minority myth remains measured, but it is not easily declined. The policing that Asian America faces from within stems largely from fears that its unruly subjects will jeopardize the limited benefits that accrue from this place of slight advantage. Living up to the myth's demands is desirable for many, tenable for some, but oppressive for all. The uneven ways Asian Americans are situated in proximity to or distance from the model minority myth's ideals unevenly incentivize its defense or dismantling. Herein lie the grounds for intraracial discord.

The model minority myth's rise in the 1960s is often explained by indexing the attainment of middle-class status among many Asian Americans in the generation following World War II. This phenomenon owes itself to the repeal of the Chinese Exclusion Act in 1943; the Immigration and Nationality

Act of 1952, which allowed people of Asian descent to apply for naturalized citizenship; and the Hart-Celler Act of 1965, which abolished national quotas for immigration. Meanwhile, the mainstream media's coverage of rebellions headed largely by African Americans, Latinxs, and Native Americans to redress race-based and settler colonial abuses stoked the fears of many white Americans. Asian Americans, in fact, were involved in these movements but have received less visibility for their participation.[1] The ways Asian Americans versus other people of color were regarded at this moment exacerbated historical fissures between them. What often goes unaddressed in the above changes enabling Asian American upward mobility is U.S. militarism. By "militarism," I do not mean an entity pertaining to only the armed forces. Rather, the term signals a broader economy, culture, means of state governance, and worldview that supports, infuses, and naturalizes military influence in all aspects of quotidian life. As with other racial groups, the GI Bill benefits for veterans returning from war allowed Asian Americans to gain a foothold in middle-class life.

In addition, given that twentieth-century U.S. wars with Asia have spurred influxes of Asian arrivants, we cannot discount the influence that militarism has held over Asian American immigration. The question of who can be trusted as an ally versus who falls under suspicion as a terrorist adds another dimension to the model minority myth that draws distinctions within racial groups. The wars with Asia have prompted the U.S. collective imagination to dichotomize Asians into friendly and enemy forces. However, even when "good Asians" come to and settle in the United States as a result of empire and multinational conflict, there always lingers the taint of their racialized contiguity to the bad. They may compensatorily perform in response to suspicions of imperfect assimilation, or they may refuse to engage with an impossible situation. And they can choose alliances among themselves—which are sometimes surprisingly queer—to redress the capitalist and imperialist underpinnings of the United States.

Sticky Rice unravels the contrarian pleasures of the desire it names in the face of whiteness, upward economic mobility, heteronormativity, and collusion with empire. The field of Asian American studies presumes that Asian American activism emerged from racial liberationist movements upholding heteropatriarchy that were only later challenged by feminism and queer thought. I argue instead that Asian American men were never uncritical, yet failed, aspirants to normative masculinity. Rather, they have always been strategically queer. They express same-sex desire within racial lines to encourage reconciliation among Asian America's internal factions. In this book, I provide a sustained analysis of the "sticky dyad" in some of the most widely read Asian American literary texts: John Okada's *No-No Boy*, Monique Truong's *The Book of Salt*, Philip Kan Gotanda's *Yankee Dawg You Die*, H. T. Tsiang's *And China Has Hands*, and Lois-Ann Yamanaka's *Blu's Hanging*. Most of these narratives would not be considered queer by any stretch. Some may convey staunchly heterosexist—or even homophobic—ideas. Yet we see in them calls for coalitional urgency through Asian American men who love, long for, and have sex with other Asian American men. At the same time, I do not want to relegate sticky pairings to that of rhetorical device only. These literary iterations of desire occur alongside contemporaneous discourses of sexual deviance, gender non-normativity, gay activism, and homonormativity that have real-world consequences for actual LGBT people. For these reasons, it bears historicizing the above texts in this way and heeding the distinctions between homosociality and queer acts and identities, even as they blur.

THE SEXY LURE OF RACE AND RICE

The video artist Nguyen Tan Hoang's *7 Steps to Sticky Heaven* (1995) is a twenty-four-minute video that is part ethnography and part homage, showcasing the voices, culinary strategies, and kinetic sex of gay Asian American men who prefer intraracial intimacies. The artist interviews his informants about why they are "sticky," desirous of other Asian-raced men. Responses range from the serious to the lighthearted. Several suggest that being sticky can overcome internalized racism. Another subject mentions that he simply finds sex with Asian men more meaningful. One humorously extols the benefits of not having to interrupt sexual activity to pick body hair out of his mouth, as he presumably would with white men. Yet another, after a thoughtful pause, calls out the aspirations to normativity behind the question itself: "What made me turn sticky? That's like asking me what made me turn gay."[2] His racial preference is not an aberration begging an etiology. Throughout the interview sequences, Nguyen's voice from behind the camera probes with follow-up questions. He flirts with his informants.

The locations where Nguyen conducts the interviews are informal. They include the seating areas of bars, cafés, and restaurants and the interior of homes. Some of the ambient sounds—such as voices at nearby tables, the clink of silverware on plates, street noise, and background music—can make it difficult to hear the dialogue at times. The movement of Nguyen's handheld camera is subtle but noticeable as he inserts himself as an active participant in the interchanges. These elements, which place the process of creating *7 Steps to Sticky Heaven* outside the more formal realm of studio film, complement the unscripted, sometimes halting dialogue and spontaneous shows of affect. Together, they lend an endearing candidness to the testimonies.

The interviews are interspersed with recurring scenes of the video artist eating rice. These interludes have no audio, and their silence provides a jarring contrast to the low to moderate din in most of the interviews. Nguyen begins by neatly cradling a ceramic bowl in his left hand in accordance with Asian table etiquette while his right hand works a pair of chopsticks. As the narrative progresses, he scoops the rice into his mouth with increasing urgency and speed. At the halfway point, he abandons the chopsticks to push the rice overflowing from his lips back with his hands. By the video's end, the partially masticated mouthfuls of rice have become impossible to contain, and they spill onto his bare chest in this frenzied meal. The artist ecstatically rubs the rice into his skin and writhes on a bed. The scenes where Nguyen begins to eat more quickly are uncomfortable for the viewer as his mouth fills with rice at a rate faster than that at which he can swallow. As he endures what looks like a self-administered force-feeding, our uneasiness increases. What seems like compelled behavior then erupts into a rapturously orgasmic finale.

The scenes of Asian-white or Asian-Asian sex portrayed in the video exist beyond a hierarchy of acceptability. The tangle of bodies and dim lighting flatten phenotypic and other distinctions. Voiceovers where the interview subjects confess inclinations shaped by socialization into white gay cultures accompany a scene featuring Nguyen and a white lover identified as "X-boy-friend." As Nguyen's partner playfully spanks and tops him, an informant can be heard relaying these words amid the slaps and moans:

> I think, I think you go through a period where, you've been foisted with all these images of . . . the gay community where you see mostly white, queer men, the white-dominated community. . . . I think everyone falls for that, that whole desirability process where, you know, these images of white men with tight bodies, six packs, and bulging biceps. And, you know, I fell for that. . . . You know, the whole dominant trip.

Another voice joins in, reporting, "I mostly like rough sex with Caucasian men, but with Asians I tend to get more *[pause]*, um *[pause]*, pretend there's meaning to it." Despite these strategically placed interview segments, the reciprocal joy conveyed by both men in the scene quells any tendency to pathologize the sexual pairing of white top-Asian bottom as simply evidence of the Asian American man's internalized racism. Nguyen, the auteur, holds the camera in some of the shots, including those in which he is on his back while being penetrated. The viewer is positioned accordingly, with his point of view in a way that, Glen Mimura claims, undermines the "stereotypical coding of Asian men in mainstream, commercial gay porn," because Nguyen retains control of the representation.[3] In subsequent scenes that feature Asian-Asian pairings, Nguyen portrays himself in scenarios that imply more sexual versatility. His partner is behind the camera in some shots, suggesting a co-authorship between him and the other man. No voiceovers from the interview material exist in aural counterpoint as before. However, rather than regard these instances of intraracial sex as egalitarian correctives for the former, the expressions of pleasure among all lovingly reveal a mutual give-and-take. We are left to understand that separating acts and partners into neat categories of "good" or "bad" is simplistic.

A bridge between the sex scenes and one depicting the eating of rice occurs when a shot of Nguyen fellating his partner cuts to one similar in composition. Head bowed over a bowl and with chopsticks in hand, Nguyen insists on shoveling the rice into his mouth, despite his inability to ingest it as quickly as he feeds himself. The pleasures of rice are ambivalent. There may be expectations within collectives of politicized gay Asian American men to congress within one's race that are restraining. (The 1990s-era term "politically correct" comes up twice during the interviews.) These imperatives can reprise doctrinaire forms of social justice from the past that relied on essentialist notions of race. Yet that pressure—the buildup and explosion of rice in its overabundance—can also produce states of unanticipated possibility and bliss, as the climax of 7 Steps to Sticky Heaven suggests. In the end, the video leaves us with the tender kissing and embracing of two Asian-raced men who are slightly conscious of performing for the camera even while they show genuine affection for each other.

Nguyen's video covertly references a slightly earlier film, Marlon Riggs's Tongues Untied (1989), which makes a similar proclamation about intraracial love. The film, which originally aired on PBS, blends elements of documentary, performance, and found-object pastiche. It ends with the declaration, "Black men loving Black men is the revolutionary act," each word in white lettering flashing in sequence silently on a black screen.[4] Riggs asks us to think about what can be accomplished by something as ordinary as love when it flourishes among African American men. "What is it that we see in each other that makes us avert our eyes so quickly?" a voiceover asks when recounting a story about crossing paths with another African American man in the Castro District of San Francisco. "Do we turn away from each other not to see our collective anger and sadness?" This refusal to recognize gay black bodies and subjectivities stems from both internalized racism and respectability politics. The film's concluding polemic makes a case for a radical intraracial erotics that intervenes on both counts.

A shot in Tongues Untied of an illustrated, heavily muscled black male figure with an oversize penis conveys African American men's alienation when encountering products meant for white consumption. The recurring image of the impossibly endowed black body persists in the Western imagination because of historically sedimented discourses that cast blackness as corporeal excess. This excess is commonly focalized at the site of the genitals. Under chattel slavery, black men were emasculated because of their inability to conform to European-descended standards of normative masculinity. They remained powerless to protect black women from the sexual violence perpetrated by white slaveholders. Upon emancipation, the archetype of black hypermasculine pathology emerged to justify the subjugation of black men through lynching and castration. An oft-cited claim from Frantz Fanon declares, "The Negro is eclipsed. He is turned into a penis. He *is* a penis."[5] Black men are reduced to their genitals. Correspondingly, the elevation of whiteness within a Cartesian modernity privileges the mind's purported capacity to restrain the body's beastly urges. Although present-day African American men can harness some clout within U.S. white gay cultures because of the valorization of masculinity therein, these partially enabling avenues to sexual access are troubling. They can turn into jarring reminders of the racial hierarchies that marginalize black participants.[6] Riggs urges his brethren to avoid these unpleasantries by prioritizing the loving of other black men.

A counterpoint to Riggs's polemic might be Samuel R. Delany's novel *The Mad Man*. Published in 1994, it similarly immerses itself in the milieu of the pre-1996 antiretroviral therapy era. Instead of the highly aestheticized optics that *Tongues Untied* presents, *The Mad Man* confronts its reader with a dogged anti-aesthetic, refusing to serve a portrayal of intimacy that appeals to the PBS-loving crowd. This does not invalidate Riggs's vision of revolution. There are multiple voices that speak to the viability of intraracial desire. The African American protagonist of *The Mad Man*, John Marr, seeks erotic and sexual connection mostly with white homeless men. Repeated utterances of anti-black slurs pepper their role-playing, and Marr's indulgences include the consumption of piss, shit, and snot. According to Darieck Scott, these acts incite their sexual charge precisely because they embroil themselves in a history of unequal power relations between black and white men. The domination Marr craves, when granted, "gives him pleasure . . . that opens the way to his most powerful ecstatic experiences."[7] As a point of contrast, Marr takes offense at being called "boy" by his professor, Irving Mossman, a straight white man for whom he feels no sexual inclination.[8] Riggs may upend the respectability politics of heterosexual African American cultures, but Delany turns even Riggs's oppositional consciousness on its head.

The relations Marr maintains with white men allow him to explore an identification with an Asian American one. Marr, a graduate student in philosophy, pursues research on Timothy Hasler, a fictional Korean American philosopher whose brilliant career was cut short by murder outside a gay bar in New York. As Marr and his adviser, who conducts overlapping research, learn more about the reclusive philosopher's life, Marr's interest piques while Mossman expresses alarm. Marr signs a lease in the same apartment building where Hasler lived and tries to retrace his steps in every way, including through sex with some of his former lovers. Meanwhile, Mossman abandons his project not because of the subject's sexual identity but because of "the *kind* of gay man he was. . . . He was an obnoxious little chink with an unbelievably nasty sex life."[9] The professor's inability to reconcile his admiration for the late philosopher's work with his disgust for the newly unearthed information about his personal life turns the intellectual of color revered for his success in a field dominated by white men into a "chink." Marr's inquiry into his subject, conversely, opens the door to joyously hedonistic erotic experiences. The intimacy Marr craves with Hasler is not sexual in our traditional understanding of the concept. He does not appear to long for a tryst with the dead philosopher. Rather, his desire mediates itself through their mutual ties with the economically transient world outside academia's exclusivity, throwing all pretense of respectability to the wind. Delany speculates that if the model minority Asian American, who earned recognition on white America's terms, found pleasure turning away from it, his African American doppelgänger might, too. Ultimately, the cathartic effects of Marr's transgressions go beyond racial identity in partner choices. Simply rejecting whiteness appears tame in light of the boundaries Delany encourages us to push.

THE EXPERIENCE OF QUEERNESS
FOR MEN OF ASIAN DESCENT

Despite the differences among Nguyen, Riggs, and Delany on the question of intraracial love for men of color, we need to keep in mind that whiteness often remains an irresistible lure, according with North America's normative logic. Nguyen's playful celebration of Asian and Asian American men who stick with one another does not exclude other pairings. Rather, it reveals that they can be sexy in the face of white economies of desire. The white men in Riggs's film are domineering, unsympathetic figures, suggesting that more equitable connections can take place only among African American men. Delany complicates whiteness as the definitive source of power when he creates white homeless characters who contrast sharply with his middle-class African American protagonist. The differing perspectives among these authors attests not to a ranking of radicalness but to a constantly shifting set of hopes and dreams about what consorting among one's own can or should accomplish.

This multiplicity of types and degrees of enthusiasm for intraracial bonding informs my treatment of the literary texts in this book: John Okada's *No-No Boy*, Monique Truong's *The Book of Salt*, Philip Kan Gotanda's *Yankee Dawg You Die*, H. T. Tsiang's *And China Has Hands*, and Lois-Ann Yamanaka's *Blu's Hanging*. Whereas Nguyen qualifies his enthusiasm for the value of Asian American men loving one another with his wish to prevent these sexual choices from being reductive, my measured endorsement of such intimacies stems more from a skepticism about the utopian fantasies they generate. I have selected the above texts because of their foregrounding of the often difficult and sometimes treacherous waters of intraracial discord. When these narratives introduce a queer dyad to air and reconcile differences, the gesture may be compelling, but it does not always hit the mark. Some examples may inadvertently solidify entrenched inequalities. Others may overlook the gender specificity of this male-centered model. Latent or overt homophobia issuing from the narrative voice, the characters themselves, or the reader might thwart their efficacy. In instances where the sexual activity is coded through figurative language, the effect can reproduce silence about same-sex desire. Rather than jettison this pairing because it is imperfect, I probe at what makes it useful, even transformative, in the midst of forces that relegate Asian Americans to states of internal division.

The trope of intraracial reconciliation through queer male desire unfolds in the context of Asian-raced men's gendering in the United States. Because of colonialism, slavery, labor exploitation, and other inequities, nonwhite men inhabit a space outside sanctioned ideals typified by Anglo-American heterosexuality. This fact remains apart from how they may identify sexually on an individual level. White, middle-class models of kinship, domesticity, and sexual comportment valued in the United States historically have remained off-limits to people of color. Conditions that have divested them of the requirements—such as self-determination, property ownership, recognition of full human status, citizenship, and other factors—for achieving those mandates ensure it. Despite the collective positioning of men of color across racial categories outside the charmed circle of Anglo-American heterosexuality, there are variations in how Anglo-America perceives them.

Riggs's unpacking of the gendering of black men calls attention to the distortions they face because of post-emancipation fears of black sexual excess. In contrast, Asian American men are gendered differently because of the historical circumstances of migration from Asia to North America. The immigrant population, especially from countries such as China, the Philippines, and India, was largely male. Ethnic enclaves were thought of as "bachelor societies," even though many men who lived in them were married to women who remained in Asia. The residential arrangements of Asian immigrant men existed outside the domain of Anglo-American propriety. Even before the Page Act of 1875, which barred entry into the United States of women from China, the gender ratios in Chinatowns along the West Coast were skewed such that women constituted only 7.2 percent of the population. That figure had dropped to 3.6 percent by 1890.[10] The labor into which Asian men were tracked after the railroad and mining industries declined was associated with women: laundry, food service, and domestic work. The connection between Asian male bodies and femininity comes from this past. Present-day gay Asian American men participating in sexual cultures that celebrate traditional norms of masculinity cope with the disadvantages of this association. Instead of excess, they are marked by lack. The filmmaker and cultural critic Richard Fung observes that gay pornography "privilege[s] the penis while always assigning Asians the role of the bottom." Thus, he argues, "Asian and anus are conflated."[11] If Asian-raced men are consigned to phallic/ penile absence within a racialized optics that centers the (white) masculine top, it is not difficult to imagine why broaching the topic of Asian American male-desiring men loving one another is subversive.

Because of the gendered immigration and labor histories that have rendered Asian masculinity non-normative in the United States, Asian immigrant men were perceived as deviant, often violently so. Unbalanced ratios between men and women in early ethnic enclaves created contradictory anxieties in the U.S. popular imagination about Asian men's potential to disrupt public safety. As Victor Jew, Mary Ting Yi Lui, and Nayah Shah have shown, Asian-raced men throughout the late nineteenth and early twentieth centuries were demonized because of their imagined propensity for sexually assaulting white women and men. A judicial system increasingly preoccupied with Asian defilement of white bodies responded to and fed into these fears.[12] On the other side of this contradiction, Jennifer Ting claims that early Chinatowns were considered "non-reproductive and non-conjugal," which cast Chinese men as hyposexual and, therefore, safe for employment in white households where women and children lived.[13] These early Asian migrants existed at a remove, albeit in different ways from that of the figure of the sexual predator, from respectable kinship, domestic, and intimate formations. For this reason, David L. Eng proposes that Asian Americans' "historically disavowed status as . . . U.S. citizen-subject[s] under punitive immigration and exclusion laws" scripts them as "queer" apart from the specificities of sexual identity or practice.[14]

It may be useful to parse the vexed and very imperfect overlap between the deviant and the queer in portrayals of Asian-raced masculinity. Whereas the U.S. cultural imagination and penal system joined in the vilification and criminalization of Asian male immigrants at the turn of the twentieth century, these men—as I discuss in detail in Chapter 4—invented intimacies outside conventions of Anglo-American middle-class life. Certainly, Eng's attempt to recuperate notions of Asian sexual deviance by invoking queerness presents us with a double-edged sword. On the one hand, it permits the imagination of different modes of affiliation that go beyond what white America can perceive or accept. These alternate relationalities can be sites of resistance and transformation. As Judy Tzu-Chun Wu argues, we should not fall prey to a reproduction of heteronormative assumptions when we challenge racist immigration laws.[15] On the other hand, Jinqi Ling warns that, in our care not to replicate patriarchal values when critiquing the subjugation of Asians, we should not "risk . . . decontextualizing Asian American men's deeply felt historical injustices toward them."[16] These discriminatory practices, Ling reminds us, had real-world consequences, such as the passing of antimiscegenation laws and the instigation of physical attacks by private citizens. The dislocation between the deviant and the queer lies in the degrees and types of agency men had in structuring their lives in the midst of conditions not of their own making.

Most contemporary scholars respond to the familial, erotic, and sexual entanglements of historical Asian lived experience by proposing more capacious racialized masculinities. They view the temptation to reassert heteropatriarchy as a replication of gender and sexual hierarchies that weaken, not bolster, claims to racial liberation. Jachinson Chan avers that we not disavow Asian effeminacy but, instead, recognize a multiplicity of legitimate gender comportments for men.[17] Celine Parreñas Shimizu prescribes an alternative order of values that challenges parameters of masculine viability. She argues that multidimensional Asian American men assert "the presence of both vulnerability and strength [and] . . . forge manhoods that care for others." Also, they "invest in the most rewarding of relations beyond propping up the self."[18] This interdependence, which cuts against Enlightenment notions of agency, appears in Nguyen Tan Hoang's scholarship, which complements his video art. Returning to Richard Fung's observation about the link between "Asian" and "anus," Nguyen does not renounce this association. He calls for a commitment to "bottomhood," defined not narrowly as anal receptivity alone but as a worldview that disperses the abjection attending femininity and queerness.[19]

Proponents of sticky politics rescript the historical sexualization of Asian men under the white male gaze. White desires for Asian bodies, when occurring among men, operate in much the same way as they do in iterations of normative heteromasculinities vis-à-vis Asian and Asian American women. This dynamic presumes the former's agency in the face of the latter's docility. According to Eng-Beng Lim, colonial-era narratives about the "white male artist-tourist on the casual prowl for inspiration and sex" in Asia invoke "the native boy . . . [as] a sign of conquest, the trope of an Asian male or nation infantilized as a boy, a savage domesticated as a child, and a racially alienating body in need of tutelage and discipline."[20] Joseph Allen Boone shows the extent to which this object of desire persists in the erotic longings of European men traveling to North Africa.[21] These asymmetrical white-Asian pairings from the past shape present-day sexual relationships between Asian American and white men. In his ethnographic work, C. Winter Han reports on micro-aggressions issuing from gay white men, known as "rice queens," who actively pursue Asian Americans because they understand their sexual power over them in a context in which whiteness is prized.[22] Given the predominant whiteness of mainstream gay economies of desire, Asian American men have many incentives to align themselves with whites rather than with one another, whom they often view as competitors instead of potential partners.[23]

Together, the imperatives of sticky politics and erotics comprise three intertwined goals. The first revises North American standards of physical attractiveness; the second contests Asian American men's relegation to subordinate roles that buttress white paternalism; and, finally, the third dispels entrenched patterns of Asian American intraracial rivalry. The structures and thinking that result from colonialism and racism form the backdrop against which Asian American men proclaim desire for one another. Because these inequities persist in making whiteness appealing, intraracial pairings can be, in many cases, transgressive.

STICKY'S LONG FETCH IN
COALITION BUILDING

My reading of 7 Steps to Sticky Heaven frames my treatments of intraracial queer desire in Asian American literature from the 1930s onward. The distinctiveness of Nguyen's film lies in its refusal to aspire to a transhistorical universalism. The self-consciously casual recording of the footage exposes the seams of the video's production, revealing its status as a crafted object situated in time and space. However, I argue that in the context of Asian American literature's political project, men have long been bonded erotically to one another. The extensive fetch of this trope attests to its persistence, malleability, and flexibility and its relevance to a multitude of structural conditions. In effect, desire among Asian American men has been par for the social justice course for a long time. Sticky is part and parcel of the language of revolution, and those articulations of social change take myriad forms.

This book does not merely replicate Nguyen's implied claim in *7 Steps to Sticky Heaven*; nor does it contradict it. To be sure, I find Nguyen's proposition for intraracial love compelling in that it urges its viewer to see what makes it enjoyably validating. However, what interests me most about the idea of two Asian American men entwined in a loving embrace is not so much the rejection of whiteness therein, although that remains a part of it. Instead, the crux of *Sticky Rice* lies in uncovering the significance of this intraracial dyad for a population that historically has struggled with coalition building. In these texts, the mere existence of Asian American men loving one another is often presented as unremarkable. These moments do not always hide under an oppressive heterosexuality. They tend to exist in tandem with it. What *is* unspeakable, however, are the political stances these moments extol, because they unsettle notions of acceptability within populations marked by race and ethnicity. Keeping this in mind, I claim that male same-sex intimacy emerges as the vehicle through which potentially divisive ideas can be aired and debated in the service of intraracial cooperation.

The bonds between men in *Sticky Rice* blur the boundaries among the homosocial, the homoerotic, and the homosexual in ways that lie beyond our concepts of modern gay identity. In fact, none of the instances of same-sex contact in the literature I read—with the probable exception of one—would be considered gay in the familiar sense of the word. My intention, however, is not to transcend a presumably limiting focus on gay specificity. It is to show how the thought and action founded by real-life intraracially desiring Asian-raced men can inform how we read the refusal of multiple normativities in Asian Americanist discourse. In her pioneering work *Between Men*, Eve Kosofsky Sedgwick wrote about the "radically discontinuous relation of male homosocial and homosexual bonds" in middle-class Anglo-European cultures.[24] This stands in contrast to, following Adrienne Rich and Carroll Smith-Rosenberg, a continuum of intimacies among women. The differences between male and female same-sex closeness lie in the divergent levels of access to power that men and women possess and the investment the former has in mobilizing bonds among themselves to maintain their position over the latter. Sedgwick's schema changes, however, when we consider social locations that are informed by racial and class oppression. I do not claim that Asian American cultures remain free of the motivation to protect heteropatriarchy. Rather, I argue that the homosocial, homoerotic, and homosexual connections among men in Asian America look very different from the types that Sedgwick covers in Renaissance and Victorian literature. Asian

American men's access to the gendered and classed power presumed in *Between Men* historically has been limited.

A productive friction between acts and identities emerges as a persistent, if not always primary, undercurrent throughout *Sticky Rice*. Some of the queerest agents in this intraracial same-sex configuration are heterosexual. These very characters can also be the perpetrators of active homophobia. In one of the texts I examine, *Yankee Dawg You Die*, the most conservative, if not reactionary, of the characters is a self-identified gay man. The most legibly gay of sexual encounters in *The Book of Salt* exists in imperfect relationship, because of colonial subject status, with the timeline of gay history recognized as the master narrative. A contextualization of these texts accordingly with that history reveals the extent to which they, too, embed themselves in events that produce uneven conditions for populations defined by sexual difference. This is an analytical maneuver that begs more exploration in Asian American studies. Can we locate *No-No Boy* in an era of McCarthyist panic about the connection between homosexuality and threats to national security? Can we regard *Yankee Dawg You Die* as a cultural product of the HIV/AIDS crisis of the 1980s? Does *And China Has Hands* urge us to rethink the storied narratives about gay life in New York City in the early twentieth century? My answer to these questions is a resounding "yes," even if the sexual identity of the characters sometimes makes it counterintuitive to think this way.

This thorniness around questions of identity in general lies at the heart of Asian American activism. Asian America, as a panethnic project, consolidated in opposition to the identitarian tendencies that previously stood in the way of a sustained and collective effort of social critique and redress. Organizing across categories of ethnicity, gender, class, and other valences of difference can be difficult, even though Asian American people inhabit a shared social location as nonwhite subjects in a country where whiteness has defined one's standing with the state. Whether it is in the context of immigration, citizenship, property rights, or other de jure factors, Asian Americans occupy a position in relation to whiteness that marks them as other. Although collective action may seem easy to espouse, coalition building remains an uncomfortable and often counterintuitive endeavor. Bernice Johnson Reagon has famously declared that one should not expect to feel safe, nurtured, or at home while doing it.[25] Instead of providing a space that validates sameness and unity, a coalition forces its participants to confront their differences. The process of pursuing shared interests, in fact, defines those interests. A coalition is always an entity in progress—never a fait accompli.

Barriers exist that threaten intraracial cooperation. Because of colonial and other types of international conflict within Asia, Asian immigrants may be suspicious of others whose regions of origin are or have been in opposition with their own. The United States' selective militaristic interests have long instigated or exacerbated clashes among nations in Asia, an effect that then reverberates in Asian diasporic populations. For instance, K. Scott Wong sheds light on the nonchalance with which the United States addressed Chinese Americans' concerns about imperial Japan's encroachment on China in the 1930s, an inaction that alienated Chinese Americans and increased resentment between them and Japanese Americans.[26] Lack of interest by the United States dissolved, of course, as soon as Japan attacked Pearl Harbor. Josephine Nock-Hee Park further expands on the role of U.S. militarism in stoking intraracial conflict. The dealings with the Soviet Union that led to the Korean and Vietnam wars and the division of Korea and Vietnam into two states—a communist north and a democratic south—fell in line with a mode of conceptualizing Asians as either friendly or dangerous. Yet Park shows that the transformation of Asians into U.S. allies and, later, immigrants is always incomplete, for the "mere fact of their American existence recalled often calamitous U.S.-Asian relations, which confounded the liberal trajectory from outsider to citizen."[27] Wong's and Park's work addresses the relevance of nation-state origin in intraracial interactions. Yet even among people who share a regional or nation-state identification, dissimilarities in socioeconomic class, generation, immigration history, English language proficiency, citizenship status, and political affiliation can present difficulty. As with all race-based social justice movements, hierarchies defined by gender, sexuality, and ability status create further unevenness. Women of color feminists have long observed that raising issues germane to these vectors of difference tends to elicit charges of detracting from racial liberation.

Sticky Rice immerses itself in the terrain of Asian American coalitional politics described in Lisa Lowe's well-known article "Heterogeneity, Hybridity, and Multiplicity." According to Lowe, social justice initiatives must recognize variations among people of Asian descent, avoid dictating an imaginary cultural purity, and acknowledge disparities that result from unequal social locations within Asian America. One can gloss over difference to foster solidarity, but doing so can "short-circuit potential alliances against the dominant structures of power in the name of subordinating 'divisive' issues."[28] Insisting on sameness in the name of political organizing also unwittingly replicates hegemonic misconceptions of Asians as an undifferentiated mass. By recognizing these heterogeneities within Asian America and, more important, understanding that multiplicities have real-world consequences, activists can avoid replicating inequality in their efforts to redress racism. Lowe's cultural theory exists alongside Yen Le Espiritu's ethnography, which argues that organizing across ethnic categories remains absolutely essential and that it benefits all Asian Americans. However, even though panethnic movements are powerful in theory, the interests of dominant subgroups often prevail in practice. Activists who occupy disadvantaged positions often wind up working, with increasing frustration, for interests that benefit those who already have greater leverage. The "needs of subgroups have often been subordinated to the interests of the larger entity, resulting in a loss of autonomy for these communities and declining power for their leaders. . . . [T]he gradual consolidation of group boundaries is often met by a counter-tendency toward intergroup divisions."[29]

Published in 1991 and 1992, respectively, Lowe's and Espiritu's texts arrive after two decades of heated exchange between male writers in the cultural nationalist tradition and their feminist peers. (Lowe cites this debate directly. Espiritu references it obliquely.) The two most prominent players in the debate, Frank Chin and Maxine Hong Kingston, typify the intraracial, intergender conflicts in Asian American coalitional politics. The extensive literary-critical work on the Chin-Kingston debates has more than adequately shown how a narrowly defined commitment to racial liberation has overlooked gender disparities within Asian America.[30] Asian American sexism arose in part from a compensatory reaction by Asian American men to U.S. immigration policies that blocked their access to heteronormative family structures. Because feminist writers such as Kingston challenged this misguided misogyny, thus exposing cracks in what cultural nationalists wanted to project as a unified front, they were denounced by Chin and his colleagues for working at cross-purposes with antiracism.

What if we decenter the conversation on Asian American coalitional politics from the familiar schema of cultural nationalism versus feminism and turn our attention to other instances that beg intraracial resolution? Some of the conflicts examined in this book are not obscure or unexpected. The debates between Japanese American men who volunteered for military service and those who resisted the draft during World War II, which informs the plot of *No-No Boy*, is a well-known and well-researched phenomenon in Asian American studies. The same is true of the material disparities between East Asians and Filipinos in Hawai'i that plantation capital instilled, conditions that give the controversy behind *Blu's Hanging* its weight. The intergenerational tensions between old and young Asian American actors, as *Yankee Dawg You Die* explores, has not received as much attention as the other two examples. Neither has the faction between pro-labor and pro-capitalist Chinese immigrants in the early twentieth century, the setting for *And China Has Hands*. The recent burgeoning of work in Vietnamese American studies has fostered a lively debate about reestablishing ties with the homeland, which tends to divide refugees who believe in it from those who do not. *The Book of Salt* comes out of this state of affairs. These instances of intraracial partition have in common the presence of a male-male dyad in the fictional texts most closely aligned with their representation.

TACTICS FOR READING

My methodology reflects the primordial commitments of Asian American literary studies. Practitioners in the field have discussed at length the misguided tendency, especially on the part of white readers, to approach literature by Asian American authors as ethnography. By consuming these texts, one presumes to gain epistemological ownership to a racial minority group and come away with a culturalist knowledge of it.[31] This reading practice overlooks the creative capacity of Asian American authors in crafting fiction. It also divests them of their agency as intellectuals who mobilize literature to intervene in the world. As it is assumed, Asian Americans cannot imagine, critique, shape, or strategize. They can only be. One formative piece of Asian American literary scholarship presents a solution to this problem. Donald C. Goellnicht—writing in 1997, during deconstruction's wane in North American English departments—argues that a liberatory reading practice must regard the imaginative literature of Asian Americans and other people of color as intellectual production. We need "to read Asian American texts as theoretically informed and informing rather than as transparently referential human documents over which we place a grid of Euro-American theory in order to extract meaning."[32] Goellnicht's lens, which regards literature as theory, dismantles artificial generic barriers and shows how they are racially inflected. Texts by Europeans and white Americans fall into the realm of philosophical tract, while the same by Asian Americans and other people of color are mere ethnographic artifact.[33]

The intervention Goellnicht made in 1997 remains relevant long after its appearance. A more recent generation of Asian Americanist scholarship expands on the theorizing potential of literature and calls attention to creative writers' mitigation of their misreadings in a racialized literary marketplace. Stephen Hong Sohn speculates that the present-day proliferation of Asian American literature featuring protagonists who do not align with the ethnoracial identity of their authors discourages autobiographically or autoethnographically informed interpretations. Moreover, in refusing a one-to-one ethnoracial correlation between protagonist and author, these texts prompt readers "to consider both the relational and the asymmetric nature of social difference and associated inequalities."[34] The fictional worlds these authors craft position Asian Americans as only one part in a multifaceted system in which racism, capitalism, and settler colonialism converge. Min Hyoung Song challenges us to rethink literature as that which is merely derivative. Literature is not just a transparent document of its times; its role in theorizing lies in its ability to imagine a different order of things. It "has the capacity to make worlds that might seem otherwise not to be possible, and in showing in concrete detail what such a world looks and feels like, literature can point to ways of being and becoming that we haven't yet considered."[35] The theorist and fiction writer Viet Thanh Nguyen's declaration about wanting to "write fiction like criticism and criticism like fiction" shows that even if we still choose to maintain a boundary between one and the other, we can allow the characteristics that define each to permeate the barrier in generative ways.[36]

I write from the vantage point of someone who has held positions in two English departments, and I have witnessed that creative writers are institutionally marginalized in ways similar to those of us who specialize in critical race and ethnic studies. (Some practitioners straddle the two categories, so these groups are not mutually exclusive.) Our fields are presumed to be less rigorous and less serious than those in areas that enjoy a greater amount of cultural capital. We expend more energy justifying the validity of our work in everyday conversation and in official communication related to renewal, merit raises, tenure, and promotion. Although the line between creative writers and critics in the discipline of literature in English was very porous during the early part of the twentieth century, the boundaries between one and the other began to solidify after the mid-century and have only grown thereafter. My interpretation of the literary texts in *Sticky Rice* aligns with the reading practices elucidated above that regard them as theory. Insofar as theorists challenge sedimented patterns of thinking or make transparent the workings of power hidden in plain sight, creative writers do the same. Literary texts often contain an argument, even if it is implied and not offered bluntly in the form of a thesis statement. Their claims, like those advanced by cultural and literary theory, are nuanced. They support themselves with evidence, rhetoric, persuasion, and narrative progression—the same components in scholarship, even if our respective articulations take dissimilar forms.

I will add that when we categorize, and thus read, literature as theory, we need also to remember that theory is not rarefied gospel. It is polemic we approach critically. Its ideas open themselves to agreement, validation, amendment, problematization, debate, dispute, indifference, or collaboration. Its claims may be useful, or they may not. It can call much needed attention to what has been neglected, but it can also fall short or unwittingly replicate hegemonic assumptions. We should acknowledge our intellectual debts to creative writers when appropriate, bringing them into our citational communities when warranted. Correspondingly, we should be diplomatically honest about the oversights of their work. Ultimately, the range of responses to creative writing should run the gamut of those we bring to scholarship.

By examining representations of same-sex desire in some of the most widely read pieces of Asian American literature, Sticky Rice is not a recovery project that attempts to "diversify" a body of work. It does not add heretofore unknown or underappreciated texts that disrupt a supposed majority. Rather, it shows how a slice of the existing canon has always been queer.[37] My analyses are indebted to Daniel Y. Kim, who demonstrates that even within the narrow gender and sexual comportments that Asian American literary cultural nationalists espouse, we can look for moments of nonconformity. Kim identifies a sexually inflected homosociality "so extravagantly on display" when masculinist agency appears to be most salient.[38] These moments of male same-sex desire express a wish for penetrative intimacy with the trappings of white masculinity. In a reading of a nonfictional essay by Chin about working on a railroad, Kim interprets the depiction of Chin's body merging with the train as coded sexual desire for his white male colleagues. According to Kim, Chin "prise[s] open a boundary . . . between the homoerotic and the homosexual . . . that resembles and is yet somehow different from the more literal coming together of male bodies that occurs in gay sex."[39] Chin's infamous championing of an Asian American manhood that accords with North American standards inadvertently destabilizes it.[40]

In the midst of these discourses about Asian masculinity, I take up the contradictions that Kim identifies in historical strains of racial liberatory thought and revise them in two ways. First, rather than assume that slips in heteropatriarchy betray evidence of the impossibility of gender and sexual normativity, especially for men of color, I read these breaches of sanctioned models of masculinity in multifaceted ways. Kim catches users of homophobic language with their drawers down, so to speak. I, instead, regard them as agential envoys of queer thinking whose challenges to traditional masculinity may also be connected to their seeming advocacy of it. I do not cast an overly optimistic light about this paradox, however. Some invocations of queerness seem deliberate, purposeful, and maybe even playful. Others are accompanied by a panic that reveals the phobic underpinnings of their consequent disavowals. Still others may be emotionally and affectively neutral about their nestling within the realm of sexual non-normativity. Second, whereas Kim points to Asian American men's inclination for white men or masculinities in his creation of a queer counternarrative, I direct attention to the transhistorical centrality of *intraracial* desire in these and other instances of self-actualization and coalition building.

At the same time, however, I stake a bridled claim about the efficacy of proposing intimacy between men in Asian America. A glorified vision of intraracial love may inadvertently stifle tough questions about internal power differentials. Some of the Asian-Asian pairings in this study initiate restorative justice. Others replicate the elisions that weaken coalitions. All of them could be problematized in some way. Ignoring internal conflicts for fear that their notice will be divisive inadvertently deepens the fissures their sweep under the rug was meant to curtail. For this reason, I organize the chapters in this book not according to chronology but in a sequence that reflects the trajectory of my argument. *Sticky Rice* first excavates the presence of sticky principles most optimistically before it complicates their pleasures. Chapters 1 to 4 lay out examples of reconciliation through male same-sex social/erotic/sexual bonding. They achieve their goal in varying ways and to varying extents. Chapter 5 warns against monolithic veneration of intraracial connections by examining their failures or missed opportunities. In addition, the arrangement of the chapters, which renders temporality non-linear and privileges argument over chronology, lays bare what recent queer theory asserts about the relationship between time and sexuality. (I address this body of work in depth at the end of Chapter 4, which imagines a temporally flexible origin narrative for Asian America.) In this way, *Sticky Rice* is performative, queer in its structure, insofar as its form conveys its content.

OVERVIEW

Chapter 1, "Veterans and Draft Resisters," reads John Okada's novel *No-No Boy* (1957) as a polemic proposing a cease-fire between Japanese American draft resisters and enlistees in the wake of World War II. Debates in Japanese America about whether or not to join the army when federal officials began recruiting in internment camps created bitter divides that persisted long after the war. I claim that *No-No Boy* effects healing through a figurative sexual interfacing between the two main characters—one a disabled veteran and the other a draft resister—that represent the conflict's opposing sides. I also uncover the queer inclinations behind Asian American cultural nationalism's recuperation of *No-No Boy* during the 1970s. The novel had languished in obscurity during Okada's lifetime. Frank Chin and Lawson Inada's rediscovery of it a generation later catalyzed their Asian American literature recovery project. Chin and Inada's longing for Okada bespeaks an erotic attachment to this early figure of dissidence.

Chapter 2, "Learning to Love Ho Chi Minh," continues to reconcile disparate political positions within ethnic groups. Monique Truong's novel *The Book of Salt* (2003) fictionalizes the story about a Vietnamese cook hired by

Gertrude Stein and Alice B. Toklas. Although the novel is set in Paris during the 1920s, I read it as an allegory about contemporary geopolitical concerns tied to the Vietnamese diaspora. I position the protagonist as the metaphorical incarnation of the South Vietnamese refugee who, during an evening of cruising in Paris, meets a stranger later revealed to be Ho Chi Minh in-becoming. The fleeting sexual encounter between the two intervenes in prevailing Vietnamese American anticommunist sensibilities, especially in light of late twentieth-century reforms by the Socialist Republic of Vietnam that encourage the diaspora to return migrate. This consummation of sexual interest between the figurative South Vietnamese refugee and the leader of North Vietnam in *The Book of Salt* also challenges popular expectations about the gratitude that refugees are expected to express to the United States.

Chapter 3, "Rebellion and Compromise," covers Philip Kan Gotanda's *Yankee Dawg You Die* (1988), a play about two Asian American actors working across generational differences. One is an older man who played exploitative roles early in his career when opportunities for Asian American actors were limited, and the other is a younger man who came of age immersed in Asian American politics and exclusively works in independent productions. The resolution at the play's end, where the actors accept gigs that push against their respective comfort zones, shows that the poles of rebellion and compromise are more nuanced than the previously doctrinaire positions the two men maintained. However, the downplaying of sexual difference between the characters elides the significance of anxieties about HIV/AIDS that demonized gay men in the 1980s. The play's simultaneous invocation of homoeroticism and depoliticization of gay identity imposes a facile resolution to the conflict between the characters. It also suggests that cultural visibility for Asian American male actors will rely on this erasure.

Chapter 4, "Desire and Resistance," addresses pleasurable occasions for contact among men in H. T. Tsiang's *And China Has Hands* (1937), a proletarian novel set in New York. The main character appears to conform to early twentieth-century archetypes of the (hetero)sexually frustrated Chinese immigrant man whose interactions with women are unsatisfying. However, what often gets overlooked is the longing that Tsiang's protagonist develops for his male co-ethnics, which proves more intense than that for any of the female characters. This desire nurtures bonds that challenge contemporaneous intellectual production about Asian masculinity, particularly in the budding field of sociology. However, these same-sex yearnings are not entirely liberating or even innocuous. There lies potential for deception, too, as shown in the protagonist's financial downfall after he succumbs to a co-ethnic loan shark. At the same time, this loss spurs his pro-union activities and allows a prototype of Asian American politics to emerge.

No discussion about fraught examples of intraracial sexual contact in Asian America would be complete without an unpacking of Lois-Ann Yamanaka's *Blu's Hanging* (1997). Chapter 5, "Intrasettler Conflict," addresses this controversy-ridden novel about the rape of a Japanese boy by a Filipino man. I argue that the reproduction of the myth of the Filipino rapist, which has existed in Hawai'i since the plantation era, undoes the types of reconciliations proposed by the texts in the previous chapters. Moreover, I claim that another dyad, an idealized co-habitation between two middle-class local Japanese women coded as lesbian, naturalizes the conditions that have privileged East Asians in Hawai'i at the expense of other groups. Together, the pairings in the novel—one physically violent, and the other ideologically so—uphold intraracial conflicts in Hawai'i that erase the interests of indigenous people, who are absent from the narrative. Chapter 5 serves as a reminder that, as compelling as sticky principles may seem, we need always to refrain from regarding any erotic or sexual dyad as unqualifiedly good, progressive, or liberating.

Readers familiar with these texts may wonder how some of them, in which there is little to no sexual activity, factor into an analysis that relies on a pattern of intraracial sex between men. This needs some explanation. First, among the narratives in which sex occurs as part of the plot, the coupling tends to take place beyond the reach of the prose. The narration cuts away before it happens, as it does in *The Book of Salt*. One can imagine a filmic equivalent in which a slow fade to black appears, the action resuming only after the couple has finished. Second, some of the sex in the texts is figurative, as it is in *No-No Boy*, conveyed in metaphors that beg recognition and elucidation. These instances of nonliteral sex can vary from the overt to the subtle. In *And China Has Hands*, the author coyly performs both the former and the latter evasions: a metaphorical act of sex presumes to transpire *and* its details are met with an absence of portrayal. Third, a character (like one in *Yankee Dawg You Die*) can make impassioned declarations of love using language associated with erotic ecstasy, but he may balk when presented with an opportunity for actual sex. Although the reluctance to represent sexual activity could be read as part of a larger sensibility that forces a sex-negative modesty, the lacuna is an absence that signifies.

I do not want to discount the extent to which traditional concepts of closeting may be responsible for the hiding, coding, or skirting of sexual representation. Doing so would deny the differences in levels of cultural acceptability of and institutional support for heterosexual versus same-sex relationships. The unwillingness to recognize homophobia is, in fact, homophobic. At the same time, to read the unrepresentability of sex only as closeting risks reducing it. If the sticky encounters between men in my archive propose coalition building, the lack of portrayal suggests the "not yet arrived" or "never will arrive" nature of coalitional success. It may be tempting for individuals to wish for an achievable future of lockstep solidarity once the messy particulars of managing and mediating difference resolve themselves. However, that messiness always clings stubbornly to a process that never ends. Because a coalition fully actualized is an impossible ideal, and wanting it to be so makes it ever more untenable, the vehicle used to portray it—a sexual pairing between Asian American men—remains correspondingly elusive.

This book does not offer a solution to the thorny processes of coalition building in Asian America. Rather, it presents an unpacking of the thematic centrality of male same-sex contact in the imaginative literature that addresses it. My analyses should be read not as an endorsement of intraracial couplings but as a prescriptively neutral exposition of a recurring strategy that has already been proposed across time by creative writers. The sticky pairings featured here garner their rhetorical force through the contrarian nature of their inclinations. They take place in a world informed by the valorization of whiteness and heterosexuality. They stand defiantly outside socially sanctioned norms. They reject capitalism, socioeconomic segregation, cultural erasure, heteropatriarchy, and a host of other factors that standardize, regulate, and surveil. In the end, there is a range of pleasures, dangers, declarations, omissions, movements, and inertias associated with intraracial sexual contact for Asian American men.

Sticking with one's own, even in the face of an enticing whiteness, must be regarded as politically variable, contingent on context. It should not itself be cause for celebration or validation, given how power can replicate itself intraracially. It should not be a litmus test in outmoded appeals to authenticity; nor should it police anyone's desires or affiliations. However, I do not dismiss entirely the optimism it can generate. Anyone who has inhaled a kitchen's aromas while waiting for a rice cooker to finish its magic knows the anticipation and craving that attends this act. Only when we understand that stickiness alone is not good enough—there is more work to do, more joy to have, more pain to redress, more truth to tell, and more love to make—will its promises materialize.

I

VETERANS AND

DRAFT RESISTERS

Very little conveys American patriotism more strongly than service in the military. Asian Americans, perceived as perpetual foreigners, gain traction in their claims to national belonging by suiting up in uniform. Military service also provides a path to legal citizenship for those who do not already have it. Many immigrants have successfully acquired U.S. citizenship through this route. However, the military's promise of delivering full cultural citizenship often falls short. Veterans of color experience disillusionment when they discover that they continue to experience racism. In addition, service during wartime carries the risk of disability or death and the obligation of perpetrating the same on others.

At no point in history has military service been as fraught for Asian Americans as during World War II. For Japanese Americans, the weighing of benefits and drawbacks when deciding whether or not to enlist took place in a context of unjust incarceration. The mass relocation and imprisonment of people of Japanese descent from the West Coast, spurred by the Japanese military's attacks on Pearl Harbor, invoked the face of racialized terrorism to justify itself. If Japanese Americans could be urged to fight for their country, might that dispel the falsehood that they threatened national security? Could that be the ultimate test of patriotic love? It appears that most of the eligible men in the internment camps believed this to be the case. Many more enlisted than refused.

One might think that the central conflict in this context, defined by the wish to project an image of respectability, occurred between a misunderstood, minoritized ethnic group and a racially unmarked general American public. Certainly, the intention to prove the U.S. nation-state's white supremacy wrong motivated many Japanese American men. What better way to stick it to the government than by calling out its mistake? Yet the situation was more complicated. Some Japanese Americans would come to feel, vastly more poignantly, not the doubt cast on them by the larger national body politic, but the internal hostility within Japanese America as the community debated the merits of this strategy. Many Japanese American servicepeople adopted a compensatory enthusiasm for their roles in the war effort. Most were assigned to the U.S. Army's all-Japanese 442nd Regimental Combat Team, which was highly decorated. Long after the war, they continued to direct vitriol at draft resisters, the antithesis of the image of the good patriot they so desperately projected.

For these racialized soldiers, what might motivate them to think critically about the measured privilege they received as a result of their service? What might allow cracks to form in the full-throated holler of "Go for Broke!" the 442nd's slogan celebrating military fearlessness? What might inspire a reach across the divide between veterans and draft resisters, an olive branch to those on the other side? John Okada's *No-No Boy* (1957), a novel written by a Japanese American veteran that portrays sympathetically the interiority of a draft resister, raises these questions. Both the novel and its reception provide insights into how Japanese America grappled with its internal rifts and, by extension, its place in the nation in the years following World War II. This chapter sets the stage for the other chapters in this volume, functioning as an urtext through which we can think about how affiliations and reconciliations form across divergent structural locations in Asian America. For a Japanese American veteran in the postwar era, turning away from the rewards of military service seems contrarian. Taking pleasure in it is perverse. *No-No Boy* proposes a resolution of the wartime conflicts within Japanese America by doing both. The drawbacks to challenging the legitimacy that comes from military service are real. Okada's novel attempts to quell disputes between veterans and draft resisters through an intraethnic homoerotics. It urges Japanese Americans who have been conditioned to punish noncompliance from within to withdraw their lateral aggression and, more important, to enjoy the queer act of doing so.

No-No Boy is a landmark text in Asian American literary studies. The novel, which narrates an account of a friendship between a draft resister and a disabled veteran, has remained a staple in Asian American studies curricula for decades. It stands among the texts in the Asian American literary canon that have generated the greatest volume of scholarship. This chapter begins by providing a brief précis of Japanese immigration to the United

States and an exposition of the conflicts among Japanese Americans about military service during World War II. It also unpacks the cultural significance of war injury. Next, it isolates and works through moments in *No-No Boy* that signal sexually and erotically charged intimacies between the two characters that represent the opposing sides of the draft debate. I locate this expression of desire in contemporaneous anxieties about homosexuality and political leftism. Later in the chapter, I address the implications of the characters' homoerotic longings in the context of the novel's rebirth and reclamation by cultural nationalists in the 1970s. In doing so, I show that an undercurrent of intraracial queer male desire has long accompanied Asian American activism, even in its most heteropatriarchal forms.

INTERNMENT, CONSCRIPTION, AND CONFLICT

The incarceration of Japanese Americans during World War II had its lead-up in events informed by U.S. expansion that spanned a century. After the end of the Mexican-American War in 1848, large numbers of Chinese immigrants entered the United States to fulfill labor needs in the newly acquired territory. Because of Anglo-American fears about a growing nonwhite workforce, the practice of recruiting from China eventually became unpopular. The Chinese Exclusion Act of 1882 barred all immigration except for certain exempted classes. Immigration from Japan to the United States surged after this restriction because of the ongoing need for cheap labor. Although the Japanese were initially welcomed as a more favorable replacement for an abject population, they would come to face discrimination, too. As with the Chinese, Japanese immigrants were subjected to legislation—such as the Alien Land Law of 1913—that thwarted their economic development because of concerns that they competed unfairly with whites. These factors ultimately resulted in the passage of the Immigration Act of 1924, which all but ended immigration from Japan.

Hence, anti-Japanese sentiment in the United States existed even before the cataclysmic attack on Pearl Harbor on December 7, 1941. Fear of Japanese Americans' economic encroachment was only later accompanied by their depiction as a national security threat when conflicts between the United States and Japan escalated. Doubts about Japanese Americans' loyalty to the United States became so strong that in 1941, the federal government commissioned an investigation into whether or not they were seditious. The study, known as the Munson Report, concluded they were not. However, the results became so controversial in the days following Pearl Harbor's bombing that they were suppressed. The report was largely forgotten until the

1970s, when the liberatory movements that redressed state abuses against people of color called public attention to the document and the civil rights implications of its silencing.[1]

Franklin D. Roosevelt's passing of Executive Order 9066 on February 19, 1942, authorized the removal of all people of Japanese ancestry from the West Coast. The War Relocation Authority called on leadership in the Japanese American Citizens League (JACL) to ensure a smooth evacuation. These leaders complied to project an image of Japanese Americans as dutiful citizens. Even before the internment, the JACL had aligned itself with assimilationist politics. The organization was founded in 1930 by professionals who promoted the values of individualistic class ascent through education and career advancement.[2] Evacuees were moved first to temporary relocation centers at racetracks and other facilities to await the construction of ten internment camps farther inland. Once the camps were built, evacuees boarded trains for long-term confinement in remote locations. Some who owned houses and businesses asked trusted non-Japanese friends and associates to tend them for the duration of the war, but the internment was as much about the federal government's seizure of property from Japanese Americans as it was about their incarceration.[3] In all, the camps imprisoned almost 120,000 people, many of them U.S. citizens by birth, without due process in the form of a trial.

In early 1943, the War Relocation Authority circulated a questionnaire, which came to be known colloquially among Japanese Americans as the loyalty oaths, to all inmates inside the camps age eighteen and older. Two questions in particular caused concern among the camp population. Number 27 asked respondents whether they were willing to serve in the U.S. Armed Forces, if ordered, and number 28 asked whether they were willing to forswear allegiance to any foreign power, including the Japanese emperor. The questions had the most serious ramifications for men who were Nisei, or second generation—that is, children of immigrants—who were young adults at the time of the internment. Issei, or first-generation, men had largely aged past their eligibility for the draft at the time of the war, because as of 1924, immigrants (who were mostly young adults) no longer arrived from Japan.

Although many respondents felt reluctant to volunteer for a war fought by a country that had stripped them of their constitutional rights, they reasoned that a "yes" response could affirm their patriotism and offset the misconception that Japanese Americans were enemy aliens. The War Relocation Authority had already won the trust of the JACL, which had earlier facilitated the internment to project respectability. The league's accommodationist leadership later worked hard to convince internees to volunteer for the U.S. Army. Answering "no" to the questions or refusing to answer at all subjected respondents to more stringent surveillance. These dissenters were spurned by their co-ethnics, who believed that their resistance stoked the public's fears about Japanese American treachery. The federal government relocated them to Tule Lake, a special camp designated for potentially seditious Japanese Americans, from which they awaited their court date. Known informally as "no-no boys" for their negative responses to the two key questions on the loyalty oaths, draft resisters underwent perfunctory trials and served two- to three-year prison sentences in federal penitentiaries such as Leavenworth and McNeil Island.[4] For the Nisei who served, many were assigned to the Army's segregated 442nd Regiment, consisting entirely of Japanese Americans. They fought in the European theater, sustaining numerous losses and injuries, and the 442nd eventually went on to become the most highly decorated military unit in U.S. history.

THE GENDERED LOGICS OF DISABILITY IN MILITARY SERVICE

The nuanced portrayal of one of the main characters in No-No Boy, a disabled Japanese American veteran, reveals the representational instability of racial and physical difference in discourses of masculine military valor. John Okada was not a draft resister himself, having served in the U.S. Air Force during World War II. Although he made the socially acceptable decision to enlist, his authorship of a novel portraying his subject, a no-no boy, with multidimensional complexity led him to be ostracized by his co-ethnics. Originally from Seattle, Okada moved to the Midwest after the war to escape the anti-Japanese sentiment that remained strong on the West Coast. For many Japanese Americans, the hope that military service would change the public's impression of them did not pan out. Okada settled in Detroit, where he worked as a technical writer for the automobile industry. He wrote No-No Boy in his leisure time.

No-No Boy opens with the reunion of the protagonist, Ichiro Yamada, with his family and community in Seattle after he is released from prison for refusing military service. Even though Ichiro is shunned by many Nisei men who had served in the war, he discovers an unlikely friend in Kenji Kanno, a veteran with an amputated leg. Ichiro receives sustained hostility from those of his own ethnic group, including family members. Conversely, Kenji may have the cultural and economic status of a wounded war veteran, but his injury will not heal properly. The foreshadowing, in the form of repeated surgical amputations to contain an infection that will not heal, signals his impending death. The escalation of tension among Nisei men comes to a head when a fight leaves a minor character dead. The lack of closure at the novel's end suspends the ethical dimensions not only of the death itself but also of the larger, intraethnic conflicts that remain unresolved among Japanese Americans in the postwar period.

The loyalty oaths were exceptional in that at no other point in U.S. history have people of color been separated so resolutely into the diametric opposition of "patriot" or "enemy" on the basis of their willingness or refusal to take up arms. This binary logic erases the porosities of the artificial divide between the two categories. Ichiro and Kenji reveal the incoherency of these absolutes in *No-No Boy*, each floating in the non-space between "yes" and "no." Their queerness lies in not only their homoerotic desires for each other but also the ambiguity with which they occupy externally and imperfectly imposed categories.[5] The World War II era in the Japanese American past may have underscored the link between the soldier and the citizen most explicitly, but it also follows a well-worn path through which racialized subjects have gained a masculine form of recognition by the nation, as well as by the state. The pinnacle of this recognition turns on the significance of the wounded body of the soldier of color. At the same time, these bodies do not remain free from the insidious concepts of disability imbricated in popular understandings about the intersection of race and gender.

No one has more cultural capital than Kenji in *No-No Boy*. His veteran status and amputated leg place him above all others in the hierarchy of acceptability in Japanese America's postwar world. The elevation of the wounded soldier of color was not new to World War II. The earliest examples can be found in representations of African American disabled veterans that date back to the Revolutionary War. According to Jennifer C. James, an abundance of African American writers have foregrounded the contributions of black soldiers in strategic ways. Laudatory accounts of military bravery "permitted black men the opportunity to benefit socially and politically by creating idealized representations of black masculinity."[6] However, the valorization of the veteran in fiction did not correlate to equality on or off the battlefield. The conditions under which these men served revealed discrepancies in treatment among the races. In addition, glowing portrayals of the African American soldier in fiction did not open up sufficient space for critiquing the horrors of war. The image of the injured veteran also had the capacity to reinforce Anglo-American beliefs about the black body as already impaired or inherently disabled.[7] Because of the complexities of how race, gender, and ability status played out, African American writers found themselves walking a very thin line on multiple fronts.

The ambivalence about the figure of the disabled veteran of color comes through in Okada's portrayal of Kenji, albeit in ways that do not completely overlap with the mitigation of historical modes of dehumanization specific to African Americans. Instead, we see an engagement with a nascent, but emerging, Asian American consciousness that stakes a claim to the nation for these so-called perpetual foreigners at the same time that a subtle condemnation of the terms on which that claim is possible emerges. In his reading of *No-No Boy*, Viet Thanh Nguyen focuses on the economic discrepancies between the two main characters, noting that consumerist trappings of middle-class life are possible for Kenji in a way they are not for Ichiro because of the material benefits of the GI Bill. The issue of consumer culture and property looms large for Japanese Americans, because Japanese immigrants were barred from citizenship and, therefore, from owning property as a result of the Alien Land Law. Hence, the contrast that Okada sets up between Kenji and Ichiro suggests that the "reward . . . for loyalty is the participation in America's bounty of plenty."[8] It matters little that both are U.S. citizens by birth. Nguyen's unearthing of the connection among race, citizenship, and ownership shows a historical deprivation of these state-issued rights to Japanese Americans.

Building on Nguyen's insights, I call attention to one particular commodity in *No-No Boy*: the automobile, which Kenji calls a "present" from "Uncle Sam."[9] The automobile already occupies a vaunted place in the collective American imagination as a marker of economic success. Significantly, Okada has chosen to spotlight the adaptive capabilities in Kenji's car: "Ichiro turned so that he could see Kenji better and he saw the stiff leg extended uselessly where the gas pedal should have been but wasn't because it and the brake pedal had been rearranged to accommodate the good left leg" (59). In this depiction, Okada suggests not only that disability is not a barrier to one's enjoyment of the fruits of U.S. patriotism but also that it is actually its precondition, especially for Japanese Americans. The irony behind this convergence of race, veteran status, and disability in the figure of the automobile is that Franklin D. Roosevelt, who authorized the internment, was himself disabled and closely associated with his vehicle.[10] A polio survivor, he maintained an unspoken agreement with the press that cameras would refrain from capturing the moments when he entered and exited his car. Instead, iconic photographs of the dapper president show him smiling from his Lincoln convertible, a relaxed hand on the wheel. He is sometimes waving to the crowd, sometimes holding an upturned cigarette between his teeth. The distance between the Japanese American veteran and the white president who incarcerated him cannot be stressed enough in these varying depictions with a treasured possession.

As a veteran, Kenji reaps some of the rewards of military valor's gendering in line with U.S. culture's sexism. However, war injuries, particularly those that are visible, such as Kenji's amputation, symbolically register in ways that create friction. As David Gerber points out, disability is also associated with emasculation. Okada's portrayal of Kenji certainly conveys ambivalence about the disabled veteran's gender comportment. These opposing discourses place the disabled veteran in the liminal space between embodied manliness and effeminate victim. The soldier's injury reminds us of his own ability to injure, making him at once victim and aggressor. According to Gerber, these contradictions stem from the slipperiness of gendered expectations that accompany warfare, on the one hand, and debility, on the other.[11] Given these paradoxes, it is not surprising when David Serlin finds that veterans' rehabilitative projects in the aftermath of World War II were endeavors to restore normative masculinity. Technologically advanced prosthetics, meant to facilitate a smooth reentry into civilian workplaces, offered a promise of rehabilitated masculinity through self-reliance and renewed autonomy. Those traits would allow men to reclaim patterns of labor and consumption that aligned with sanctioned models of heterosexuality. Correspondingly, the rehabilitation of the veteran became an analogue for the rehabilitation and remasculinization of the nation.[12]

The allure of Kenji's body in *No-No Boy* sits within these broader traditions of representing the wounded soldier as the quintessential patriotic citizen and the veteran of color as evidence of the nation's success in incorporating nonwhite subjects into its fold. While Japanese Americans were considered suspect during World War II because of their ethnic proximity to the enemy, Kenji's characterization subverts this logic by drawing on an existing link between war injury and patriotic sacrifice. His racialized, injured body affirms the U.S. nation-state's presumption of consensualist assimilation and validates its militarization in the service of empire building. A triangulation of racial difference, disability, and pro-Americanism coheres in his characterization as a wounded soldier. Even so, these invocations of patriotism ultimately fall short of their intended goal: the uncomplicated harnessing of cultural citizenship for the veteran of color.[13] Ichiro, the nondisabled draft resister shunned by his co-ethnics, recognizes and craves the respect Kenji's body garners. However, both men remain aware of the physical and psychological toll the repeated operations on Kenji's leg and his knowledge of impending death take.

Kenji becomes a complex figure on which multiple contradictions converge. As a Japanese American subject, he embodies the phenotypic traits that Anglo-American society associates with threats to national security. However, as a veteran with an amputation, what Serlin calls "visual shorthand for military service," he transforms himself into the national hero par excellence.[14] As a well-disciplined consumer whose home contains the trappings of his GI Bill benefits, Kenji exhibits a middle-class lifestyle that signals ascent into triumphalist narratives of postwar prosperity. At the same time, his reluctance to consummate his romantic interest with a Nisei woman indicates a breakdown in his performance of normative masculinity. Although it is tempting, following Serlin's logic, to read Kenji's failure to restore heteromasculinity as a metaphor for Japanese America's failed attempts to raise its civic status through military service, I want instead to examine the homoeroticism in Kenji and Ichiro's friendship, which provides a way out of the impasse between compliance and resistance.

A HOMOEROTICS OF INTRAETHNIC HEALING

The plot in *No-No Boy* organizes itself not by the teleological passage of events traditional to the genre of the novel but around an unanswerable question that Ichiro tries to unravel with Kenji: "Would you trade places with me?" (62). The question is impossible because it reveals the absurdity of choosing between social death and a dead body. The third-person omniscient narrator never stakes a definitive claim to either of the positions that Kenji and Ichiro exemplify, instead laying out their circumstances by saying:

> So they sat silently . . . one already dead but still alive and contemplating fifty or sixty years more of dead aliveness and the other, living and dying slowly. They were two extremes, the Japanese who was more American than most Americans because he had crept to the brink of death for America, and the other who was neither Japanese nor American because he had failed to recognize the gift of his birthright when recognition meant everything. (73)

The inversion of living and dying and American and Japanese hints at the near-equivalence of these pairings, but Okada's prose refuses to make that connection exactly parallel. If the living-dying dyad is problematized by an uncomfortable relationship to a dichotomous binary, so, too, is the coherence of national identity organized around America-Japan. Within this logic, the structuralist tendency to equate "American" with "life" and "Japanese" with "death" destabilizes, too. The imperfection of these parallels is what makes Kenji's answer unconvincing when he buckles and admits that he would not trade places with Ichiro. His response proves anticlimactic because of these almost, but not quite, hierarchized binaries. This gesture toward a conclusion seems purposefully designed to generate frustration.

The novel's refusal to resolve the question of which identity, veteran or draft resister, remains more unfavorable signals its refusal to explain the circumstances that led Kenji down one path and Ichiro down the other. Jinqi Ling finds that Okada "speak[s] the ideologically unspeakable while keeping his narrative position usefully ambiguous."[15] Picking up on this ambiguity, Elda E. Tsou argues that it signifies the Japanese American subject's inability to express itself under the strictures imposed by the loyalty oaths. The "coercive representation and the ruse of consent that is implied by these acts of intending, questioning, responding, and refusing to speak" convey themselves through the opacity of Okada's prose.[16] Although I tend to agree with both Ling and Tsou, I argue that this existential stasis between loyalty and treachery does not leave the reader hanging. It finds release in the covert sexual desire between the two main characters.

Even though homophobia is palpable in the predominantly male social world in which *No-No Boy* takes place, an equally palpable homoerotic undercurrent governs the friendship between the two main characters. We see this in Ichiro's interior monologue as he thinks about Kenji's body:

> Give me the stump which gives you the right to hold your head high. Give me the eleven inches which are beginning to hurt again and bring ever closer the fear of approaching death, and give me the fullness of yourself which is also yours because you were man enough to wish the thing which destroyed your leg and, perhaps, you with it but, at the same time, made it so that you can put your one good foot in the dirt of America and know that the wet coolness of it is yours beyond a single doubt. (64)

Nguyen points out that Ichiro's silent wishes render Kenji's amputation as a phallus. The physical integrity of the racialized body needs to be sacrificed to obtain a symbolic power for Japanese American men within codes of U.S. masculinity.[17] Certainly, the Freudian allusions of this symbol cannot be missed, especially when we consider the portrayal of Ichiro's mother. An overbearing and castrating figure, she dominates both her son and her husband.[18]

Unlike Nguyen, I do not posit Kenji's stump as only an abstracted signifier for male social and psychic vitality. If we read the passage literally and regard Kenji's leg as a corporeal materiality that Ichiro relishes sexually, other possibilities emerge. The trove of amateur and professional pornography featuring amputees that Tim Dean has unearthed grounds more literally these declarations of desire for Kenji's stump. This vast archive includes numerous incidents of amputees anally penetrating their partners. Rather than condemn this genre for objectifying people with disabilities, Dean convincingly makes a case for its potential to establish "a fundamental kinship between bodies that are but artificially segregated into disabled and nondisabled. When these bodies come together, we see not that they're the same but that their conjunction dissolves the invidious disabled/able-bodied binary."[19] Similarly, Okada's fictional world dismantles the artificial barriers between veterans and draft resisters by eroticizing Kenji's amputation and making room for critiques of the social order. The coupling of Kenji and Ichiro symbolically links the heroic soldier with the maligned draft resister, showing how they are not opposing figures in the Cold War Japanese American cultural landscape. They may not be the same, but it becomes obvious that both have been subjected to the injustice of internment; both have come under the nation-state's coercion to recruit them into its war machine; and both continue to experience the indignities of race-based discrimination.

In Ichiro's interior monologue, the imperative "Give me the stump" is neither one of phallic jealousy between men nor of threat of castration but an invitation to initiate a penetrative embrace, one accompanied by an erect positioning of the head. Quite the size queen, Ichiro admires his friend's "eleven inches" in a manner that removes the leg from the realm of medicalized pathology and into a space where pleasure flourishes. The language that follows is the most erotically charged in a novel that otherwise regards both sexual activity and romantic love with cynicism. Ichiro thinks about Kenji's stump "hurt[ing]" and pushing him to an "approaching death" and "destr[uction]," using language evocative of orgasm. He recognizes the multiplicity of insertions Kenji's disabled body can effect as he thrusts with either his stump or his "one good foot." He solicits the "fullness" of Kenji's "man[hood]," from where he can initiate a decisive plunge into "wet" "dirt." Although the reading that Nguyen proposes casts the comparisons that Kenji and Ichiro make about their respective struggles as masculinist contest—"'Whose is bigger?' . . . 'Mine is bigger than yours in a way, and then again, yours is bigger than mine'" (64–65)—when we examine the erotic elements of these interchanges, they transcend phallic competition.[20] The libidinal longing that Ichiro possesses for Kenji's stump converts it from an immaterial phallus, as in Nguyen's reading, into something more resembling a flesh penis.

In this declaration of erotic longing, the nation becomes the receptive partner in its relationship with the war-injured Japanese American veteran who eases his foot into its soil. In a twist, it would appear that Ichiro indirectly conflates himself with "America," which receives Kenji's body, when he expresses that he wants to be similarly penetrated. His claim to intimacy with the nation comes in the roundabout form of an erotic wish to be entered by his friend's disabled body in an implied three-way encounter as it is being "dirt[ied]" inside America with his other leg. However, in this erotic triangle, the two acts of receptivity are not analogous. Whereas the nation that pulls the racialized subject into its embrace alters, consumes, and eventually annihilates him, the penetration that Ichiro wants turns these forces on their head by refusing well-worn trajectories of assimilation into bourgeois heteropatriarchy. Insertions into the nation are dangerous and often fatal, as Kenji's fate shows, but insertions that reverse the nation's teleologies can be symbolically enabling.

My observations about Ichiro's receptive pleasures echo Kathryn Bond Stockton's argument about Freudian frameworks in a reading of Toni Morrison's *Sula*. According to Stockton, the intellectual or medico-scientific productions of Europeans are not inherently irrelevant for a text about African American experiences. Rather, the limitations of Freud's work can reveal, rather than uphold, the racial specificity of master narratives of growth and maturation. In Morrison's fictional neighborhood, which alludes to anal pleasure in its name "the Bottom," the characters who refuse white, middle-class ambitions possess qualities akin to Freud's anally fixative subjects: undeveloped, stalled, and infantile. However, sublimating these desires into dominant values and rejecting anal impulses only results in political stasis.[21] Nguyen Tan Hoang takes up the privileging of bottomhood in ways that are related to but also different from Stockton's. Bottoming, Nguyen argues, is not merely a sexual practice involving anal receptivity but an expansive worldview that "undermines normative gender, sexual, and racial standards" and "reveals an inescapable exposure, vulnerability, and receptiveness in our reaching out to other people."[22] In all, Freudian discourses that pathologize bottoming and Anglo-American concepts of assimilative heteromasculinity are connected. Okada's rich description of Ichiro's anal-erotic desires anticipates a bottom-affirming politics almost two decades before Morrison's *Sula* and five decades before Stockton's and Nguyen's critical theory. Ichiro's unruliness in the eyes of the nation-state, his postwar class regression, his indulgence of queerness, and his anal desires together create an alternative to the virulent displays of compensatory patriotism and masculinity among other Japanese American men. The homoerotic desire Ichiro directs at Kenji becomes the vehicle through which Okada's prose conveys a rejection of multiple normativities.

The loyalty oaths tore a cleavage within Japanese America. The redress movement in the 1970s made inroads toward reconciliation, but the gulf that divided veterans and no-no boys ran deep even after that. Okada's decision to tell a story that provides a multidimensional portrayal of a draft resister enacts an interaction mirrored in the novel. As an Air Force veteran, Okada reaches across the divide between enlistees and resisters to imagine what in 1957 was an as-yet-unrealized coalition of politicized Japanese Americans. He functions in a capacity similar to that of Kenji, who, in the act of protecting Ichiro from the hostility of other Japanese American men, uses the cultural capital of his veteran status to ameliorate these conflicts.

A REVOLUTION MEANT
ONLY FOR MEN?

The homoerotics of anal receptivity that Ichiro declares becomes the solution for Japanese America's misguided aspirations in the postwar era. It bypasses the predictable path—as charted in Eve Kosofsky Sedgwick's *Between Men*—of triangulating a relationship between two men through a woman. The structuring of same-sex intimacy in *No-No Boy* makes it much more appealing than any of the heterosexual pairings in the novel, which are invariably unfulfilling. Unlike Sedgwick, who reads "male heterosexual desire . . . [as that which] consolidate[s] partnership with authoritative males in and through the bodies of females," Ichiro and Kenji exhibit an attraction for each other that not only makes women irrelevant but also regards their very presence as a barrier to the intimacy they forge.[23]

When Kenji, who courts a Nisei woman named Emi, attempts to consummate his relationship with her through Ichiro because his leg aches too much for sex, he receives only anger. On an evening when all three socialize together, Kenji retires for the night, leaving Ichiro alone with Emi after hinting at what he expects of the two. Ichiro becomes indignant. "So you're sending in a substitute, is that it?" he demands (89). The source of Ichiro's emotion is ambiguous. Does it stem from his sexual jealousy of the desire Kenji feels for Emi when he believes he is the rightful recipient of it? Is it the omniscient narrator's critique of Kenji's lingering reverence for heterosexually inflected assimilation? Okada's prose remains coy about the matter. Although Kenji may previously have admitted to a disinclination to trade places with Ichiro, this scene hints at the possibility of the situation being otherwise. He may want to harness Ichiro's political dissidence, "substitut[ing]" in his friend's place, without the strain of social isolation it would cause. The thwarted attempt at heterosexual surrogation reverses Ichiro's earlier wish to acquire cultural citizenship vicariously through Kenji's war injury. Although Ichiro's longing for the comforts of Kenji's position is easy for the novel's intended reader to perceive, the converse is not immediately legible. It may even be incomprehensible. This failed pairing between Ichiro and Emi brings it to light.

The following scene finds Ichiro and Emi in a nonsexual encounter. The dialogue is the most accommodationist in the novel. Emi commands Ichiro:

Next time you're alone, pretend you're back in school. Make believe you're singing "The Star-Spangled Banner" and see the color guard march out on stage and say the pledge of allegiance with all the other boys and girls. You'll get that feeling flooding into your chest and making you want to shout with glory. It might even make you feel like crying. (96)

The remedy Emi imagines for Japanese America's failure at assimilation is not a refusal of its terms but more impassioned efforts. Her language of patriotism is erotically charged, invoking rapturous love that "flood[s]" and compels "shout[ing]" or "crying." Emi's enforcement of normative affect and Kenji's encouragement of normative sexuality become foils for the opposite—the link between dissident politics and queer desire—elsewhere in *No-No Boy*. Emi's description of political emotion is consistent with Sara Ahmed's claim about increased emotional expenditures in displays of loyalty when the nation "fail[s] . . . to 'give back' the subject's love." According to Ahmed, the "subject 'stays with' the nation, despite the absence of return and the threat of violence, as leaving would mean recognising that the investment of national love over a lifetime has brought no value."[24] However, the advice Emi offers borders on camp. The scene suggests that the overt physical abuse Ichiro suffers from Japanese American men finds its subtler form when meted out by seemingly benevolent women. We might also read, as James Kyung-Jin Lee does, Emi's words not as evidence of naïve consensualism but as an expression of the ambivalence with which racialized subjects must always function in American life.[25] Regardless, neither Kenji's nor Emi's strategies are effective. Ichiro does not sleep with Emi; nor does he become an instant patriot; and the two male characters continue to bond with each other without a female go-between until Kenji's death.

This is not to say that sexual pairings between men and women have no place in a critique of the nation-state. Okada tentatively broaches this possibility at the beginning of the novel but fails to explore it fully. Ichiro has just been released from prison when he decides to visit his friend and fellow draft resister Freddie. As he gets off the bus at the designated stop, he sees a dilapidated apartment building that contrasts sharply with the middle-class home where Kenji lives with his family. He hikes up a flight of creaky stairs and meets a Nisei woman across the hall from Freddie's unit. Okada's portrayal of her, as with his heavy-handed depiction of the dwelling's conditions, is not meant to elicit desire. Ichiro knocks on Freddie's door, and the neighbor responds to the tapping:

A plump, young Japanese woman peered into the hall and asked not unkindly: "What you want?"

"I'm looking for Fred Akimoto. He lives here, doesn't he?"

The woman opened the door wider, inspecting him in the added light. Her housecoat was baggy and dirty and unzipped down to her waist. A baby cried far inside. "Freddie's sleeping. He always sleeps late. You can pound on the door until he hears you, or," she grinned at him, "you're really welcome to come sit in my place and wait." (45)

The nameless woman's sexual desires are pathologized within normative frames of heterosexual propriety. She sleeps with Freddie while her husband is at work, and Freddie's declaration that he stays "there all day until the old man [comes] home" (47) signals her failures of wifely chastity and implies neglect of her motherly duties. This scene also suggests that Japanese American men's heterosexual capital is tied to their ability or willingness to conform to the nation-state's scripts for cultural citizenship. Freddie admits that before the war, he could afford to be "so damn particular about dames" (47), but his current status as a pariah has changed those circumstances. His admission, problematic as it is, that his former social status afforded him options no longer available, exposes the link that binds male sexual desirability to jingoistic compliance. It also reveals the gender-specific standards of physical appearance to which women are held. "She's nothin' but a fat pig" (47), Freddie declares, which inspires Ichiro to imagine how the coupling would play out. He "pictured Freddie with the fat woman . . . and couldn't resist a smile" (48).

However, this emphasis on the woman's anatomical difference, her corpulence, does not mean that female agency within heterosexual economies rests solely on normative standards of physical beauty. Although the scene implies that Japanese American men's sexual desirability depends on their embrace of the masculinist cultures of warfare, *No-No Boy* suggests that their female counterparts can be evaluated with similar criteria. Much of what makes the nameless woman's portrayal off-putting to the intended reader is her lack of sexual restraint. That she appears to be indiscriminate in her appetite, even to the extent of her willingness to consort with no-no boys, may in fact be a coded indication of her political alignment with the most reviled sectors of Japanese American society. Freddie claims that she "don't care who I am or what I done or where I been. All she wants is me, the way I am, with no questions" (48). However, her democratic willingness to have sex with ostracized figures, far from not "car[ing]," *does* appear to be a loaded statement. This politicizing of partner choices becomes all the more visible if we consider, as in the passage in which Ichiro wishes to be penetrated by Kenji's stump, how world making enacts itself through sexual play. Yet the spirit behind the nameless woman's sexual choices does not provide a corresponding hope in the way Kenji and Ichiro's pairing does. When Freddie teases Ichiro about the advance his neighbor made on him, he does not imply that Ichiro would find the opportunity appealing. Her desire is stigmatized and leaves little room for women's revolutionary potential.

The unfavorable depiction of Freddie's neighbor remains a missed opportunity for No-No Boy to develop heterosexual forms of eroticized political resistance that parallel Ichiro's same-sex yearnings for Kenji. The furtive sexual activity to which Freddie resigns himself differs diametrically from the extended passages that describe in lush, glowing detail Ichiro's longing for Kenji's stump. The discrepancy with which the novel represents heterosexual versus queer articulations of eroticized political critique may result from the lack of Japanese American women's prominence in debates about how best to respond to the loyalty oaths. Denied a public platform for vocalizing her opposition to the nation-state, Freddie's neighbor asserts it through sexual congress with men whose behavior is more legible as resistance.

When the loyalty oaths were distributed, every member of the camp population older than eighteen, regardless of gender, was required to fill it out. However, women's participation in the military was voluntary. The phenomenon of Japanese American female veterans from World War II needs more exploration. Brenda Moore uncovers this little-known aspect of history in her study of Nisei in the Women's Army Corps and Army Nurse Corps. During the early days of the war, these gendered labor niches (the Women's Army Corps consisted largely of clerical workers) had been off-limits to women of Japanese descent in a way that they were not to German American and Italian American women. As the conflict wore on, military officials recognized the benefit of having more workers on hand and supported Japanese American enlistment. As a group whose service was elective, Japanese American women had more leverage in setting the terms for their participation than did their male counterparts. They opposed the formation of segregated units similar to the 442nd Regiment. However, they also revealed the racial specificity of their vision of integration when they insisted on serving in white units and not among African Americans.[26]

Despite these aspirations to assimilative patriotism, many Japanese American women, as with the men, felt ambivalent about serving in the military.[27] Records show that a number of women answered "no" to one or both of the fraught questions on the loyalty oaths.[28] Interviews with female veterans indicate that many enlisted with significant reservations.[29] In tandem with Okada's underdeveloped Nisei female character, whose sexual inclinations show dissidence in the face of rabid militarism, these historical records and testimonies reveal cracks in mainstream accounts of the successful disciplining of Japanese American subjects into normative cultural citizenship.

They also prove that women, often assumed to have been silent or simply not invested, actively participated in conversations about weighing justice against civic duty in matters related to the wartime draft.[30]

Yet in the fictional world that unfolds in *No-No Boy*, no sexually charged revolution for women exists that would correspond to the relationship between Ichiro and Kenji. Nothing allows opposing positions they may embody to reconcile through same-sex desire. The reader is left either with the brash, laughable Americanism that Emi trumpets or a nascent resistance more easily read as sexually indiscriminate apathy, which Freddie's neighbor embodies. Likewise, no impetus arises for political transformation in Ichiro's mother, whose rejection of assimilation is a delusional refusal to believe that Japan has surrendered. The novel hints repeatedly that Ichiro's evasion of the draft may have stemmed from maternal piety to Mrs. Yamada, whose sexist portrayal is even less favorable than that of Freddie's lover. As with Freddie's neighbor, no redemptive potential emerges from Mrs. Yamada's non-normativity. Her suicide at the novel's end, unlike the martyr's death granted to Kenji, leaves her even more abject. Whereas the penetration that Ichiro craves with Kenji's body is celebrated without reservation, the lack of similar erotic opportunities for reconciliation between women reveals the male-specificity of the intraethnic coalition that *No-No Boy* proposes.

POSTWAR SEXUAL
AND POLITICAL DISSIDENCE

The bodies of scholarship on the Cold War era in Asian American studies and sexuality studies rarely come into dialogue with each other. They tend to have completely separate citational communities, an indication that scholars in one field do not read and engage with those in the other. What Asian American studies and sexuality studies mean by the "Cold War" can appear so divergent from each other that one sometimes wonders whether they refer to the same entity. The research in Asian American studies about the period immediately after World War II typically foregrounds the upward class mobility, cultural assimilation, suburbanization, and increasing alignment of Asian Americans with whites. It also addresses the significance of ongoing U.S. military intervention in Asia and the Pacific, particularly in Korea and Vietnam, which would lead to the Korean and Vietnam wars. It explores the events of multinational conflict between the United States and the Soviet Union played out through the proxy of Asia. In these contexts, the figure of the Asian-raced subject wavers between the proto-model minority and the enemy to the state.[31] Sexuality studies' inquiries into the postwar period guide us down a different path. It sheds light on the significance of panics about homosexuality in the context of the Red Scare. It focuses on fears about the potentially treasonable threat of racially unmarked subjects whose difference becomes all the more unsettling because of its perceived invisibility. In Asian American studies and sexuality studies, we can find common threads in the form of questions about Americanism, patriotism, and conformity. Whether the dissidence surveilled is defined primarily by race or by sexuality, the scholarship on the Cold War era reminds us of the abuses that lurk beneath the cheery veneer of postwar prosperity.

Because the secondary literature on *No-No Boy* has overlooked male same-sex desire, the novel does not immediately beg a historicization that places it at the convergence of homosexuality and political critique. On account of my close readings, however, we need a contextualization of its emergence at a time when sexual difference and leftist leanings linked tightly together. The conformist pressures of postwar America weigh heavily on Kenji and Ichiro even if Okada's critique of these patriotic consensualisms is only hinted at and never voiced. That the friendship between the two men stops short of actual sexual contact mirrors the novel's own political intervention. It is present but frustratingly lacking in an explicit articulation that would make it more recognizable as protest.

David K. Johnson corrects a common misconception that the purge of federal employees who were or were suspected of being gay or lesbian during the 1950s remained a mere addendum to the more extensive ousting of communists. The surveillance of potentially communist and queer subjects during the McCarthy era went hand in hand. Both entities were deemed national security risks. One line of reasoning posited that homosexuals, along with others "especially vulnerable to blackmail," were not inherently disloyal or seditious—only that they could potentially compromise the bulwark the nation needed to maintain against the Soviet Union because of their need for secrecy.[32] Others, such as Senator Joseph McCarthy, took a more medically deterministic stance, claiming that "homosexuality . . . was the psychological maladjustment that led people toward communism," thus conflating mental and political difference.[33] Johnson argues that it was the very extensiveness of these Cold War sweeps of the federal government that eventually led to a critical mass of gays and lesbians willing to mount organized resistance against discrimination.[34] Robert J. Corber also rethinks the periodization of the modern gay and lesbian rights movement. The tendency, Corber avers, to characterize the Stonewall riots of 1969 as the pivotal moment that initiated the shift from a politics of middle-class accommodation (germane to organizations such as the Mattachine Society and the Daughters of Bilitis) to one of revolutionary protest needs revision. Leftist thought was very pervasive among gay cultural producers in the 1950s, who worked hard to "challeng[e] the discourses and institutions that naturalized the construction of gender and sexual identity."[35] Post-Stonewall social changes became part of an ongoing timeline of protest, as both Johnson and Corber claim, that built on the previous generation's critical yoking of non-normative sexual expressions and challenges to capitalist conformity.

Although we might not readily imagine Okada commingling with the authors Corber examines in his literary criticism—Tennessee Williams, Gore Vidal, and James Baldwin—who have been institutionalized into a recognizable gay canon, Corber himself remains reluctant to ascribe an uncomplicatedly gay specificity to these authors, writing that they "tended to treat homosexuality less as a category of identity resembling other categories of identity such as race and ethnicity than as a form of oppositional consciousness. . . . [These identity-based models] hindered the formation of the broadly based coalitions that were needed to overcome the racist, sexist, and homophobic structures of postwar American society."[36] The simplistic assumptions behind movements structured around racial liberation aside, Corber provides legitimacy to my placement of Okada in these discourses. Okada does not need to be gay-identified to rub political shoulders with his contemporaries or to have his work read alongside theirs. Insofar as *No-No Boy* emphasizes a politics of coalition over a politics of identity, the novel's emphasis on a shared opposition to patriotic conformity, regardless of one's tracking into the categories of "veteran" or "draft resister," resonates with the sensibility of the texts in Corber's archive. Like the characters in Williams's, Vidal's, and Baldwin's fiction, neither Kenji nor Ichiro conforms to sanctioned postwar mandates of middle-class heteromasculinity. There may be stark differences between Kenji's and Ichiro's households, whereby the former's luxury trappings stand in contrast to the latter's material dearth. However, both men retain a queer bachelorhood in opposition to the consumerist heterosexual domesticity characterized by the postwar period. Kenji and Ichiro alike refuse wedded, biologically reproductive normativity.

Tina Takemoto's research uncovers a real-life counterpart to Okada's queer draft resister. Her case study using materials from the Gay, Lesbian, Bisexual, Transgender Historical Society provides an account of Jiro Onuma, a pre-Stonewall Japanese American figure who eschewed the cultures of heterosexuality and flourished in the homosocial spaces of young, working-class men, where he maintained same-sex lovers throughout adulthood. The lure of heterosexual respectability among Japanese Americans remained strong in the period leading up to the war because it allowed them to feel superior to other Asian ethnic groups not similarly structurally positioned. Whereas the Page Act stymied the formation of heterosexual pairings among Chinese Americans because of its ban on the entry of women, Japanese immigrant men were encouraged to bring wives or send for them later. Onuma, an immigrant, arrived in the United States from Japan in 1923. During the war, he was interned at Camp Topaz.[37] He initially answered "no" to questions 27 and 28 on the loyalty oaths but changed his answer to "yes" on number 28 four weeks later. Takemoto notes that the available evidence makes it impossible to discern what caused him to reconsider, but she speculates that Onuma wanted to remain at Topaz rather than be transferred to Tule Lake to await trial. His partner, however, was relocated this way (presumably because he answered "no" to both), and the two were separated for the remainder of the war.[38] Although the fictional characters in *No-No Boy* are not gay in the sense that Onuma and his partner (whom Takemoto, unable to track down a last name, identifies only as "Ronald") appear to be, these separate examples—one fictional, and the other historical—show an overlap pertaining to sexual dissidence in the face of Japanese American draft resistance.

CULTURAL NATIONALISM'S DESIRES

It has become commonplace in Asian American studies to state that cultural nationalism relied on a model of anti-racist agency that reproduced normative masculinity. The gendered underpinnings of the movements in the late 1960s and 1970s can be explained in part by a reaction against the feminization of Asian male immigrants in the late nineteenth and early twentieth centuries. The conformist climate of the 1950s may have given Okada the cold shoulder so that he died without being recognized for his work. However, the following generation found a belated interest in *No-No Boy*. Jeffery Paul Chan, Frank Chin, Lawson Inada, and Shawn Wong, the four cultural-nationalist writers who founded the Combined Asian American Resources Project (CARP), rediscovered the novel; they edited the first major anthology of Asian American literature, *Aiiieeeee!* (1974), which contained an excerpt from *No-No Boy*.[39] Thereafter, it gained a critical mass of readers. Eventually, CARP reissued *No-No Boy* in its entirety in 1976, during the early stages of the Japanese American redress movement, which sought reparations for the internment. This time, it received great acclaim, and it has not gone out of print since.

Okada wrote a second novel that was never published. In the afterword to *No-No Boy*, Frank Chin reports that, after Okada's death in 1971, he and his fellow CARP editor Lawson Inada visited Okada's widow, Dorothy. During the meeting, she explained what had happened to the missing manuscript. Shortly after her husband's death, she took his files to the Japanese American Research Project at the University of California, Los Angeles (UCLA), hoping they might be of use for researchers. The archivists rejected the materials, presumably due to their controversial nature. They also encouraged her to destroy them, a directive that she heeded. According to Min Hyoung Song, this tale of obliteration belongs to the recurring "trope of the lost manuscript" in Asian American literary history. These disappearances reveal the presence of "narratives by Asian Americans that were not, or could not, be written and published, the many stories one is sure were there to be told but were not."[40] Chin reacted to hearing about Dorothy Okada's destruction of her husband's second novel by fighting an urge to "kick her ass around the block" and "burn UCLA down." Implied in his declaration is that the archivists, "these champions of Japanese American history," and the compliant widow were one and the same.[41] To be sure, Chin reassured his readers that he did not, in fact, act violently. What followed instead was a heartfelt conversation with Dorothy about the elusive author, whom Chin and Inada missed meeting in person by a few months. Chin's anecdote recounts the actions of a woman dutifully following institutional authority to the detriment of an unruly male figure. It unnervingly mirrors the fictional interaction between an accommodationist Emi and a resistant Ichiro.

This parallel between Chin's true-life tale about meeting Dorothy Okada and the interaction illustrated in John Okada's fictional narrative also rests on their twinned homoerotic resonances. Kenji and Ichiro, using Emi, mount an attempted but ultimately unneeded triangulation. They bond with each other directly instead of mediating their desire through a woman. Meanwhile, Chin and Inada wish to access the deceased Okada by going through his widow, a modification of the Sedgwickian model of erotic triangulation. We can think of Dorothy Okada as the conduit through which Chin and Inada sought to achieve that closeness with the dead author. However, she is also portrayed as the obstacle to that intimacy because of her destruction of his second novel. When Inada tells his own story about the same visit, he expresses his pain about the missed connection, both textual and corporeal. The intensity of his words sounds like that of a lovelorn suitor:

> It hurt to have [Dorothy] tell us that "John would have liked you." It hurt to have her tell us that "you two were the first ones who ever came to see him about his work." . . . It hurt to have her tell us that all she had to show of his "other work" were a few technical brochures for business corporations, which is how he made his living. It hurt to have her tell us that "you really didn't miss meeting him by very long."[42]

In this loss, consummation came tantalizingly close. Inada declares the experience of reading *No-No Boy* an acceptable substitute for the author's flesh-and-blood presence. He professes, "You can feel him as you read this book, the very *heart* of the man throbbing within you, making you stand up and move to others, filled with the passion and compassion of being."[43] Inada's sexually inflected language casts him, the reader, as the receptive partner while Okada, the author, penetrates him—mirroring the positions Kenji and Ichiro took. Inada reels internally from Okada's "throbbing within," and this sensation prompts him to become similarly erect, or to "stand up," as he becomes "move[d]" to a greater plane of communion with other politicized, "passion[ate]" readers. In line with triangulated homoeroticism's codes about the prohibition on actual sexual contact, the strength of Inada's response to *No-No Boy* may be possible only insofar as the potential for real sexual intimacy with the author disappears. Unlike the bonding between Kenji and Ichiro, which is hindered and not facilitated by a woman, Inada can take sexual and erotic pleasure in Okada's absence through his widow precisely because it remains an absence.

When we read these testimonies of how CARP's editors crafted a usable past by recovering *No-No Boy*, their excessive heteromasculinity suddenly begins to look very queer. There is no suppression of male-male desire here. The queerness becomes patently obvious for anyone willing to put aside common assumptions about the gender and sexual politics of literary cultural nationalism. Critiques of the sexism underpinning cultural nationalism have been so ubiquitous that they are unremarkable. With a few exceptions, there has been a dearth of work that addresses its professed homophobia. Whereas an earlier scholar such as David L. Eng may have laid crucial foundation by exposing the disavowal of homosexuality among Chin and similar writers,[44] subsequent research has shown that this tendency comes with a corresponding same-sex libidinal attraction.

Daniel Y. Kim finds that Frank Chin's oeuvre paradoxically reveals an overwhelming preoccupation with male homoeroticism, more so than any of the authors he condemns in his polemical tracts. As Kim observes, the disdain that Chin feels over the purported pandering of certain Asian American writers to a white readership expresses itself by likening it to sexual receptivity with white men. Ironically, Chin himself possesses a sexual investment in an idealized white masculinity, seeming to want to glean his own virility through erotic congress with those who exemplify its ideals. He expresses an "interracial mimetic desire . . . 'consummated' in highly eroticized moments of intersubjective commingling that are depicted as carnal in a virtual rather than literal sense."[45] Daryl J. Maeda identifies additional moments of queer desire in Chin's work that push it in another direction. Maeda's reading of *The Chickencoop Chinaman* echoes some of Kim's observations about the role of cross-racial relationships among men, but he focuses on the significance of blackness. In a scene where the two main characters of the play discuss segregation in the South, "Chin links Asian American men to black men through their penises" when the characters recount a story about using Jim Crow restrooms with African American men.[46] Unlike Kim's reading of Chin's yearnings for white masculinity, Maeda's treatment of the erotic energy between Asian American and African American men sees the exchange as reciprocal. Although Asian American activism is commonly criticized for being only derivative of Black Power movements, Maeda's reading of the interchanges between the characters in *The Chickencoop Chinaman* shows a two-way traffic of support and influence: "Asian American men regain their masculinity by taking hold of their phalluses along with black men doing similarly."[47]

I diverge from Kim and Maeda by calling attention to the fact that Chin misses the possibility of male same-sex desire working *intraethnically* within Japanese America as dissident politics. The erotic intimacy between Kenji and Ichiro breaks down the hostility between veterans and draft resisters that stands in the way of anti-militaristic critique. To someone like Emi, Ichiro appears frustratingly stalled and regressive in his insistence not to participate in the affects of patriotic nationalism. His refusal, in Emi's words, to "do something" (95) eerily mirrors the narrative's own stasis as it, too, refuses traditional novelistic development and teleology. However, as an anally fixative subject, Ichiro embodies the precise characteristics that allow Japanese America to shape a commitment to redress and intraethnic coalition building. Far from not "do[ing] something," Ichiro possesses a powerfully unruly inertia. As Judith Halberstam avers, these failures expose the fictions on which the ideology of heterosexist capitalism stands.[48] Ichiro's anal desires and the regressive tendencies that accompany them become the basis on which alliances form among Japanese Americans that contest the militaristic avenues through which economic stability is attained.

In this sense, the cultural nationalism of the 1970s seems to anticipate Halberstam's early twenty-first-century critique. If we understand cultural nationalism as a movement or set of movements that emerged from working-class communities of color to upend the capitalist-imperialist foundations of U.S. society, then CARP's championing of a maligned novel whose revolutionary potential rests on teleological failure and the allures of male same-sex attraction is not improbable or ironic. Given the grounds on which *No-No Boy* proposes to resolve Japanese America's internal cleavages, the master narrative about the emergence of an Asian American literary vanguard in the 1970s needs to be rethought. Because the shepherding of Okada's novel was a major component of CARP's creation of a recognizable arts and culture movement, it could be said that intraethnic same-sex desire stood at the heart of Asian American organizing from the onset. Nestled between an introduction by Inada and an afterword by Chin, the novel proper carries the imprimatur of these writers who have gone on to establish a distinctive cultural nationalist bent to their work. This endorsement of a homoerotics of intraethnic healing urges a rethinking of how we have come to understand the relationship, often cast as contentious, between the racial liberatory movements of the 1970s and queer sexuality. In *No-No Boy*, it is through misguided appeals to heteropatriarchal capital that Japanese Americans attempt to raise their social profile. This valorization of gender and sexual normativity in the wake of the war's emasculating effects coalesces in Kenji's amputated leg. As heteromasculinity upholds itself as a barometer of Japanese American cultural citizenship, Ichiro's homoerotic investment in his friend's disabled body becomes the corrective for these tenuous claims to the nation.

However, my revision of Asian American cultural nationalism's heteropatriarchal origins and its championing of *No-No Boy* still leaves intact its male-specificity. The novel initiates a sexual logic that blurs the lines between male veterans and draft resisters, but there is no corresponding means for women to participate in this vision of coalition. It may be that cultural nationalism remains a strictly male domain, whether that space is queer(ed) or not. The novel implies that women cannot actualize a cohesive and legible anti-integrationist politics in the way that men do through erotic attachment with one another. In the end, it overlooks possibilities for dissent that do not align with the male-centered intimacy Kenji and Ichiro have built for themselves. We often say that Okada was writing before his time. However, as his two male leads await conditions more amenable to the alternatives they have fashioned, the women they leave behind relegate themselves to greater social invisibility.

LEARNING TO LOVE

HO CHI MINH

The novelist Monique Truong sparked her inspiration to write *The Book of Salt* (2003) when she learned that the modernist writer Gertrude Stein and her partner, Alice B. Toklas, hired cooks who were (in the parlance of their time) Indochinese while living in Paris. The protagonist of Truong's novel is a fictional composite of two Vietnamese employees refashioned from Stein's accounts in *The Autobiography of Alice B. Toklas*. Truong's protagonist, Bình, delivers his story in a first-person narration that shifts back and forth between the present in France and the past in Vietnam. Although he understands his position as a hired hand in the Stein-Toklas household and receives treatment accordingly, his labor escapes alienation. The novel is replete with mouth-watering depictions of Bình preparing French cuisine. These moments show the cook brimming with pride in his work, but an uneasy tension informs the relationship between the hypervisibility of the products of his labor and the invisibility of his subjectivity to those around him. Bình's queer desires appear so frequently that they are unremarkable to the reader, but they remain imperceptible to the other characters around him.

For a Vietnamese American novelist at the turn of the twenty-first century, how might a story line that unfolds in 1920s France appeal? When Truong was asked this question in an interview, she responded wistfully that the past allowed her to explore a world unfettered by the overdetermined ways that Vietnamese America has been cast in the long wake of the Vietnam War: "There are no military conflicts in my novel, there are no soldiers, there are no weapons. I suppose it is no coincidence that the first long-distance flight of my imagination as a writer would take me to a time when Vietnam was more or less at peace. When you are a child of wartime, peace is the all-consuming fantasy."[1] This imaginary world looms large in *The Book of Salt*. Yet I also want to read slightly against the grain of Truong's words by asserting that the novel reveals as much about the U.S. present as it does about that French past. The two unfold side by side and rely on each other for their legibility. In this way, the novel's nonlinear plot is a metacritical commentary on how it intervenes in contemporary understandings of Vietnamese America. Bình, while living in Paris, repeatedly directs his memory to the home he left in Vietnam, collapsing past and present and here and there. By extension, the text prompts its readers to do similarly in conceiving of imperialism transhistorically—across time, space, and context.

The long aftermath of the Vietnam War solidified popular understandings of colonialism in Vietnam that overshadow occupations predating the country's war with the United States. The French incursion into Indochina, spurred by imperial competition with Great Britain, was regarded by colonial officials as a benevolent, civilizing mission, in contrast to the violent, conquering sort exercised by the rival country.[2] Catholic missionaries had traveled to Southeast Asia since the seventeenth century. France's professed goals in the region were the building of churches, schools, and infrastructure and the defense of the indigenous population from Chinese and other invaders, rather than the extraction of natural resources and the appropriation of labor. This is not to say that the French refrained from forms of colonialism that are more easily recognized as capitalist, only that they justified their occupation by invoking altruism. The discourse of protectionism with which the French proceeded in these earlier times resonates with post–Vietnam War concepts undergirding the United States' relationship with the South Vietnamese. The passage of the Indochina Migration and Refugee Assistance Act (1975), which allocated funds for the evacuation and resettlement of Southeast Asians displaced by the war, emerges out of a sensibility that resembles that of past occupations. This time, the imperial rival for global domination was the Soviet Union, not Great Britain, and the brutal violence of war was impossible to overlook. The cultural logic of salvation remains, however. The casualty for South Vietnamese refugees thus saved by the United States was the legitimacy of their longing for the homeland.

This chapter examines portrayals of male same-sex pleasure in *The Book of Salt* that heal the conflict between the Vietnamese diaspora and the Vietnamese state. This reconciliation fosters diasporic connectivities and challenges the foundations on which the United States justified the Vietnam War. Unlike the intensely homoerotic yet physically unconsummated relationship in John Okada's *No-No Boy*, the sexual contact in *The Book of Salt* is actualized. Bình's encounter with a nameless Vietnamese man during an evening of cruising in Paris may be brief and fleeting, but his thoughts return to it repeatedly. The stranger is known as "the man on the bridge" before the novel's end reveals him as Nguyễn Ái Quốc, the man who eventually adopts the name Ho Chi Minh and becomes the leader of the independence movement in communist Vietnam. The novel's consummation of intraethnic desire, I argue, issues a plea to contemporary Vietnamese diasporans to resolve their internal disputes and open themselves to transnational affiliations with the lost homeland. Bình and the man on the bridge represent the South Vietnamese refugee and the Socialist Republic of Vietnam attempting reunion in the face of Vietnamese American red-baiting at the turn of the twenty-first century. These conflicts unfold amid an ongoing American exceptionalism that casts the refugee as the grateful recipient of U.S. magnanimity while the violence of historical military encroachments remains obscured. My reading of the intraethnic healing in *The Book of Salt* suggests that the embrace of transnational ties goes hand in hand with the critique of refugee gratitude.

Although the Vietnamese diaspora in the United States has become increasingly friendly to financial and cultural investment in the homeland, a spirit of anticommunism still troubles transnational connections. Like the draft debates that split Japanese America during World War II, internal disputes have divided Vietnamese Americans into those who are sympathetic to leftist politics and those who are suspicious of anything that resembles communism. These two sides remain unequal in terms of their relative cultural and material capital. Similar to how the Japanese American pro-enlistment stance was much better supported than that of the resisters, anticommunists among Vietnamese Americans are much more organized and better financed than their critics. Yet we need to refrain from overstating the extent of these divisions. Just as many Japanese American veterans expressed ambivalence about military service, many Vietnamese American anticommunists do not necessarily replicate normative, pro-American values. At the same time, because of the ostracizing of those who have chosen to step outside the community's politics of respectability, we need to take these factions seriously. *The Book of Salt* initiates dialogue across the divide.

The argument I assign to *The Book of Salt* may seem specious, given the level and type of profile it has attained. Unlike *No-No Boy*, which could never be marketed to a mainstream audience and was slow to find a readership even among Asian Americans, *The Book of Salt* has enjoyed widespread acclaim. It is one of the most commercially successful novels by a Vietnamese American writer, and Truong received a large amount of exposure following the book's publication. National Public Radio's Liane Hansen interviewed her on *Weekend Edition.* The *New York Times, Village Voice, Chicago Tribune, Los Angeles Times,* and other major media outlets positively reviewed the book. It received numerous honors, including a Bard Fiction Prize, a PEN Oakland/ Josephine Miles Literary Award, and a Stonewall Book Award. This debut novel paved the way for a positive reception of Truong's second book, *Bitter in the Mouth* (2010).

The commercial success of *The Book of Salt* revisits old questions that circulated among writers and scholars in Asian American literary studies when the field was still in its infancy. Wary of fiction capable of reaching a mainstream audience, some authors and critics expressed reservation about texts by well-received names such as Maxine Hong Kingston, Amy Tan, and David Henry Hwang. Their concerns about market-driven multiculturalism raised persistent questions. Does the author who garners popular acclaim necessarily pander to white Americans? Does she or he replicate troubling ideas about racial difference? Is social justice or political critique elided to make that work palatable? Although one might expect these questions to have faded with the doctrinaire forms of racial liberation that engendered them (i.e., cultural nationalism), they persist, even if they have become more nuanced.[3]

The Book of Salt does not uncomplicatedly bow to commercial taste cultures in ways that might raise concern about its politics. The novel actually speaks to two potential audiences: first, consumers of products and services, such as travel and cuisine, associated with Anglo-American leisure and, second, a fractured Vietnamese American community negotiating its relationship with the homeland. Although the former may be more obvious because of the novel's circulation and reception, the latter is revealed with a closer look at the cultural backdrop that informs the Vietnamese presence in North America. There are two stories in *The Book of Salt*, each targeted at these respective audiences. One story is normatively alluring (but, as I show, still disquieting), and the other is stridently polemical. Furthermore, the overwhelming visibility of the former at the expense of the latter is performative. The novel mirrors the protagonist's actions, thoughts, and affects as he carefully negotiates the terms of his presence and invisibility in a society that will not recognize his rebellion.

The first part of this chapter performs a reading of Truong's novel that establishes the protagonist as the metaphoric incarnation of the South Vietnamese refugee. I propose that we read the novel allegorically, as a coded narrative that conveys a critique that cannot yet be directly expressed about the demands of U.S. culture and society on the Vietnamese diaspora. From there, I explain how this interpretation of the novel turns the instance of intraethnic queer sex into a call for bonding between diasporans and the Vietnamese state. These subversive readings contest two predominant ideas:

first, that refugees will enter into a relationship with the U.S. nation-state in ways that demand a display of gratitude and, second, that conflicts among Vietnamese Americans about anticommunism are either a failure of assimilation on the part of the unruly or evidence of lingering war trauma on the part of the compliant. As I note in Chapter 1, conceiving of intraethnic divisions in simplistic dichotomies deflects attention from the forces of war that subjugate racialized populations collectively, regardless of any political claims that may be voiced individually. Finally, I place *The Book of Salt* within the temporal milieu of its publication in the post-9/11 time period with a close reading of a passage that provides a meta-discursive exposition of how the novel delivers resistant messages in ways that penetrate normative taste cultures.

WHERE IS THE VIETNAM WAR IN THE 1920S?

According to Isabelle Thuy Pelaud, the Vietnamese American literary canon quickly and strategically emerged in response to demands for representation that accompanied the arrival of refugees from the U.S. war in Vietnam. Produced under the pressure of expediting a collective voice, these texts foreground the experience of military conflict, displacement, loss, poverty, and racism. The transparency of these ethnographically inflected narratives existed in "dialectical relationship" with an American reading public that was still coming to terms with its national wounds following military defeat.[4] Some recent Vietnamese American writers have expressed concern about the expectation that they will continue to conform to realist verisimilitude or that they need to portray the war at all, stating that to do so would restrict artistic choices and reproduce negative perceptions of refugees. However, Pelaud maintains that the wish to transcend the war *is* limiting because the war's effects remain present. The insistence to move on is just as binding as the expectation to keep writing about it. Moreover, it risks depoliticizing this work.[5]

Because of the recurring themes that have defined past Vietnamese American literary production, *The Book of Salt* seems to be an aberration. The story unfolds in what is, for this body of work, a temporally and spatially unusual location. The plot departs from topics that have preoccupied earlier writers. In my reading of Truong's novel, I probe at the beginnings of resistance that are buried in this vision of Paris in the 1920s, despite Truong's observation that this was "more or less" a time of peace. I link this moment to the Vietnam War's long aftermath contained within it in coded ways. In the story line, the war is not slowly brewing only to erupt several decades later. It has already happened, and its effects linger with us.

The events in *The Book of Salt* take place before the Vietnam War, but its presence emerges in the connection between the protagonist's exile and the pleasures that he, a working-class diasporic subject, finds with men he meets while cruising for sex in public. Bình's moments of unsanctioned, non-heteronormative leisure occur under the radar of what those who are more advantageously located can perceive. Like South Vietnamese migrants in the United States, he must delicately manage his need for pleasure with demands to conform to popular conceptions of the despondent refugee. The fact of male homosexuality is regarded as rebellious—even if, to Bình, it is quotidian—in the novel, and the fact of an ungrateful refugee is just as queerly unsettling. These two entities sit alongside each other and mutually constitute their possibility. The refugee, portrayed in the U.S. collective imagination as a passive object in need of rescue, becomes the repository for a host of affirmations the United States has generated to rationalize its place in the world. *The Book of Salt* intercedes therein by invoking same-sex desire.

The different instances of homosexuality—gendered, racialized, and classed—in *The Book of Salt* reveal hierarchies within its scope and its varying propensities for critique or accommodation. Meg Wesling reveals the vast racial, material, and respectability discrepancies between Stein and Toklas, on the one hand, and Bình, on the other hand. A chasm divides Stein and Toklas's white, partnered, domestic, class-privileged lesbianism and Bình's economic and sexual transience. Furthermore, Stein and Toklas's comfortable standing is made possible only through the labor of colonial subjects such as Bình, signaling "the continued racialization of categories of 'free' and 'unfree' as the basis for bourgeois European understandings of public and private, the market and the domestic."[6] The novel opens with Bình arriving at Stein and Toklas's apartment to begin work. After being ejected from his home by his father for maintaining a sexual relationship with the male head chef at a colonial official's house, Bình traveled all over the world—further honing his culinary skills in the kitchen of a freighter—before arriving in France and into the employ of Stein and Toklas. The narration makes it clear that the homophobia that precipitated his migration did not originate from indigenous peasant superstition, barbarism, or premodern ignorance in Vietnam from which its victims need to be saved. It is a direct consequence of French imperialism. Truong points her finger at the transport of French Catholicism to the Vietnamese colony when she identifies the reason for Bình's exile. This imperially installed religious practice mirrors the United States' intervention much later that similarly created intraethnic discord.

The cultural violence of French Catholicism and the physical violence that issues from Bình's father have a causal relationship. In the first of many internal monologues that posit the father as the addressee, Bình states:

"Sometimes, I cannot give enough thanks to your Catholic god that you, my dear and violent father, are now merely cobbled together from my unwavering sense of guilt and my telescopic memories of brutalities lived long ago." He references punishments such as "a slap in my face and a punch in my stomach" to which he was subjected while living in his father's household.[7] Bình's father is a stock figure in postcolonial novels, the elite colonial subject recruited to perform the direct work of subjugation. In line with that archetype, he becomes more immediately oppressive than the Europeans because of his awareness of his subalternity. He plays a key role in the church by finding new converts, who tend to be locals in distress, and therefore vulnerable. He wields his patriarchal authority over his wife and children with an iron fist, but the novel's characterization of his cruelty always lays the blame on French Catholicism.

Upon acclimating to Paris, Bình sees that the church functions in tandem with the nation-state as a regulatory system that demands his docility. In place of his father's brute force, the control in France relies on subtler means:

> Most Parisians can ignore and even forgive me for not having the refinement to be born amidst the ringing bells of their cathedrals, especially since I was born instead amidst the ringing bells of the replicas of their cathedrals, erected in a far-off colony. . . . As long as [they] can account for my whereabouts in their city or in one of their colonies, then they can trust that the République and the Catholic church have had their watchful eyes on me. (17)

These architectural reproductions of religious authority in Vietnam do not skew themselves to destabilize colonial power in the manner of imitation described by Homi K. Bhabha.[8] The notion of the colonial subject mimicking imperfectly the language of imperial rule locates subversion in the distance between the original and the copy. In this case, however, replicas (as opposed to mimics) miss the mark not strategically but feebly. The lack of "refinement" of this failure renders Bình safe and unthreatening to white Parisians and expatriates, who would otherwise worry about the sexual safety of their daughters: "I have no interest in your little girls. Your boys . . . well, that is their choice" (17). Yet even if the Vietnamese cathedrals' shortcomings do not signal a playful disavowal of colonial authority, Bình's own movements while in France tell a different story. Perceived as an incompletely actualized subject of (rather than menace to) French rule, Bình remains neutralized. An unsuccessful replica of a Frenchman, he needs no policing because it is assumed that he self-polices compensatorily. Like the invisible, unobtrusive labor he provides for Stein and Toklas, his desire and behavior go unnoticed as he turns the streets of Paris into his cruising ground.

WAR, EXILE, AND REFUGEE GRATITUDE

A casual reader might be tempted to regard Bình's arrival in Paris, with its presumably more sexually permissive culture, as a liberating event. However, we need to parse the reasoning whereby a displaced person seeks refuge in the metropolitan center of colonial power that instigated his expulsion. This logic naturalizes the conditions under which South Vietnamese asylum seekers entered the United States following the Vietnam War. During the Paris Peace Conference of 1919, the nationalist independence leader Nguyễn Ái Quốc (later known as Ho Chi Minh) appealed unsuccessfully to Woodrow Wilson to intervene in France's occupation of Indochina. However, Vietnam did not register as significant enough to factor into consideration in Wilson's vision of self-determination for all nations. The United States' passive collusion with France in Wilson's inattention eventually gave way to more active involvement in the form of arms and other aid. Vietnam successfully fought France for its independence, and in 1954, the country was divided into a communist North and a democratic South. In the midst of the Cold War, the United States feared the encroachment of the North, supported by the Soviet Union and China, and escalated its presence in South Vietnam as part of a larger communist containment strategy.

Like the Korean War, the Vietnam War was fought between the United States and the Soviet Union, along with allies of both nations, on a foreign battlefield, using the militarized labor of the local population. The colonial appropriation of the bodies and resources of South Vietnam went largely unchallenged by Americans during its early years, when fears about communism were ubiquitous. As the military conflict wore on, it became increasingly unfavorable with the American public, which had wearied of a long, protracted occupation in which its young citizens risked lives for an enterprise that had been exposed for its ethical lapses. The war was so unpopular that by 1974, Gerald Ford had withdrawn many of his troops and aid. The mass withdrawal of U.S. support in South Vietnam all but guaranteed North Vietnamese victory. In the days leading up to and following the fall of Saigon to North Vietnam, the South Vietnamese began to flee the country.

The expulsion of South Vietnamese and other ethnic groups affected by the wars in Southeast Asia and the fictional expulsion Bình experiences in *The Book of Salt* both result from colonialism. The erasure of this externally generated intraracial violence in Southeast Asia forms the basis on which the logic of refugee gratitude coalesces. Yen Le Espiritu impresses on us the need for a "critical refugee study" to counter these normative forms of knowledge production about Vietnamese Americans.[9] These racialized U.S. allies, seen as forlorn and desperate, are not recognized as escapees from a genocidal environment created by multinational war. They are imagined as the recipients of an enlightened U.S. altruism that redeems them from the barbarisms wracking a global South. Incorporating war refugees into the U.S. body politic creates what Mimi Thi Nguyen calls the gift of freedom—that is, "a world-shaping concept describing struggles aimed at freeing peoples from unenlightened forms of social organization through fields of power and violence."[10] However, the act of giving within these imperial structures turns the gift into an imposition of debt. This paradoxically generates its own encumbrance because "the obligation to remember and return the value of the gift means that freedom is imperfect, and alarmingly so."[11] Nguyen suggests that the largely conservative leanings of Vietnamese Americans may not necessarily stem from a failure to disburden themselves of pre-migration intraethnic conflicts or post-migration trauma. Instead, she claims that refugees' brandishing of conservative politics is the performance of a script that responds to a nation-state demanding their compliance, conformity, and thankfulness as payment for a debt that cannot be repaid.[12]

Migrants handed these expectations would understandably take measures to make a livable set of conditions for themselves. In a deft examination of Vietnamese diasporic popular cultures, Nhi T. Lieu shows that images evoking glamor and high society disrupt and intervene in hegemonic conceptions of refugees as despairing, poverty-stricken subjects. The display of consumerism in popular-culture productions such as music videos, variety shows, and beauty pageant contests is an attempt to contest the heavily sedimented signs that would "pathologize [Vietnamese Americans'] experiences in American society" and yoke them to a discourse of loss.[13] Nguyen and Lieu, respectively, show that placating the nation-state by acting out refugee gratitude and securing pleasure on one's terms are not mutually exclusive. They often coexist as these subjects delicately manage their enjoyment to conform to the social expectations of war-traumatized victims rescued by the United States.

CLINICAL REHABILITATION IN THE METROPOLE AND COLONY

If Bình, the figurative South Vietnamese refugee, becomes disruptingly queer because of his pursuit of pleasure without the gratitude expected of colonial subjects, how does his behavior register within the coded polemic

contained in Truong's novel? The difference between Bình's sexual non-
normativity and Stein and Toklas's privileged lesbianism may be a false one,
given what Ann Laura Stoler contends about a formative intellectual history
of sex. (Yet I do not want to jettison the distinction entirely.) Stoler notes a
curious absence in Michel Foucault's widely read account, *The History of
Sexuality*, which traces the emergence of the European middle class in the
eighteenth and nineteenth centuries through the state's active managing
of the sexual behavior of its citizens. The rapid proliferation of knowledge
about sex during this time went hand in hand with the consolidation of the
European bourgeoisie. In this context, Foucault states, "Sex was not something one simply judged. It was something one administered."[14] Stoler points
out that Foucault's genealogy of bourgeois modernity, signaled by the rise
of the European welfare state, coincides with a general history of European
imperial expansion. The rational, white European subject may have been
constructed through its conceptual opposite, the so-called primitive or savage, but the "sexual discourse of empire and of the biopolitic state in Europe
were mutually constitutive: their 'targets' were broadly imperial."[15] However, even though sexual governance in the colony and the metropole may
have been connected, "deeply sedimented discourses on sexual morality . . .
re[drew] the 'interior frontiers' of national communities, frontiers that were
secured through . . . the boundaries of race."[16] In sum, Stoler calls attention
to the close, yet paradoxical, link between incorporation and exclusion in the
colonial/nation-building project of sexual health, which Foucault overlooks.

Stoler's analysis alternatingly illuminates and clouds a scene in *The Book
of Salt* that illustrates the frictive logic of refugee gratitude whereby the very
source of imperial power is meant to palliate its consequences. In a flashback
set in Vietnam, the colonial official's French-educated Vietnamese chauffeur confronts Bình about his relationship with the head chef. He begins by
referencing his knowledge about recent clinical trends:

> "When I was in medical school, I heard about treatments for your
> condition."
> "Condition?"
> "Yes, your condition. There are doctors. . . . [T]here's been extensive re-
> search done in England and in America. . . . I can help you." (127)

In the doctor-chauffeur's reference to homosexuality's recent medicalization,
Truong casts Bình's impending absorption into the spatial origin of colonial
control as a dizzying, yet not fully realized, triad of punishment, correction,
and salvation. Whereas the Catholic dogmatism of Bình's father comes with
physical violence, the subtle regulating forces of European medicine gently

seep into the colony. At the same time, the doctor-chauffeur's offer of treatment gives way to accounts of a recreational culture that feeds the "condition" it is meant to cure. He "prided himself on being cosmopolitan, a man
of the world via Saigon and Paris. So he began telling me about all the cafés
and dance halls in Paris that are filled, he said, with men like me. . . . He
had . . . read about them in the writings of those doctors who were trying to
find a cure" (128). At this intersection of multiple possibilities, ranging from
clinicalization to indulgence, Bình dismisses one while pondering the en-
ticements of the other. To the chauffeur's recommendation that "garlic, gin-
ger, and other 'hot' spices" be avoided, Bình opines, "What a quack!" (128).
His rejection of his pathologization comes about by favorably appraising the
aromatics that, not coincidentally, are most readily associated with Asian
cooking. Kyla Wazana Tompkins shows that spices were identified by Anglo-
American dietary reformers during the nineteenth century as responsible
for sexual ills because of their association with foreign, racialized bodies.[17]

Bình's premigration defiance also reveals a not-yet-understood dislocation between the elite colonial subject's educational credentials and his position in the economic hierarchy:

> "Never mind my condition. What is wrong with you?" I demand-
> ed to know. . . .
> "What do you mean 'wrong' with me?" the chauffeur asked.
> "Well, there must be something. Otherwise, why would a doctor
> make his living as a chauffeur?" (127)

After his graduation from a French medical school, the doctor-chauffeur
found that opportunities available to French citizens with similar credentials
(acquired through the state's biopolitical disbursements) remained off-limits
to him.[18] Instead of putting his training into practice as intended when he
returned to Vietnam, he was appointed by colonial officials as a veterinar-
ian. This placement echoes the inability of Bình's older brother to secure a
promotion to head chef, a position eventually filled by the Frenchman who
becomes Bình's lover. The racialized tension between inclusion and exclusion, made visible in the administrative center of colonial governance, calls
attention to the contradictions of the life-giving state in imperial Europe.

Correspondingly, Bình never becomes threatened, so to speak, with the
clinical treatment designed with bourgeois French citizens in mind; nor does
he visit any of the "cafés and dance halls" (128) learned of in this interchange,
which are also meant for whites. On some level, he understands that these
procedures and places do not have him in mind. He cruises on the street,
avoiding institutionalized leisure, and his homosexuality remains beyond

the medical and cultural epistemological fray. It might seem that, following Foucault, the supposed prohibition against sex that Bình faces in the colony might be a productive one in that it attempts to write him into European biopower's plan for creating healthy citizens. In actuality, Bình's indulgence cannot be corrected, as Stoler would contend were she to read *The Book of Salt*, due to race-based assumptions about the intended recipients of the state's coercive care. In this sense, Truong suggests that the very illegibility of Bình's pleasures within scientific medicine protects them from regulation. Biopower, like any other form of control in modernity, is not totalizing.

Therefore, Bình—symbolizing the South Vietnamese refugee negotiating pleasure under the indebtedness and resignification that Mimi Nguyen and Nhi Lieu lay out—also escapes regulation per Stoler by refusing France's pull of sexual incorporation. What, then, does it mean that he meets and enjoys an evening of sex with a stranger the reader later learns is Ho Chi Minh in-becoming? This question bears contemplation (and I address it in detail shortly) because this encounter is so highly treasured even though it takes place over a shorter time span than the relationships Bình maintains with less favored lovers: one a Frenchman living in Vietnam and the other a biracial African American man passing for white in Paris.

Blériot, the head chef at the colonial official's house in Vietnam, happily congressed with Bình in private, but his flaunting of whiteness in public establishes boundaries between himself and the racialized colonial subjects under his supervision. When he shops at the marketplace, Bình accompanies him, along with three street children hired to help carry the provisions. "He walked three steps ahead, keeping enough distance between us to say, We are not one. Yet he was still close enough to relay his exclusive control over the four Indochinese who followed him" (122). Bình would ordinarily be regarded as securely working class because of his skilled labor, but his proximity to the homeless children at this moment collapses this economic distinction under the colonial gaze. Their collective constitution as racialized natives laboring under the white head chef renders Bình and the children one and the same. Yet this colonial ordering of racialized bodies also places Blériot at the bottom of a hierarchized whiteness for being what Stoler calls a "recalcitrant and ambiguous participant . . . in imperial culture."[19] French citizen-nationals in the metropole had a low opinion of the subaltern whites dispatched to the colonies. They, too, numbered among the bodies that colonial power sought to manage. Following Stoler, it could be said that Blériot's sexual transgressions are indicative of his placement in Vietnam.

That Bình's and Blériot's flirtations are obvious to the homeless children, who "recognized [them] . . . and . . . laughed . . . as if we had embraced in front of them and kissed each other with our mouths open" (123), while racialized queerness remains invisible to Stein and Toklas reverses predominant notions of epistemological access in the colonial relationship. As Edward W. Said claims, the Orient remains completely knowable to the West. More so than "military or economic power . . . [t]o have such knowledge of such a thing is to dominate it, to have authority over it."[20] However, rather than achieve greater transparency under the colonial gaze, the natives in *The Book of Salt* see and comprehend in the other direction, upstream against the current of power. They effortlessly understand white subjects. Reading Truong's novel as a reflection of the contemporary moment, one dominated by an accommodationist queer politics of inclusion and state protection, David L. Eng foregrounds the incongruity of Bình's sexual libertinism with his environment. "Queer Asian migrants remain subjects in waiting," unable to mobilize the structural resources that ensure the comfortable life exemplified by Stein and Toklas.[21] Similarly, they cannot harness the cultural resources that would make them knowable to Eurocentric master narratives of teleological history, because they are immobilized by the dynamic that Said describes.[22] As a not quite queer subject who exists in a perpetual state of arriving, Bình finds himself both conspicuously visible as a racialized body and conveniently disappeared as a pleasure-seeking or rebellious agent. His scripting into the role of the imperfectly assimilated and therefore perpetually self-policing colonial subject makes it so.

Bình's positionality as, in Eng's formulation, the colonial subject stuck in time and unable to enter the space of sexual freedom emblematic of modernity allows a crucial violation on Stein to occur. Stein and Toklas do not perceive the substance of Bình's relationship with Lattimore, an American expatriate in Paris, and they assume Lattimore hires Bình to cook for him on his day off—hence, his absence from their apartment on Sundays. They remain so oblivious that Lattimore's theft of Stein's manuscript, using Bình as his tool, could never be anticipated or suspected. Similar to how Blériot's haughty inability to see actual Vietnamese people in the marketplace makes him an unsuspecting target for pickpockets, Stein's failure to recognize the sexual dimensions of Bình and Lattimore's connection, a function of her privileged location, obscures this relationship's potential to violate her.

The characterization of Lattimore in *The Book of Salt* is already queered by an intertextual allusion to the unnamed protagonist of James Weldon Johnson's *The Autobiography of an Ex-Colored Man*. Like Lattimore, the protagonist of Johnson's novel subsists on a trust fund established by his biological father in exchange for silence about his paternity. A white male companion extends this economic exchange in adulthood by hiring him as a live-in musician during his sojourn in Europe. Siobhan Somerville's reading of Johnson's novel historicizes its emergence as a cultural artifact arriving on the heels of the medicalization of homosexuality. The clinical invention of the homosexual and anxieties about the slippery racial boundary between black and white arrived simultaneously. Hence, "questions of race—in particular the formations of 'whiteness' and 'blackness'—must be understood as a crucial part of the history and representation of sexual formations."[23] These characters' experiences in both U.S. and European societies are informed as much by sexual as by racial ambiguity.

In his dealings with his companion, Johnson's protagonist may be, according to Somerville, a "naive participant in his own economic exploitation," as well as "skillful at securing his power through its very erasure."[24] However, his counterpart in Truong's novel reverses this economic relationship in his interactions with Bình. *The Book of Salt* contains numerous scenes of Bình working in Stein and Toklas's kitchen. However, no depiction of him cooking for Lattimore exists, even though this presumably is what he has been hired to do. Instead, we get sex scenes. Once Lattimore receives Stein's stolen manuscript, he disappears. Bình remains with half of the bill for a portrait Lattimore insisted they have taken—an instance that led him to believe it was a gift—which stiffs the payments he received for his labor, be it sexual or culinary. The two characters whose whiteness is troubled by settlement in the colonies (in Blériot's case) or by hypodescent (in Lattimore's case) claim it ever more fiercely because of its imperfection. Bình's encounters with damaged whitenesses set these two figures up as foils for the celebrated intraracial sex with the man on the bridge.[25]

ANTICOMMUNISM
IN VIETNAMESE AMERICA

Before addressing the significance of the pairing between Bình and Ho Chi Minh in-becoming, I need to lay out the cultural terrain that informs Vietnamese American anticommunism. We should be careful not to ascribe the aversion to communism and political positions that resemble it to a simplistic and reactionary stance in the wake of war trauma. Also, the fact that Vietnamese American anticommunism seems to be at odds with the leftist political movements engendered by the Vietnam War begs explication. Asian America consolidated itself during the late 1960s and early 1970s when activists of Asian descent organized across ethnic and racial lines to contest racial and economic inequality in the United States and imperialism abroad. These movements attempted to reverse post–World War II assimilationist trends that had started to align people of Asian descent structurally with whites. These were divide-and-conquer strategies that more firmly entrenched inequality for non-Asian people of color. For many activists during this time, Asian American or otherwise, professing allegiance to North Vietnam's leader, Ho Chi Minh, became conceptual shorthand for resisting the actions of the U.S. government, domestic and international.

Asian Americans who rejected the mechanisms that distanced them from African Americans and Latinxs pointed to the presence of Southeast Asian populations, which included not only Vietnamese but also Hmong, Mien, Laotian, and Cambodian Americans, to challenge claims that people of Asian descent uniformly thrived economically. Activists reminded the public of these largely poor and working-class refugee groups to dispel the model minority myth. The irony was that many Vietnamese Americans repudiated leftist politics in line with this critique. Viet Thanh Nguyen exposes this contradiction further by calling attention to the atrocities performed by South Vietnamese soldiers at the behest of the United States. Two of the most widely circulated photographs of the Vietnam War era—one showing the execution of a suspected North Vietnamese spy by a South Vietnamese general and the other depicting civilians, many of them badly burned, fleeing a South Vietnamese napalm attack—remind us that many of these U.S. allies were "not only victims but also victimizers," according to the politics embraced by the Asian American movement.[26] Downplaying the violence committed by South Vietnamese soldiers paints an incomplete picture of the Vietnam War. More insidiously, as Nguyen argues, the well-intentioned exhortations from the U.S. left that excuse acts by the South Vietnamese because of their domination by the United States deny them full status as ethics-bearing subjects, "keep[ing] the minority and the other in their places, the role to suffer and then to be saved by the powerful majority."[27]

The presence of anticommunist sentiment in the Vietnamese diaspora stems directly from the military actions of the United States during the Vietnam War. However, we also need to remember that those who embrace anticommunism do so agentially, with a complex range of motivations. A volatile divide remains in Vietnamese America between those who repudiate communism and those who ascribe to leftist politics. The former position tends to be associated with an older, migrant generation and the latter, with younger members born in the United States or who were very young when they arrived. Anticommunists are also more visible and socially acceptable within Vietnamese American circles than political leftists. To a certain extent, this divide can be explained because of the older generation's persecution by communist Vietnam, but this risks simplifying the bifurcation. Although the suffering from exilic displacement is real and the horrors of reeducation camps cannot be discounted, the scholarship shows that we cannot relegate causes of anticommunism solely to unresolved loss leveled by North Vietnam and, later, the Socialist Republic of Vietnam.

In her work on the binds of nonmaterial debt, Mimi Nguyen claims that Vietnamese Americans' professed conservatism is the performance of a role into which they have been coercively cast. Other scholars find that the fostering of anticommunism serves purposes that go beyond appeasing hegemonic concepts of the grateful refugee. In fact, much of the work in Vietnamese American studies indicates that beliefs about the function of the state in society actually take a back seat in discussions about communism. Thuy Vo Dang's research shows that displays of anticommunism became a vehicle for Vietnamese Americans to correct the misinformation and erasures that inform U.S. histories of South Vietnam. Anticommunism can also be a source of community pride and a means through which Vietnamese Americans mourn their losses in the face of exile. Intergenerational transmissions of memory take place through these sentiments. Over the course of her research, Dang found that many informants can distinguish between opposition to communist ideology more generally and critique of specific practices by the current Vietnamese state.[28]

Beyond the community-building potential of anticommunism, some instances of red-baiting may simply be opportunistic. According to Kieu-Linh Caroline Valverde, accusing someone of being a communist can offer recent migrants who have lost their position in the homeland a way to gain the respect of their co-ethnics in the United States. Red-baiting arises among business owners who attempt to stain the competition. It is also often used to shore up expressions of sexism.[29] Lan Duong and Isabelle Thuy Pelaud show that anticommunism tends to rear its head during moments of hostility directed at women. In 2009, they curated an exhibition of Vietnamese American art in Santa Ana, California, that closed early because of pushback from anticommunists. Red-baiting accompanied the sexism directed at the female curators.[30]

Although the differential prevalence of anticommunism in Vietnamese America is perceived to be generational, this explanation needs some nuance. In her ethnographic work, Karin Aguilar–San Juan finds that inadequate cross-generational consultation with elders when young community leaders make decisions and speak on behalf of Vietnamese Americans may be more of a sticking point than actual differences in political beliefs. In the context of conflicts between an older generation with limited English proficiency and a younger generation that communicates more easily with the non-Vietnamese world, anticommunism becomes the vehicle through which displeasure about representation and process is voiced.[31]

One report suggests that intraethnic divides created by anticommunism may actually be overblown. In 1999, an angry crowd besieged a video store in California's Orange County to protest the owner's display of a picture of Ho

Chi Minh and the flag of the Socialist Republic of Vietnam. Thousands of protesters gathered to denounce the store's owner, and four hundred police officers outfitted with riot gear were dispatched to control the crowd. The Hi-Tek Incident, named in reference to the store, lasted several weeks. What often goes unmentioned is that the owner actively elicited a response; he had had the image and flag up for some time without any effect.[32] Even though Vietnamese Americans are generally understood to be living under heightened vigilance associated with earlier forms of the Red Scare, provocative gestures such as these sometimes require prompting before they receive any reaction.

BRIDGE BUILDING

How might divisions within Vietnamese America, even as nuanced as they are, be bridged? Whether consciously provoked or not, the internal cleavages wrought by anticommunism remain stressful for Vietnamese Americans. Anticommunism generates distrust and stifles dialogue on many topics, despite the enabling forms it sometimes takes. These conflicts are an ongoing concern as Vietnamese Americans fear the possibility of being accused of or exposed for sympathizing with the Vietnamese state by their co-ethnics. In the wake of national and international changes that have enabled U.S. nationals to travel to Vietnam in recent decades, these fears hamper transnational contact between the state and the diaspora. In 1986, the Socialist Republic of Vietnam enacted a series of market reforms known as Doi Moi, which facilitated the transmission of capital and culture in and out of the country. These policies shepherded an increased openness to financial investment and cultural innovation from foreigners in an attempt to reverse postwar economic downturns. Lan P. Duong points to 1986 as the moment when the Vietnamese government began to compromise between a professed desire for sovereignty and its need to join the global economy.[33] Doi Moi, combined with the United States' lifting of its embargo in 1994 and the normalization of U.S.-Vietnam relations in 1995, attracted venture capital from affluent Vietnamese Americans, lured Vietnamese American entertainers to the homeland, and allowed the export of Vietnamese cultural productions to the diaspora.[34]

The Book of Salt, published only four years after the Hi-Tek Incident and in the midst of strengthening ties between Vietnamese Americans and the Socialist Republic of Vietnam, seems neither an overt attempt to provoke nor an apologia for the capitalist motivations behind U.S. nationals' homeland investments. Instead, it appears to be a call for anticommunism to dissipate in order to recognize Vietnamese Americans' complex and growing diasporic connectivities. A key scene invokes sex between men to make that case.

One evening, Bình encounters another Vietnamese man while strolling on a bridge over the Seine. This event takes place three years before the narrative present. The idealized sexual encounter between Bình and the man, whom he never refers to by name, provides a moment of comfort when contrasted with the unsatisfying, even exploitative, relationships that occur throughout the narrative. This intraethnic relation is portrayed as healthy, satisfying, and egalitarian—unlike Bình's interactions with Blériot and Lattimore.

Throughout the narrative, Bình refers to the lover he meets over the Seine as "the man on the bridge," marking the location where they encounter each other while absorbed in reflection. Bình begins the conversation:

> "Well, friend, are you lost or are you thinking? In my experience, when a person stands on a bridge, it usually means one or the other.
> "'Am I lost or am I thinking?' That, friend, is a question worthy of a philosopher," the man on the bridge replied. "I believe the answer is . . . I am thinking about being lost."
> "An answer also worthy of a philosopher," I said. (87)

Bình's pick-up line and the man's deft engagement with it lead to conversation about their migrant histories, and they are delighted to learn they have similar stories about their arrival in France. The man had also worked on a freighter. The two depart the bridge together to dine at a restaurant and later retire to a secluded spot in a park. Throughout the remainder of the narrative, Bình reminisces about this encounter fondly.

The man on the bridge reenters the story, but only in the form of a visual image. Toward the end of the novel, Bình visits the photography studio to settle the half-paid bill for the portrait Lattimore wanted. To his astonishment, he sees a picture of the much cherished man there. He learns from the photographer that the man had worked as his assistant and that his name is Nguyễn Ái Quốc, what Ho Chi Minh was called while advocating for Vietnamese independence during his stay in France. Once the narrative reveals this, the earlier dialogue gains a new significance. Given that Bình possesses the characteristics of a South Vietnamese refugee in the wake of resettlement, we see that *The Book of Salt* could be a coded polemic proposing intraethnic reconciliation in the service of a Vietnamese transnation:

> "I have always liked bridges," [the man] suddenly resumed. . . . "And you, friend, how about you?"
> This time silence on my part told him that, even in this setting, that was an odd thing to say.
> "Bridges belong to no one," he continued on anyway. "A bridge

belongs to no one because a bridge has to belong to two parties, one on either side. There has to be an agreement, a mutual consent, otherwise it's a useless piece of wood, a wasted expanse of cement. Every bridge is, in this way," he explained, "a monument to an accord." (92)

Bình initiated contact, but as the conversation becomes increasingly familiar, the man shifts their flirtation to a discussion about "agreement," "mutual consent," and "accord." The dialogue about the bridge turns its materiality into an ethics of intraethnic healing. Before any erotic coupling occurs, trust and good faith is established. In this neutral zone, belonging alternatingly to "no one" and the "two parties," Bình and the man find a common purpose. Their sexual encounter, portrayed very differently from those that traverse racial boundaries, proposes reunion between the South Vietnamese refugee and the Vietnamese state. By extension, it calls for reconciliation among Vietnamese Americans who remain divided on the hot-button issue of communism.[35]

I stop short of valorizing this figuration of the bridge because conflict resolution is never simple. Often, the will to heal entails the suppression of history or the overlooking of difference. We cannot view bridge metaphors in the context of coalitional politics without thinking of the iconic anthology *This Bridge Called My Back*, edited by Cherríe Moraga and Gloria Anzaldúa. In the front matter, the editors and other contributors provide a multifaceted account of the possibilities and drawbacks of bridge building for women of color. Moraga stands clear on the need to organize across identity categories. She asserts that, if "we are interested in building a movement that will not constantly be subverted by internal differences, then we must build from the insideout, not the other way around."[36] Donna Kate Rushin finds that demands for bridging, when not accompanied by active engagement from those issuing them, can be another way to maintain power. Expressing her concerns in verse, she writes: "I've had enough / I'm sick of seeing and touching / Both sides of things / Sick of being the damn bridge for everybody."[37] Rather than the "monument to an accord" (92) that Bình's lover claims, the speaker in Rushin's poem enacts a chremamorphism, turning herself into a reluctant bridge, to speak her frustration about translating across race, gender, generation, or politics. "I'm sick of filling in your gaps," she says. "I must be the bridge to nowhere / But my true self."[38]

Given bridge building's difficulties, it may be useful to further probe the sexual congress between Bình and the anonymous man.[39] Unlike the homoeroticism in *No-No Boy*, never consummated but accompanied by overtly sexual language, the sex in *The Book of Salt* occurs, but its depiction remains so demure that it materializes only as a gap on the page. The reader does not gain access to the action beyond Bình's intimation after dinner, "There is a quiet place that I know in the Jardin du Luxembourg," to which the response is the man's smile before a section break occurs. The other side of that double space between paragraphs simply shows the two men parting:

> "I will walk you to the train station."
> No, he shook his head. "Train stations are terrible places for good-byes."
> I returned to the bridge alone.
> I always do. (100)

The lack of actual sex in the prose, or having the sex occur only in the break on the page, becomes the absence that signifies. Although none of the sex portrayed in *The Book of Salt* ever gets explicitly depicted, a complete and conspicuous lack of representation informs the most satisfying encounter. Truong's evasion of the physical intimacy in this scene resembles that in another piece of fiction from another literary tradition. Tennessee Williams's short story "Hard Candy" also uses a blank space between paragraphs to portray queer sex. Williams's non-depiction of what occurs in a movie theater when Mr. Kuppers, an elderly man, initiates an economic transaction with a male youth in return for sexual favors can be interpreted as evidence of the closet's overwhelming forces. The effect is further compounded by the fact that there is no direct acknowledgment of Mr. Kuppers's queerness anywhere. However, Robert J. Corber's take on Williams's refusal to portray sex in "Hard Candy" paradoxically recovers its protagonist from the realm of shameful secrecy. The circumvention, Corber claims, restores Mr. Kuppers's humanity (which is important in light of his family's cruel rejection) by disabusing the intended reader of the presumption of entitlement to his subjectivity.[40]

Unlike "Hard Candy," *The Book of Salt* does not hide Bình's same-sex desires from the reader, who is welcomed into the protagonist's interiority throughout the novel. With no shroud of silence surrounding homosexuality and no mystery about Bình's subjectivity more generally, the diversion of sexual representation requires another explanation. When the novel was published in 2003, conflicts about anticommunism still overwhelmed many Vietnamese Americans. It goes without saying that the Hi-Tek Incident had occurred in very recent memory. That the sexual reconciliation enacted by Bình and Ho Chi Minh in-becoming happens in a public location but remains hidden signifies that this vision of intraethnic reunion does not yet exist outside a dreamlike utopianism wished for in secrecy. It may perhaps not ever be actualized, at least not to the extent of the idealism that accompanies this moment. The sexual activity's refusal to appear in the prose signals the absence of the referent that a would-be representation would index. The end of the chapter leaves us with only Bình by himself on that symbolic and material bridge.

ON NOT GOING HOME

The beckoning from the homeland at the end of *The Book of Salt* generates ambivalence, despite the idealism symbolized by the sexual encounter. When the sociologist Karin Aguilar–San Juan traveled to Vietnam as part of a delegation of U.S. researchers in 2006, she had the opportunity to present her work to the equivalent of the country's vice-president. At the conclusion of her presentation, he asked her how she thought Vietnamese Americans could "help Viet Nam."[41] She was flummoxed because she knew that most of her informants "would rather die" than do so.[42] Yet Aguilar–San Juan would later think more deeply about the dislocation between Vietnamese American revulsion for the homeland and the Vietnamese government's professed need for support from the very people it banished.

The continuing opposition to contact with the Socialist Republic of Vietnam takes place alongside the increasing numbers of diasporans who have return-migrated. For a Vietnam aspiring to enter the global economy, the influx of capital and talent from abroad helps the country compete with its Asian neighbors. For Vietnamese American investors and cultural stakeholders, this engagement with the Vietnamese state remains mercenary on some level. We must not downplay motivations that appeal to neoliberal capital. However, a reunification with the homeland can also provide affiliations that challenge American exceptionalism, facilitate creative forms of cultural syncretism, and enable an alternate history of the U.S. war in Vietnam to develop.[43] Rather than play the role of the grateful refugee, these return migrants reject what Mimi Nguyen would call the gifts of freedom in which the United States has attempted to ensnare its debtors.

Long T. Bui reminds us, lest we become too enthusiastic about this trend, that Vietnamese American desire for transnational connectivities "is fraught with both anguish and hope."[44] At the end of *The Book of Salt*, Bình's father retires to his deathbed, and his brother has written to ask him to return and bury the hatchet. Although Bình addresses his father throughout the novel's interior monologues as if he is already dead, this summons reveals that he is still alive, albeit not for much longer. Rather than express filial resentment to justify refusing to return home, Bình reveals a longing for the man on the bridge that encourages him to remain in Paris. His hopes of reuniting with his onetime lover keep him anchored to a place to which he otherwise would have no affinity. His reluctance in the novel's final moments mirrors the uncertainty with which Vietnamese diasporans consider regenerating ties with the homeland. There is a hesitation to return, countered by the simultaneous pull of unfulfilled longing. The possibility of reconciling with the dying father/nation creates pain. Yet so does the apparent path of least resistance—that is, staying in a metropole that dictates the affects and discourages the rebelliousness of its colonial émigrés. The ambiguous conclusion to *The Book of Salt* indicates that Vietnamese Americans' transnational attachments to the homeland, highly desired in some cases and resisted in others, will remain a source of psychic tension even as external barriers to access, whether they are imposed by nations or by co-ethnics, are removed.

This is not to say that travel to the metropole is for naught. In *The Book of Salt*, the origins of colonial power nurture a reconciliation, which the novel imagines as erotic practice. As Bình reminisces about the man on the bridge, he concedes that the

> only place that we shared was this city. Vietnam, the country that we called home, was to me already a memory. . . . Paris gave him to me. And in Paris I will stay, I decided. Only in this city, I thought, will I see him again. For a traveler, it is sometimes necessary to make the world small on purpose. It is the only way to stop migrating and find a new home. After the man on the bridge departed, Paris held in it a promise. It was a city where something akin to love had happened, and it was a city where it could happen again. (258)

The distance from the homeland makes the reconciliation of the South Vietnamese refugee with the anti-imperialist leader of North Vietnam possible. It is not Bình's docile wish to assimilate into Parisian life that prompts him to "stop migrating" and begin to think of France as his "new home." For the South Vietnamese refugee, the satisfaction in taking root within the diaspora comes from the allure of a bond with his co-ethnics that cannot occur where the effects of imperial violence are most proximate.[45]

This spatial removal from the homeland has a temporal corollary. Truong's choice to set her novel six decades before the most highly profiled incidents of Vietnamese American anticommunism tempers its message by relocating it from the heat of the conflict. As these two postcolonial exiles in 1920s Paris meet each other, the imperative embedded in their sexual encounter reaches forward in time to address Vietnamese Americans at the beginning of the twenty-first century. Build bridges, they urge. You may find yourself alone on it once it is over. But you knew that already.

UNWITTING INGESTION

In a study about food in South Asian diasporic literature and film, Anita Mannur calls food novels "commodity-comestibles" to signal how they are marketed to and consumed by mainstream audiences. These texts are commonly perceived as safe because of their celebration of culture and apparent lack of political content.[46] However, Mannur's analysis shows that these novels can and do launch critiques about race, labor, neoliberalism, and capitalism. I agree that they do, even if, as in *The Book of Salt*, these moments are coded. Truong's novel conforms to the generic conventions of the food novel in its thematization of cooking. However, it also breaks from earlier conventions of representing food in Asian American literature that Sau-ling Cynthia Wong describes in her formative study. The fare portrayed in *The Book of Salt* exists at a remove from the crudely exotic sort brandished to disgust or intimidate white readers.[47] The cuisine that emerges from Bình's hands—delicacies such as wine-soaked figs, roasted duck in port, consommé, oysters, pâté, truffles, and tarts—conforms with the terrain of normative culinary palates. We are meant to covet these meals laced with connotations of Francophilic class-based access, their gustatory pleasure available to the epicure's mouth, even if the cook's secrets remain out of reach.[48] The novel invites the reader to eat vicariously through Stein and Toklas. We dine as they do.

As the reader consumes the commodity-comestible that is *The Book of Salt*, she or he also ingests something else. The sweet, easily digestible treat contains something the epicure did not bargain for: a critique of the state's military investments abroad and the nation's willingness to collude with that violence in its discursive production of the grateful refugee. The covert planting of this ingredient alludes to Bình's statement that one of the ways disgruntled cooks act out is to ejaculate into their employers' food before serving it to them. This embedding of resistant messages in a seemingly compliant plot resembles the strategies identified in fiction by the early scholarship in Asian American literature. Critics have described it as a "surface plot" that hides a "buried plot," a "technique of indirection," or "masking."[49] Although these hermeneutic lenses may seem dated to someone who has been following the more recent trends in the field, the conclusion about the novel to which I come is still relevant, given the conditions of the Vietnam War's aftermath that make certain critiques difficult to voice.

Bình readily admits he has never subjected Stein and Toklas to the silent protest he describes. "Saucing the meat, fortifying the soup, enriching a batch of blood orange sorbet, the possible uses are endless, undetectable. But that is an afterthought. I never do it for them. I would never waste myself in such a way" (64). His restraint is not respectful deference to his employers but skepticism about small acts of resistance that, while meaningful in their own right, "waste" or do nothing to alter the conditions of labor. There *is* a bodily fluid that finds its way into Stein and Toklas's food, and it is not semen but blood. Bình links his cutting, what he calls "silver . . . threading my skin" (72), to an early memory of being cared for by his mother, an important figure in his childhood memories for how she buffered his father's abuse. The blood that occasionally infuses the exquisite meals in the Stein-Toklas household resembles the critique embedded in *The Book of Salt*, invisible to the eye but unsettlingly perceptible on the tongue. When Toklas confronts Bình about the blood—"I know what goes into my mouth" (70)—the substance of the offending ingredient is clear even if the reasons for its presence lie dormant. She believes he inadvertently cut himself while cooking because of drunkenness, a sloppy accident by a subaltern subject without the faculties of self-restraint that colonialism is meant to bestow.

Bình's cutting is a deliberate and premeditated act, even if it would, by normative medical standards, be considered impulsive self-harm. Truong does not pathologize it. In fact, she describes it with the euphoria commonly associated with sexual pleasure, potentially surrogating for the depictions of actual sex that remain absent:

> Weightlessness overtakes me moments before my vision clears, my throat unclogs, and my body begins to understand that silver is threading my skin. I am floating away, and a sea of red washes me back. . . . [W]ithout warning, my instinct and my hunger give way, dislodged by something newer, stronger. A spiral swims away from the red mud seas and grows broader and hotter, and I cannot stop it. I cannot stop it. (72–73)

Bình alludes to compulsivity in these sessions, but he wields these compulsions with control: "I want to say that it is automatic, but it is not. I have to think about it each time, consider the alternatives, decide that there are none" (65). By way of analogy, the planting of a covert critique of U.S. imperialism in *The Book of Salt* needs to be understood as purposeful and thoughtful, undergone with the same level of calculation as Bình's bloodletting. By saying this critique is deliberate, I do not appeal to a naïvely intentionalist claim about Truong's motivations while writing. Rather, by assigning purpose to the critique's presence, we grant credibility to the Vietnamese diasporans who voice it. Challenging popular conceptions of the grateful refugee is neither impulsive nor reckless. It comes from a materially grounded analysis of how militarism nurses an ongoing myth about the racialized colonial subject's need for salvation from himself. It interrogates the states of displacement in the present by invoking the past.

The critique contained in *The Book of Salt* (within the logic of its intradiegetic vehicle) comes across as both self-injury and self-soothing. Bình claims that cutting "gives me proof that I am alive" (70). Asian American subjects historically have understood that a measured amount of safety comes with avoiding political action and complying with standards of white propriety. My description, in Chapter 1, of the differential treatment of Japanese Americans who chose to enlist in the military compared with those who resisted the draft is but one example. Contesting the premises that supply this limited stability opens oneself to vilification. Troubling the well-worn narratives about the United States' magnanimity is self-injury for Vietnamese Americans who, like Japanese Americans, have benefited in small ways from displays of obedience. Yet this self-injury also transforms itself into a refusal to accept the erasures to which Vietnamese Americans are subjected when they are so cautious as to refrain from breaking their skin. By choosing not to remain silent, by not saving their own hides, they spill blood as a confirmation of vitality even if it means risking alienation from their co-ethnics. Putting this metaphor within its original context, we see that what Bình cherishes most about cutting is "the meeting and mending" (74) of skin. The cleaving of the community stings, but proof of life lies in the potential for healing and reconciliation.

NEW MILITARIZATIONS AND INTIMATE AFFILIATIONS

Published in the wake of the attacks on the World Trade Center and Pentagon on September 11, 2001, and on the eve of the U.S. invasion of Iraq, *The Book of Salt* appeared at a moment that reopened old national wounds from the Vietnam War. The specter of defeat, known as "Vietnam Syndrome," turned the Persian Gulf War of 1991 and the wars in Iraq and Afghanistan in the subsequent decade into a means through which the United States could symbolically recuperate its military loss from the past. The "retroactive victory" remains a recurring theme in scholarship on the Vietnam War. Thomas M. Hawley argues that an overzealous quest to find and repatriate the remains of every soldier who went missing in action is the United States' attempt to win a lost war.[50] Susan Jeffords claims that the assertion of normative masculinities in American culture is a means to secure victory in a post-defeat era.[51] Along these lines, Sylvia Shin Huey Chong proposes that white veterans' mastery of the body and remasculinization through Asian martial arts are intended to overcome the war's defeat.[52] Yen Le Espiritu sees the seemingly successful assimilation of Vietnamese refugees as the United States' validation of its superiority and, thus, its ultimate victory.[53] This series of U.S. conflicts with Arab nations at the turn of the twenty-first century not coincidentally took place alongside the normalization of diplomatic relations with Vietnam. In the face of a newly demonized global region, the United States traded one enemy for another. These transhistorical links between the Vietnam War and the U.S. wars with Arab nations arise not only in the collective American imagination but in Southeast Asian refugee subjectivities, as well. The trauma that accompanies militarized violence enables comparative critiques of U.S. occupations that span decades.[54]

Arriving shortly after U.S. militarism's increased reach were new conflicts among Vietnamese Americans. These have attracted less mainstream attention than those involving anticommunism, but they still show the extent to which intraethnic divides remain complex and not easily attributed to a standoff between staunch traditionalism and leftist progressivism. In 2010, a contingent of LGBT representatives and their allies applied for a place in California's Orange County Tet Parade, which inaugurated the coming lunar new year. Religious groups, headed mostly by Christian clergy, opposed their presence. One Catholic priest, Sy Nguyen, invoked an authenticity reminiscent of cultural and anticolonial nationalisms by stating, "Tet is a cultural event for Vietnamese whether in Vietnam or anywhere in the world. . . . Parading members of Vietnamese gays, lesbians, and transgender groups . . . is not only irrelevant to the meaning of Tet, but is perceived at best as a complete lack of sensitivity to the Vietnamese traditions, and at worst a cultural attack on the Vietnamese community."[55]

Van Tran, a Lutheran minister, reinforced Nguyen's claims when he pronounced that "gays and lesbians are not accepted by the Holy Bible"; nor is "homosexuality . . . accepted in 1,000 years of Vietnamese culture."[56] The clergypeople's static notions of culture overlooked the fact that Catholicism took root among Vietnamese people only with the advent of missions established by French Jesuits. The embrace of Lutheranism occurred even more recently, after resettlement in the United States when Lutheran churches took a visible role in sponsoring refugees. This diasporic community's acceptance of Christianity appears to be unremarkable and free from interrogation about its nonconformity with an imagined pre-contact Southeast Asian authenticity. Meanwhile, post-Stonewall North American customs that track sexually dissident and gender nonconforming subjects into legibility as gay, lesbian, bisexual, or transgender remain suspect.[57]

Supporters of LGBT groups' right to march criticized the opposition for a hostility that seemed at odds with the spirit of religion. Activists also affirmed their participation by appealing to conservative models of intimate affiliations that same-sex couples would adopt were it not for legal barriers that existed at the time. Thanh Do of the Vietnamese Gay Alliance stated that the most pressing purpose of visibility for his organization at the moment was "to create awareness about the gay marriage issue in Orange County."[58] Summoning the politics of respectability that accompanies marriage, Do and other supporters aligned their interests with those resisting their inclusion. The debates about the Orange County Tet Parade emerged slightly more than a year after the passage of Proposition 8, the ballot measure in California's 2008 elections that reversed the State Supreme Court's ruling that found an earlier ban on same-sex marriage illegal. However, the bringing together of the two factions at odds on the issue of LGBT participation in the Tet Parade ultimately traveled down a more familiar path toward Vietnamese American unity, one that resonated with Thuy Vo Dang's research on the role of anti-communism in the diaspora. Hung Nguyen, a parade organizer, backed the presence of LGBT Vietnamese Americans because "our community recognizes that they are human beings, too," and "we welcome anyone to celebrate with us, as long as they are not terrorists or *communists*."[59]

Despite these grumblings, the Orange County Tet Parade contained LGBT representation in 2010, 2011, and 2012 while it was under the administration of the city of Westminster. In 2013, a turn of events occurred when the city could no longer afford to staff the event. The handover in organization and funding to the private sector, the Vietnamese American Federation of Southern California, meant that parade administrators would hold more latitude in dictating the composition of participants. The banning of LGBT groups in 2013 ignited the low-level controversy that had been brewing since 2010, and the Partnership of Viet Lesbian, Gay, Bisexual, and Transgender Organizations sought intervention, but unsuccessfully, from the Orange County Superior Court. Despite the outcome, LGBT representatives that year still marched as guests of another organization.[60] For the 2014 lunar new year, activists petitioned the Westminster City Council to deny the Vietnamese American Federation a permit to hold the parade because of its discriminatory practices. The council representatives very grudgingly, but unanimously, allowed the event to go forward on the basis that refusing to do so would be a violation of the First Amendment. In the end, an extralegal vote mounted by a dissenting member of the Vietnamese American Federation was distributed among community leaders, who then ruled 51–36, with ten abstentions, against the exclusion of sexual minorities.[61] Since then, LGBT groups have been permitted in the Orange County Tet Parade.

Given these recent disagreements, it may seem that couching the rhetoric of anticommunist abatement in a same-sex encounter would not be the most amenable way for Truong to deliver the polemic I attribute to *The Book of Salt*. However, the debates over the Orange County Tet Parade show how connections between leftism and sexual non-normativity took unexpected turns as each side attempted to defend its position. Some clergy voiced Christian principle to condemn sexual difference. In response, the minoritized positionality of LGBT Vietnamese Americans became incorporated into the conservative language of marriage equality. (It goes without saying that an increasing preoccupation with marriage rights in mainstream LGBT activism had already eroded more capacious sexual, domestic, and kinship structures germane to earlier queer life.) Some activists were charged with the predictable accusation of being communist for their advocacy of LGBT representation.[62] Yet they were also brought into the fold of the diasporic family by holding them in favored contrast to other threats deemed more menacing: threats of terrorists and communists. These combined tensions show the extent to which the diaspora's claims of membership and cultural legitimacy remain malleable according to the interests of its stakeholders.

It is no accident that the figure of the upstanding LGBT subject in these debates would become the conceptual opposite of the "terrorist" in the post-9/11 era. Jasbir K. Puar unearths a troubling convergence between the U.S. occupations of Iraq and Afghanistan and the rise of an assimilationist queer liberal politics. The shift in U.S. queer activism's commitments, from anticapitalist critique in previous generations to consumerist rights-based interests in the present day, goes hand in hand with the United States' ongoing imperial ventures. These military incursions into the Arab world generate their own pliable American exceptionalisms that morph across time to fit a range of events. In response to the war on terror, gay and lesbian voices of the global North joined an Islamophobic chorus decrying homophobia in majority Muslim countries. The brandishing of purportedly greater freedoms for sexual minorities in the United States, which justifies early twenty-first-century imperial occupations, coalesces with U.S. elites' pursuit of state protection, such as same-sex marriage rights, in an exceptionalist sensibility that Puar calls "homonationalism."[63]

David Eng echoes Puar's concern about contemporary queer liberalism serving as an instrument of state control instead of challenging capitalist modernities. While Puar asserts that figurations of the brown terrorist body become queered through their pathologization in the popular imagination,[64] Eng directs his focus at the discursive function of racialized subjects in mainstream queer activism's shoring up of whiteness, property rights, and normative kinship. Racial liberatory politics are cast as regressive, vestigial formations that stand in the way of a color-blind present and future. It is not difficult, Eng claims, to see why Gertrude Stein and Alice B. Toklas have been "conscripted today as the poster children for queer liberalism."[65] They exhibit sexual dissidence simultaneously with capitalist collusion while the erotic libertinism of nonwhite subaltern characters remains illegible. Truong's contribution, Eng asserts, ruptures these power-laden notions about what can be known about colonial subjects. It does this by introducing a queered version of North Vietnamese revolt that locates its most recognizable figure, Ho Chi Minh, at its center. This alternative historicity, based not on empiricism but on subaltern theorizing, disrupts the stasis of these queer Asian diasporic subjects who wait for interpretive conditions more amenable to them.[66]

As for the indebted, grateful refugee, the victimized Asian-raced sexual outlaw-turned-queer-liberal-subject, or any other easily recognizable archetypes, they exist to validate the burden the United States believes it carries for the world. What remain hidden in these narratives of salvation and transformation are the military occupations that motivate the need for nonwhite bodies to take refuge. The exilic postcolonial subject's declaration, "I am here because you were there," applies ever more at the start of the twenty-first century with the United States' extension of its imperial reach. In his examination of the connections between U.S. assimilationist discourse and colonialism in the mid-twentieth century, Victor Bascara borrows the above pronouncement. Explaining his decision to do so, he writes, "Originally invoked by and for immigrants to England from its former colonies, that slogan erupts at the convergence of Asian American cultural politics and the emergence of U.S. imperialism."[67] Following Bascara, I transpose this statement yet again, both forward and backward in time to France in the 1920s and the United States in the post–Vietnam War era. I am here, because you were there. Or, to invoke the coercive forms of inclusion into the fold of liberal, enlightened modernity demanded of the figures above, we can shift this claim slightly: I am queer because you were there.

And, no, I am not grateful.

3

REBELLION AND
COMPROMISE

The field of Asian American literary studies generated a lot of research in the 1990s on the mother-daughter relationship.[1] This theme, though dated when seen through the lens of more recent frameworks, allowed scholars to explore a complex range of interrelated topics. They included the intersectional forces of racism and sexism, the management and appeasement of a nuclear family's patriarch, and the tensions between an older immigrant generation and a younger U.S.-born one. This interlacing of race, gender, and generation channeled itself through the emotionally intense and fraught intimacies between daughters and their mothers. Right before the cusp of this intellectual production, however, a key text written by a playwright covered similar ground but with some significant differences. Philip Kan Gotanda's *Yankee Dawg You Die* (1988) spotlights the gendered forms of racism that confront Asian American men. It also addresses the divergent ways an older generation versus a younger one mitigates their effects and how actors across a generational divide bond with each other on common ground.

The conflict in Gotanda's play occurs between Asian American male actors who accommodate gendered forms of racism in their work and those who refuse it. The conditions under which Asian American performers gain professional traction pit the interests of the cultural and the economic against each other. If theater, film, and television are products of their historical moment and cross-cut with concepts of race and gender germane to those contexts, what ethic binds Asian American actors when working with

troubling representations? One stance claims that for actors, any employment is favorable to none. By accepting roles as they come, no matter how
degrading, actors can support themselves financially and gain a foothold in
the industry. The power they wield when refusing roles remains so limited
that it is nonexistent. Other performers will eagerly fill the opportunities
they turn down. However, actors, producers, and directors in independent
theater, film, and television would assert the opposite—that to throw one's
hands up in defeat overlooks the artists who seek options beyond resigned
acceptance. Gotanda's play about Asian American actors acting provides a
metacritical commentary that embodies the aesthetics of the latter's polemic,
given its bare-bones cast of two and other minimalist elements that appeal to
theater companies with modest budgets. Its unassuming and unapologetic
specificity to the Asian American experience does not court commercial
tastes. Rather than the resistant stance that such a text might be expected to
extol, however, it proposes a moderate perspective that brings nuance to the
opposing positions. The happy medium where the actors meet conveys itself
through an expression of sexual desire between the two male characters representing these two sides.

Yankee Dawg You Die premiered in 1988 at the Berkeley Repertory Theater in Berkeley, California. The play is Gotanda's eighth and among his best
known and most frequently performed. It remains one of the standards in
the Asian American dramatic canon, along with Frank Chin's *The Chickencoop Chinaman* and *The Year of the Dragon*, David Henry Hwang's *M.
Butterfly*, and Diana Son's *R.A.W.* The questions it raises about race and representation in Asian American performance sustain their pertinence to this
day, which has seen a resurgence of discussion about opportunities for Asian
American actors.

The curtain rises showing Vincent Chang, an older actor, delivering a
monologue from a caricatured role depicting a Japanese soldier. An invisible
and inaudible interlocutor struggles to comprehend his accented English, and
the character that Vincent portrays expresses frustration over being misunderstood. As the narrative unfolds, Bradley Yamashita, a younger actor who
grew up lionizing Vincent for his Asian American trailblazer status in entertainment, enters the story. After the starstruck wonder wears off, Bradley—
who is influenced by his generation's Asian American politics and proudly
limits his acting to independent productions—criticizes the older Vincent for
his detestable professional choices. An angry outburst disrupts the budding
mentorship, but the ensuing conversations, informal theater experiments,
and moments of homoerotic play reconcile the actors' differences. At the end,
we see Vincent preparing for his first independent role and Bradley for his
first commercial one, reversing the positions from which they began. Vin-

cent happily anticipates an independent production's experimental bent, and Bradley expresses enthusiasm about the possibility of transforming the commercial industry from within. The play's conclusion recapitulates the opening monologue. This time, Vincent's standard American accent overtakes the previous one he was required to assume. The stereotyped, two-dimensional character falls away. Earnestly, he ends the monologue by asking, "Why can't you hear what I'm saying? Why can't you see me as I really am?"[2]

The eruption of the older actor's subjectivity through the façade of caricature embodies what the younger actor hopes to accomplish in this meeting halfway between rebellion and compromise. Having Vincent perform the action implied in Bradley's decision yokes the two men together across the fissure separating a pre- and post-1970s Asian American political emergence. The interests of actors—regarding dignity, fair treatment, and credibility in their desires—remain the same no matter their age or stage of career. This implied solidarity across generations hinges on a crucial, but subsequently downplayed, revelation that Vincent maintains a closeted same-sex relationship. Bradley, whose heterosexuality never falls under question (though it is troubled by homosexual panic), dismisses the relevance of Vincent's sexual difference. When Bradley, with good intention, claims that sexuality no longer matters, he erases a vast disparity between the cultural and structural locations of straight and gay men in the late 1980s. By depoliticizing sexual difference, Yankee Dawg You Die rides on the figurative potential of same-sex desire in intraracial conflict resolution, but it does so at the risk of making the coalitional mistakes I laid out in the Introduction.

This chapter begins with a first-person account of seeing a production of Yankee Dawg You Die. Following that, I provide an analysis of how the dialogue and blocking shed light on the erotic dimensions of Vincent and Bradley's relationship, mediating the sides of the debate associated with each of the actors. Next, I locate the play in the sensibility of the HIV/AIDS epidemic and address the implications of the narrative's silence about these concurrent developments in gay history. This leads to a sustained analysis of the appeal to normative heteromasculinity in a text that presents itself as more progressive and complex than the cultural nationalisms of the past. I close by questioning the gender and sexual normativities that remain intact in discussions about roles for Asian American male actors.

VIEWING A PRODUCTION OF
YANKEE DAWG YOU DIE

I became acquainted with Yankee Dawg You Die as a graduate student at the University of Michigan in the late 1990s during a seminar taught by the literary critic Stephen Sumida. He had an acting background, and when the class read Gotanda's play, he treated us to a viewing on a grainy VHS tape of a university production with himself in the part of Vincent and a student playing Bradley. After graduate school, I lived in the Twin Cities of Minneapolis and St. Paul for four years in the early to mid-2000s. It was one of a very few U.S. metropolitan areas with an Asian American theater. However, I did not then have the opportunity to attend a production of *Yankee Dawg You Die* or any of the other plays that belong to a compact but recognizable Asian American dramatic canon. The Minneapolis company devoted its efforts to new and emerging work, mostly by local playwrights, which provided a good platform for the talents of its sizable Asian American population. Although I was glad to have attended these performances, the emphasis on contemporary and little-known texts unwittingly elided an established tradition of Asian American theater. *Yankee Dawg You Die* remains one of the most iconic texts in Asian American drama, but it is surprisingly difficult to see live. An Internet search for reviews of the play turns up very little beyond a year or two after its debut.

My quest to see a live performance of *Yankee Dawg You Die* finally ended in 2014. A colleague at the University of Wisconsin alerted me to an upcoming production in Madison. Grateful for the notification, I ordered my ticket from the theater through its online reservation system, made travel plans, and packed a suitcase without delay. The Bartell Theatre is a performance space that houses five drama and dance companies, one of them the Madison Theatre Guild, which is where *Yankee Dawg You Die* had a two-week run in 2014. Located in the isthmus section of Madison that joins the affluent West Side neighborhood with the more blue-collar East Side, the Bartell Theatre is one block away from the Wisconsin State Capitol and centrally located in a well-trafficked, pedestrian-friendly downtown near other arts and culture spaces, shops, cafés, bars, and restaurants. Other plays the Madison Theatre Guild produced during the season included contemporary standards such as Paula Vogel's *How I Learned to Drive* and Moisés Kaufman's *Gross Indecency: The Three Trials of Oscar Wilde*. It also premiered a piece of local interest, a biography of Lavinia Goodell, a woman prohibited in 1876 from practicing law in Wisconsin because of gender discrimination.

That this production of *Yankee Dawg You Die* was not performed by an Asian American theater company and received as much attention as it did in a city with a small Asian American population was nothing short of extraordinary to me. The intimate performance venue, which contained approximately eighty seats, was filled to its limit on the Saturday evening I attended. The box office even turned some people away. David Furumoto portrayed

Vincent Chang, and Christian Inouye played the part of Bradley Yamashita. Afterward, the actors and the director, Betty Diamond, hosted a lively talk-back session with audience members, about a fourth of whom remained to participate. The demographics of the audience at the Bartell Theatre that night were in line with Madison's largely white population, although some visible people of color were in attendance. As I discussed in Chapter 2, *The Book of Salt* possesses a form and content that aligns, but only partially, with white, middle-class taste cultures. However, *Yankee Dawg You Die* exhibits a different kind of politics and aesthetics. It makes no apologies for its overt portrayal of Asian American experiences with injustice. It does not attempt to temper its critique, often strident, with visually or aurally appealing elements. Yet the theater still saw this kind of turnout, despite the apparent disjunction between the audience base and the text.

For this production at the Bartell Theatre, the set design remained very sparse, almost self-consciously so. The economical nature of the scenery, props, and costumes conveyed a sense of Asian American theater's origins outside the comforts and, hence, the confines of commercially supported performance. This sparseness also showcased without distraction Furumoto's and Inouye's acting, bringing their skills front and center, with little else for the audience to take in. Given that a common justification in the entertainment industries for not hiring more people of color is that the most talented ones are not well represented in the labor pool, Diamond's choice to push design to the background, to the extent it almost disappears, signals the folly of continuing to use this excuse. A review of *Yankee Dawg You Die* in a Madison media outlet praised the acting without qualification. The reviewer noted Inouye's "nice job playing Yamashita," calling attention to his "soft, measured delivery" in a poignant scene. The reviewer commended Furumoto even more ebulliently, calling him a "joy to watch" as he "infuses the character with integrity, wisdom and patience." His "portrayal of the buffoonish Japanese soldier is so good and so offensive that it's stunning. . . . [H]is subtlety is mesmerizing on stage. In fact, it's hard to take your eyes off him."[3] Excellent Asian American actors, even in majority-white Madison, are available. The directorial choice to highlight them on a minimalist stage makes that fact impossible to ignore.

ATTRACTION AND REPULSION

The two characters in *Yankee Dawg You Die* become alternatingly attracted to and repulsed by each other. Vincent and Bradley are driven together and apart twice before their conflicts resolve at the end. The diegesis opens in a party at a Hollywood mansion. Vincent stands alone, lost in pensiveness, when Bradley notices him through the crowd. Before any dialogue begins, the stage directions show the extent to which the younger actor is taken by the presence of the older one:

> VINCENT CHANG, *a youthful, silver-maned man, in his late sixties, stands on the back terrace of a balcony sipping a glass of red wine. Stares into the night air.* BRADLEY YAMASHITA, *twenty-seven, pokes his head out from the party and notices* VINCENT. *Stops, losing his nerve. Changes his mind again and moves out on the terrace next to* VINCENT. BRADLEY *holds a cup of club soda.*
>   *Silence.* VINCENT *notices* BRADLEY, BRADLEY *smiles,* VINCENT *nods.*
>   *Silence. They both sip their drinks.* (75)

The blocking for the performance at the Bartell Theatre remained faithful to the playwright's vision. In this scene, a railing is the lone object composing the stage's sparse scenery. When the lights go up, we see Vincent standing in front of it, looking comfortably lost in solitude. A starstruck and nervous Bradley approaches him from behind and beyond the range of sight of the older man. Bradley takes a few steps, falters, and musters his courage to continue. His initiation of contact leads to a loaded moment in which the two men acknowledge each other's presence through friendly eye contact. They share a space of wordless side-by-side proximity, imbibing with affected casualness, before they begin conversation.

The actors' movements, gestures, and facial expressions in this first meeting resemble the early stages of sexual or romantic pursuit. Bradley appears jittery when he approaches Vincent, knowing the older man has the upper hand in the interaction because of his accumulated experience and higher professional profile. In a context in which the younger actor stands everything to gain from the older in a highly competitive field, Bradley remains appropriately polite and unassuming. The palpable thrill of being in Vincent's presence, however, goes beyond mere careerism. Bradley is smitten. Vincent does not take Bradley's amiable introduction for granted and reciprocates his interest. When the younger actor opens the conversation, he responds affably and expresses openness to further interaction:

> BRADLEY: Hello. (*Vincent nods.*) Nice evening. (*Silence*) God. *What a night.* Love it. (*Silence. Looking out.*) Stars. Wow. Would you believe. Stars, stars, stars. (*Pause.*)

VINCENT: Orion's belt. (BRADLEY doesn't follow his comment.
VINCENT points upwards.) The constellation. Orion the Hunter.
That line of stars there forms his belt. See?
BRADLEY: Uh-huh. (75)

The ambiguity behind Bradley's marveling reveals the uneven positions between the two men in the industry. The "stars" to which Bradley refers could
be the prominent figures in acting. Because this is the young actor's first invitation to a Hollywood party, he may feel out of his element. Vincent steers
the conversation so that the figurative meaning of the word "star" drops
away, leaving only the literal one. A veteran actor, he remains unfazed by the
crowd and motions to the sky. Although Bradley "doesn't follow" at first, he
quickly becomes interested in the older actor's preferred form of stargazing.
The constellations allow the two men to begin bonding in a manner that
is demurely flirtatious but not immediately panic-inducing. When Bradley
turns the conversation to the demographics of the party's guests, it is Vincent who becomes slow on the uptake:

BRADLEY: Jeez, it's a bit stuffy in there. With all of them. It's nice
to be with someone I can feel comfortable around. (VINCENT
doesn't understand.) Well, I mean, like you and me. We're—I
mean, we don't exactly look like . . . (*Nods toward the people inside.*)
VINCENT: Ahhh.
(BRADLEY laughs nervously, relieved that VINCENT has understood.) (75–78)

What follows reveals the political gulf between the generations. Vincent responds by claiming an ascription to color-blindness. Bradley corrects his
vocabulary—"It's Asian, not oriental" (78). Their initial banter veers toward
shoptalk as the two actors discuss the film industry and gossip about their
colleagues. In an erotically suggestive moment, Vincent catches Bradley star-
ing at him. The stage directions say, "VINCENT *is not sure of* BRADLEY's
intent—perhaps he was admiring Vincent's good looks" (82). The motivation
behind the inspection turns out to be Bradley's sheepish query about plastic
surgery Vincent may have undergone, which Vincent vehemently denies.

The instant the two men face each other and gaze with curiosity, both
trying to discern something about the other, feels loaded. Vincent might
wonder whether Bradley is about to make a sexual pass while Bradley quiz-
zically inspects Vincent for evidence of having gone under the knife. The

notability of this moment becomes more significant in retrospect, when we find out about Vincent's same-sex relationship, which he keeps under wraps because of concerns about his career. His attempt to process the substance of Bradley's interest aligns with the subjectivity of someone who has learned pre-Stonewall means through which male-desiring men connected with one another. Mastering the subtle, often nonverbal cues—glances, eye contact, body language, and touch—that signal mutual sexual interest would have been a matter of survival for gay men of his generation. Vincent's angry refutation of the rumors about plastic surgery dispels the erotic energy, safely establishing a nonsexual context to what seems at first blush to be a budding romance.

The plot's vacillation between Vincent and Bradley's attraction and repulsion only to reunite them in the end follows that of a typical romantic comedy, even though *Yankee Dawg You Die* would not be considered a text in that genre. The two men's first meeting falls flat, and Bradley's hotheadedness alienates Vincent before the night is over. When the two discuss a role that Vincent played in a science fiction movie, Bradley initially does not remember him in it. After Vincent clarifies, the realization dawns on Bradley: "Oh . . . oh! You were the husband of the woman who was eaten by the giant salamander?" He guffaws in laughter. Vincent confirms and acknowledges, "It was a little hard to tell, I know. The makeup was a little heavy," which Bradley interrupts by saying, "Makeup a little heavy? Jesus Christ, you had so much hair on your face that you looked like a fucking chimpanzee!" (85). This statement issues an even more damning criticism of the older actor's choices than the one presented by the play's opening interlude. No longer human, if only a racist caricature, Vincent has been reduced to nonhuman animality, a rhetorical maneuver that, as Mel Y. Chen observes, follows an entrenched pattern of positioning the socially disenfranchised as the constitutive outside to full human rationality.[4] Bradley's insult ends the dialogue and the scene itself, but not without evidence of his continued interest in Vincent. He "*occasionally steals a glance at*" (85) him as the stage lights dim.

The play's most overtly sexual dialogue takes place during a reconciliation the following week when Vincent and Bradley meet again at an audition. After the initial awkwardness of patching the rift in their budding relationship, Bradley resumes beaming in Vincent's presence:

You know, Mr. Chang, when I was growing up, you were sort of my hero. . . . I'd be watching TV and suddenly you'd appear. . . . And at first something would always jerk inside. Whoa, what's this? This is weird, like watching my own family on TV. It's like the first time I made it with an Asian girl—up to then only white girls. . . . With this

Asian girl it was like doing it with my sister. It was weird. Everything about her was familiar. Her face, her skin, the sound of her voice, the way she smelled. It was like having sex with someone in my own family. That's how it was when you'd come on the TV. (87)

Bradley's memories about the jarring appearance of an Asian American actor on-screen at a formative moment in his youth is portrayed with language that reveals libidinal urges. Whereas the flirtation between the two men at the party remained subtle, Bradley's attachment for Vincent has become blatantly sexual. There is physiological twitching, "something . . . jerk[ing] inside." There is also a description of Vincent's presence affecting Bradley's interiority—uncanny in that it makes his familiar surroundings, his "family," strange or "weird." As if the sexual dimensions of Bradley's joy are not plain enough, they extend in ways that make themselves even more obvious. Bradley goes on to compare the experience of beholding Vincent's likeness among a sea of white faces on-screen to that of his first intraracial sexual experience. His recollection of "ma[king] it with an Asian girl" after previously having had only white lovers resembles the accounts provided by some of Nguyen Tan Hoang's informants in *7 Steps to Sticky Heaven*, as I discuss in the Introduction. In both cases, we see a dreamy emphasis on the pleasure of erotic and sexual congress with a body that looks and feels like one's own. Bradley directly links the ecstatic moment of recognition in his intraracial heterosexual experience to that of partaking in the limited opportunities for fandom directed at Asian American actors who "come on the TV." The enjoyment of seeing Vincent on-screen, Bradley declares, becomes so intense that it is akin to sexual ecstasy. The ejaculatory agency with which Bradley endows Vincent for trailblazing stands at odds with what unfolds in dialogue later about the feminized roles commonly assigned to Asian American men.

THE ERASURE OF SEXUAL DIFFERENCE

Bradley may profess an attachment, which can be read as love, sexual desire, or both, for Vincent in his capacity as an actor. However, the implications of the erotic energy between them need to be suppressed for the narrative to function. In *Yankee Dawg You Die*, sexual difference disappears while normative gender and sexual presentations come to the fore. The plot propels itself by developing the stormy relationship between Vincent and Bradley as they work out their differences. Their on-again-off-again affiliation lasts through arguments, discomfiting but welcomed reunions, impromptu theater exercises, and further disagreements. Their eventual reconciliation takes place in an exposure of the motivations underlying Vincent's compensatory masculinity. When Bradley gripes about the emasculation of Asian-raced men on U.S. television—"They fucking cut off our balls and make us all houseboys on the evening soaps" (100)—Vincent dismisses its effect on his career. He does not acknowledge the gendered dimensions of anti-Asian racism for Asian American men, proudly asserting that in one of his previous roles, he "got the woman" and "she was *white*." Bradley refutes Vincent's vehement claim that he kissed her "ON THE LIPS! ON THE LIPS!" (100) by stressing that he would have remembered such an uncommon moment on network television. This causes a crestfallen Vincent to realize that "they edited it out" (100). The relegation to the cutting room floor of Vincent's interracial kiss becomes an analogue to the figurative castration Bradley condemns, the "cut[ting] off" of Asian American men's "balls."

An interlude follows where the audience sees Vincent alone, illuminated with a spotlight, on the phone. The other end of the conversation remains inaudible, and he speaks in hushed tones: "I cannot. You know why. Someone might see us together. (*Listens*) You do not know. People talk. Especially in this oriental community and then what happens to my career? I am a leading man" (102). Another interlude shows Vincent on the phone again. This time, his interlocutor is suicidal because Vincent has broken off the relationship. "Why do you keep on threatening to do it?" he accuses. "I hate that. You know you won't do it. Besides, I am not going to change my mind. (*Pause*) We can still see each other. (*Beat*) As friends" (115). Vincent's closeting for professional reasons was foreshadowed earlier when he admitted that, as a person of Japanese descent, he changed his name to evade the xenophobia after World War II—"Hell, I wanted to work" (97)—and has since been passing for Chinese American. However, rather than see these two forms of passing, ethnic and sexual, as evidence of how Vincent has, in fact, failed himself when he closes the play with the lament, "Why can't you see me as I really am?" (127), we might regard them as strategic manipulations of his leverage in structures that value heteromasculinity and other normativities.

In the wake of one of Vincent and Bradley's fights, the former speaks of a past heterosexual marriage that ended once he buckled under the pressure to maintain appearances. His ex-wife "did not mind the idea of me playing around," Vincent reports. Elaborating, he admits that "she minded but could live with it" but what "she could not stomach was who I was playing around with" (122). The story leads to an invitation for Bradley to visit for a drink, which he politely declines. The offer and its refusal create discomfort. The dialogue that follows attempts to diffuse it, but the resolution, which rests on Bradley's dismissal of the significance of sexual difference, is an apolitical declaration that seems out of place with the character who speaks it:

BRADLEY: It's okay.
(VINCENT *doesn't follow.*)
BRADLEY: It's okay, Vincent. It doesn't matter to me.
VINCENT: I do not know what you are talking about.
BRADLEY: It doesn't matter, Vincent. People don't care nowadays.
VINCENT: I do not know what you are talking about, Bradley. I do
    not. It is late. Good-bye. (122)

The relegation of sexual difference to something that "doesn't matter" or something about which "people don't care" may be a quick way for Bradley to assuage Vincent's embarrassment at an awkward moment. Vincent's response to his unreciprocated sexual interest then defuses his target's claim that sexuality is irrelevant. However, if we place Bradley's statement within its historical context, we see that it overlooks key disparities at the time of the play's appearance. It disappears the culture of fear that surrounded gay men in the 1980s.

Far from not "matter[ing]" at the time *Yankee Dawg You Die* premiered, sexual difference was absolutely crucial, and it had grave consequences. By now, it is common knowledge that the Reagan administration initially refused to address AIDS and fund programs devoted to prevention and care because of its concentration in demographics among the most devalued in U.S. society: gay men and intravenous drug users.[5] Jennifer Brier's study of those administrative events indicates that the federal Working Group on Health Policy drafted a memo in 1985 that stressed the urgency of AIDS as a civil rights issue, but White House staff members pressed a revision that struck out that emphasis, relegating it instead to a public health emergency. The final version the president signed reflected this update.[6] To be sure, this was not the first time an unfavorable population elicited control and containment with the intention of protecting citizens favored under biopolitical regimes. Nayan Shah unearthed a similar dynamic among Chinese immigrants, disease, and state forces at the turn of the twentieth century.[7] In the homophobic climate of the 1980s, gay men's lives and the lives of the HIV-positive were circumscribed by not only a lack of access to appropriate medical care but also the absence of antidiscrimination statutes regarding employment, housing, and public services. The government's refusal to consider AIDS patients worthy of protection exposed an intention to mark them for cultural as well as biological death.

Bringing the significance of these anxieties to the Hollywood industries, *Yankee Dawg You Die* remains curiously quick to forget that Rock Hudson died of HIV-related causes a mere three years before its appearance. The play recuperates elements from the real-life actor's personal history in the fictional Vincent's story, which include a heterosexual marriage of appearances. However, the two men are diametric opposites in how their respective masculinities code in U.S. popular culture. Whereas Vincent is reduced to a montage of two-dimensional racist caricatures—despite his feeble protests of being "a leading man" (102)—Hudson embodied the iconic figure of larger-than-life heteromasculinity throughout his career. Richard Meyer notes that Hudson's height and physique (along with, I would add, his whiteness) together created a manhood stylized to appeal to heterosexual women. The discrepancies between widely circulated photographs of Hudson on his hospital bed in 1985 and publicity stills from his career during the 1950s show the extent to which the American public continued to hold on to earlier images that presented a clean, wholesome, domesticated masculinity. Far from humanizing HIV/AIDS by presenting its visual evidence in a body that looks familiar—that is, non-gay and non-intravenous drug using—the images of the dying actor were instead "imbued with a heavy (and heavily homophobic) symbolism such that Hudson's moribund body becomes both signifier and symptom of his 'almost certain' homosexuality."[8] At this historical juncture, gay men had not yet arrived as subjects worthy of biopolitical care. Hudson's performance of heterosexuality on-screen at the height of his career, despite many in the industry who knew about his male lovers, served only to increase fears about gay men's and, by association, HIV disease's insidious ability to hide.

These images of Hudson, supine and ailing, at the end of his life provide an unintended but unmistakable foil for the kineticism of *Yankee Dawg You Die*. The play seems to take place beyond the politics of the HIV/AIDS crisis, which was in full force while Gotanda was writing. A pointed disconnect remains between Hudson's body, on the one hand, and the fitness demanded of both Vincent and Bradley in the stage directions, on the other. *Yankee Dawg You Die* is a physically demanding play. Insofar as a director can interpret the stage directions in ways that involve highly choreographed and vigorous blocking for the actors, one must be in normative physical health and of normative physical ability to portray the roles. Certainly, the production I attended by the Madison Theatre Guild attests to this. In *Yankee Dawg You Die*, the animated, nondisabled gay Asian American body stands in stark contrast to Hudson's HIV-infected, debilitated white body circulated in the popular media. The optics of health presented by this contrast generates further distance between the fictional Vincent and the real-life Hudson. Meanwhile, the conditions of same-sex desiring positionality during the Reagan era are evacuated from consideration.

Bradley's assertion about the inconsequentiality of sexuality may have been diplomatic in the heat of the moment, but it remains misguided as a political strategy. More ironically, it reprises an apoliticism for which the text's narrative voice has already condemned Vincent. The rapport Bradley attempts to establish with Vincent when the two men first meet takes the form of a statement about the party's racial demographics, to which the latter professes color-blindness: "Actually, I had not noticed. I do not really notice, or quite frankly care, if someone is Caucasian or oriental or . . ." (78). Vincent expresses uneasiness about Bradley's observation about their shared racial difference in the face of Hollywood's antipathy to Asian American representation. He prefers to believe that race does not matter, but his claim to not caring about it is unconvincing to Bradley and the play's intended audience. When Bradley later states that sexuality is beside the point, the play inadvertently reproduces the naïve multiculturalism that Vincent previously upheld. His words overlook years of federal inattention to the HIV/AIDS crisis. The resolution with which the play ends may provide complexity to a long-debated question about race and the conditions of employment for Asian American actors. Yet it does so at the risk of eliding the structural ramifications of sexuality contemporaneous with its appearance.

Yankee Dawg You Die suggests that Vincent's increased openness about his relationship with his same-sex partner at the end of the play is connected to his newfound willingness to accept roles in noncommercial productions. By pushing the envelope on portrayals that avail themselves to actors of color, he also contests the expectations of compulsory heterosexuality. However, these two instances of embracing the non-normative or the non-hegemonic are not analogous. We should not regard Vincent's partner choice as a dissident element in an otherwise accommodationist life history. With his lover's emotional manipulation and repeated suicide threats, which have manifested in two attempts, the relationship is far from healthy. The play's conclusion, which shows Vincent back in his relationship, implies that the reunion—like his acceptance of a role true to the spirit of Asian American politics—is a positive turn of events. However, there is no reassurance that the relationship has changed. At the same time, rather than judge his partner, I emphasize that these stressors in the couple's relationship take place in a 1980s-era context that has already deprived gay men of the essentials for biological life. Counseling may seem like an extravagance. Even though the homoeroticism in Vincent and Bradley's encounters facilitates the characters' cease-fire and resolves the opposing stances from which they began, gay identity is evacuated for this reconciliatory vehicle to work. Bradley must insist to Vincent on the inconsequentiality of sexuality. In turn, Vincent's coming out must be less a demand for political redress following years of state neglect than a decision to proceed with the nonchalance of no longer "car[ing]" (122) to closet himself.

In addition, Vincent's growing refusal to pass as straight does not find its corollary in the ethnic passing to which he had earlier admitted. There is no coming out as Japanese American, which was a salient social location in the 1980s, given the historical moment's demonization of Japan. In this era, white Americans feared the depression of U.S. industry by Japanese imports and felt anger about the manufacturing jobs that had started to decline. Japan became the scapegoat in this economic climate. Gotanda's character is the namesake of the real-life Vincent Chin, who in 1982 was murdered in a hate crime by two working-class white men in a struggling auto-industry Detroit. They had taken out their anti-Japanese racism against someone they believed to be of Japanese descent. His killers, Ronald Ebens and Michael Nitz, never served any prison time. The case garnered widespread national attention. Gotanda's choice to assign his character a name that, at the time of the play's premiere, would still have been readily associated with this act of violence does not seem like a coincidence. The vilification of Japan during the 1980s was very real, even if its particular form departed from that of the character portrayed by Vincent in the opening scene of the play.

Vincent and Bradley's compromise also depends on the maintenance of bonds between men that are meant to provide a bulwark against women. At their first meeting, Vincent warns Bradley about certain Asian American female actors to avoid as he navigates the industry. "Don't turn your back on her," Vincent insists as they direct their attention to one named Theodora Ando. When "BRADLEY *doesn't follow*[,] VINCENT *mimes sticking a knife in and twisting it*" (79). She is a backstabber, or so Vincent implies. It is no accident that this reference later becomes the friendly joke that allows Vincent and Bradley to mend their relationship after their first fight. As they wait to be called at an audition the following week, they speculate on how they might be cast:

> VINCENT: They want me for the part of the father. I am meeting the director. We could end up father and son. It might prove to be interesting.
> BRADLEY: Yeah.
> VINCENT: Then again, it might not. (*Silence. Awkward moment.* VINCENT *studies* BRADLEY.) Maybe they will cast Theodora Ando. As your sister. Make it a *murder* mystery. (VINCENT *mimes stabbing with a knife and twisting the blade.* BRADLEY *recalls* VINCENT's *earlier reference to Theodora at the party and laughs.* VINCENT *laughs, also. Pause.*) (86–87)

The two men make peace through levity at a woman's expense. Vincent can establish his credibility with Bradley by instilling fear about Theodora, and Bradley can position himself as a protégé of the more experienced actor by participating in her denigration. The Asian American female figure here is not the sympathetic one Bradley appraises positively in his recollection of a formative sexual experience. She is one who threatens Asian American men professionally.

This echo of the most simplistic tenet of Asian American cultural nationalism, which upholds traditional masculinity and regards women as emasculating threat, undermines the refreshing break that *Yankee Dawg You Die* makes from the previous decade's hard-line politics. To be fair, Gotanda's play does display a revision of the dogma of the 1970s. It references obliquely the theme of racially abhorrent performance in Frank Chin's *Year of the Dragon* (1974), only to revise it. (Perhaps most ironically, Chin was the first Asian American playwright to achieve recognition in the mainstream theater industry.) The reconciliation between Vincent and Bradley does not foreclose the possibility that there may be moments of transformation when acting in commercial productions, even if those gains are small. The resolution to the defining conflict in Gotanda's text implies that the lines between rebellion and compromise can remain flexible.[9] However, this new moderation still carries the traces of the old separatism in its treatment of gender difference.

DISIDENTIFICATION IN PERFORMANCE

Bradley's explanation for why he changed his mind and accepted the commercial role at the play's end assumes clear, unquestioned distinctions between racist and acceptable representations in Asian American performance. He states that he intends to work cooperatively with the show's masterminds to change its substance and make the concerns of Asian American actors more visible. There is another way that performers might rework something racially abhorrent that goes beyond the purview of the logic propelling *Yankee Dawg You Die*. Rather than the intervention Bradley describes, actors can effect what José Esteban Muñoz calls "disidentification." This maneuver involves neither uncritical acceptance nor wholesale dismissal but a transformation of sedimented and often hurtful stereotypes that "recycle[s] them as powerful and seductive sites of self-creation."[10] The cultural producer or consumer resignifies archetypes for subversive ends, divesting them of their original power. This strategy can be as subtle as, for instance, the choice of the Madison Theatre Guild's sound designer to play a Muzak version of Carl

Douglas's "Kung Fu Fighting" during the play's intermission, lending camp to a song that appropriates the aura of Asian martial arts. It can also be more overt, as action performed onstage.

Gotanda does not delve very deeply into actors' ability to revise and re-deploy racist fodder in this way. At one point, he does raise the potential, only to squelch it before the joy it generates becomes too unbridled. This aborted ecstasy takes place when Vincent and Bradley re-create a scene from a fictional musical, *Tea Cakes and Moon Songs*, from Vincent's past.[11] The song is a declaration of love from a waiter named Charlie, portrayed by Vincent, to his female sweetheart, Mei Ling, whose role Bradley assumes. Vincent encourages Bradley to play his character—who has only one line, "So Solly Cholly," uttered in caricatured English—with increasing camp. He commands Bradley, "Higher! Make your voice higher!," and keeps goading, "Higher! Higher!" (93). Bradley complies with enthusiasm at first. The stage directions indicate that "BRADLEY *coquettishly hid[es] behind a fan*," and "VINCENT *urges him to make his voice more female sounding*" (93). The blocking in the Madison Theatre Guild's production showed Vincent and Bradley "*whirling around on the stage*," one after the other, an example of the animated kineticism I referenced earlier. "VINCENT *sing[s] and tap-danc[es] with BRADLEY in tow singing in a high-pitched falsetto*" (93) while flutter-ing a fan. The scene is among the play's most boisterous, the two "*getting more and more involved, acting out more and more outrageous stereotypes*" (93). The playful sequence grinds to a halt when Bradley exclaims in anger. The mood changes. The physical animation stops. "Wait, wait, wait, what is this—WAIT! What am I doing? What is this shit? . . . You're acting like a Chinese Stepinfetchit," Bradley accuses. "That's what you're acting like. Jesus fucking Christ, Vincent. A *Chinese Stepinfetchit*" (93–94). Bradley comes to his senses, levels an indictment at Vincent, and ends the scene.

Parallels emerge between the conclusion to scene one and the conclu-sion to scene two in the first act. In the former, Bradley likens Vincent to a chimpanzee; in the latter, to Stepin Fetchit. These two insults invoke anti-blackness to convey Bradley's own pain when he comes to terms with Vin-cent's past decisions. Compounding the allusion to abjected blackness lurks the threat of homoeroticism and gender non-normativity. Bradley's initial delight in taking part in the performance is obvious. At Vincent's urging, he manipulates his voice to portray Mei Ling, even if the stage directions indicate that the pitch is a strain, "*struggling to go higher*" (93). The kinetic accompaniment to the song's lyrics plays out the romance between Charlie and Mei Ling as the two actors run together in wide loops on the stage. What stops Bradley, however, is not the realization of his drag performance as a heterosexual woman, which seems too unspeakable for him to acknowledge, but Vincent's racial caricature. It becomes the scapegoat for the queer pleasure Bradley had enjoyed a moment earlier.

Bradley's refusal to accept the sexual dimensions of his and Vincent's reenactment of the song takes place not only within his subjective experience of it but also in Gotanda's authorial voice. The stage directions instruct the actors to play *"more and more outrageous stereotypes,"* but they remain mum as to what, exactly, those stereotypes are. Although playwrights commonly allow room for interpretation, the ambiguity at this particular moment anticipates the obfuscation of Bradley's homosexual panic shortly afterward. Gotanda's hinting at and eventual evasion of popular assumptions about Asian-raced men's non-normative gendering and sexuality partially uncovers itself in the interlude that follows. A spotlight appears on Bradley auditioning for a commercial featuring a Japanese tourist using a camera. He queries an invisible panel:

> What? Take the picture, then put my hand like this—in front of my mouth and giggle? Yeah, but Japanese men don't giggle. How about if I shoot the picture and like this. . . . Just laugh. (*Listens*) I'm sorry, but I can't do that. Look, it's not truthful to the character. Japanese men don't giggle. What? (*Listens. Turns to leave.*) Yeah, well the same to you, Mr. Asshole Director. (94–95)

Bradley refuses to re-create actions and affects associated with girls, such as the demure covering of the mouth and giggling, when transposed onto grown Asian men (despite his adjacent act of fluttering a fan only a moment earlier). His anger is directed at the reproduction of gendered forms of racism that emasculate him and others like him. However, one might ask what is wrong with a Japanese man who decides that giggling is an acceptable way to express pleasure. Why does an embrace of gestures associated with femininity disqualify something as "not truthful to the character"? Although the polemic in Gotanda's play appears to move beyond the separatism of the previous generation's cultural nationalism, the yoking of authenticity and normative masculinity remains intact. When Bradley decides at the play's conclusion to work inside the system to change it, the progress implied is not an amelioration of gender normativity's unforgiving strictures for Asian American men. It is a restoration of the hegemonic masculinity that historically has been denied to them.

Karen Shimakawa argues that archetypes in Gotanda's play, such as the Japanese soldier, convey more complexity when we probe under their surfaces. The overblown way in which Vincent performs the role does not necessarily solidify its racism. Rather, it renders the character unintelligible and "incapable of being understood."[12] His obliteration of the character through exaggeration becomes a quiet strategy that is neither wholly resistant nor wholly submissive. Far from being uncritically accommodationist, the Vincent that emerges in Shimakawa's reading maintains awareness of his place in an industry that relies on the commodification of Asian-raced bodies.[13] However, I want to turn her interpretive premise to the scene I referenced earlier. It is one she does not consider. Bradley's portrayal of Mei Ling is experienced differently. The actors' impromptu rendition of the musical exists beyond the reach of the market. Two friends take part in playful theater exercises on their own and without an audience other than the men themselves, who simultaneously perform for and derive pleasure from watching each other. Although Bradley may be vigilant about the real possibility of directors coercing him into portraying stereotypes he deems offensive, when institutions are out of the picture he can take uninhibited joy in embodying discomfiting roles with his idol and mentor. Josephine Lee astutely notes that in *Yankee Dawg You Die*, the "most deeply ambivalent, disturbing, and powerful moments . . . are those when the Asian American actors displayed a marked attraction for playing 'Fetchits,' and share with us as audience the thrill of being deeply inside what is shameful."[14] Building on Lee's claim, I stress that this shame indexes the loss of normative masculinity for Bradley. Initially, he happily assumes the role of a heterosexual woman opposite to Vincent, who plays his love interest, and he responds to verbal encouragement to intensify the character. Once terror about his breach of normative heteromasculinity sets in, Bradley externalizes it. He directs that anxiety about the loss of manhood at Vincent and further masks it with an accusation that invokes not queerness but antiblackness.

Discussions of sexual non-normativity in *Yankee Dawg You Die* have tended to focus on Vincent, not Bradley, which is expected, given how Gotanda has characterized his sexual identity. James S. Moy juxtaposes Vincent's subjectivity with contemporaneous gains made by queers, indicating with disappointment that this aspect of the text "crush[es] the unwitting Chinese/Japanese/closet gay into the space of aporia, subverting the most positive aspects of the play before it."[15] Shimakawa counters Moy with a more positive view, claiming that Gotanda "creates an Asian American gay man . . . coming into his own, personally and professionally, successful and content in both realms."[16] This is a stance about which, as I expressed earlier in my concerns about the health of Vincent's relationship, I remain less enthusiastic. Neither Moy nor Shimakawa discusses the possibility of straight-identified Bradley's experience of queerness. Given my interpretation of the role-playing scene, I would argue that Bradley's nonconformity is more polymorphously perverse than Vincent's and, therefore, more pleasurable and potentially more disruptive. However, it comes with a correspondingly increased panic.

Yankee Dawg You Die does problematize the doctrines of cultural nationalism, but it does not depart from those premises to a very great extent. There is a nuance to the stark poles of rebellion and compromise that did not exist in, say, Frank Chin's work. However, the idea that Asian American male actors should strive for recognition of their ability to wield traditional markers of masculinity leaves the preceding decade's gender politics intact. When Vincent closes the play by reciting the opening monologue with a twist, ending with a heartfelt plea for mainstream U.S. viewers to "see me as I really am" (127), the implied standard for realness resembles the model proffered by Chin in a well-known essay, "Come All Ye Asian American Writers of the Real and the Fake."[17] What Chin and Gotanda both claim to be fake—that is, a product of fantasies issuing from white racism—is a feminized artifice that must be eradicated before Asian American men can come into their authentic own.

THE PERSISTENCE OF UNCHALLENGED MASCULINITY

It should not surprise us that the softening of hard-line distinctions between protest and accommodation leaves unchallenged an aspiration to hegemonic masculinity. Those standards persist so strongly, and their linkage with agency and self-determination remains so intact, that it can be hard to think otherwise. Almost two decades after the premiere of *Yankee Dawg You Die*, the director Jeff Adachi's documentary *The Slanted Screen* (2006) attempts to bring the questions raised by Gotanda's play to bear on early twenty-first-century contexts. The film provides a historical and contemporary overview of the representation of Asian and Asian American men in the motion picture industries. It functions as a counterpart to an earlier documentary, *Slaying the Dragon* (1988), which addressed Asian-raced women in film and television. An intergenerational cast of experts—Asian American male actors, directors, writers, and producers—speak of their experiences, critique current states of affairs, and propose ways forward. The documentary is a recovery project, too, as it showcases early to mid-twentieth-century stars such as Sessue Hayakawa and James Shigeta, names that have been largely forgotten in mainstream accounts of Hollywood, in roles of male leads and love interests opposite white women.

Adachi's subjects exhibit an overwhelming agreement that the dearth of Asian American men in Hollywood remains a problem. Moreover, they condemn their relegation to a limited set of roles. They speak of barriers to entry. When Asian American men do manage to find work, they are often cast as minor characters that lack complexity. The word "stereotype" gets repeated across a range of interviews. A recurring bone of contention is the pressure to perform parts that portray Asian or Asian American men in such ways. Early in the documentary, the film studies scholar and director Darrell Hamamoto provides a working definition for "stereotype" to establish a context for the discussion: "A stereotype is any sort of image or portrayal that constricts, confines, or—in some cases—marginalizes a group of people. It's a generalization that unfairly is used to characterize a certain group."[18] On the heels of defining the word, various actors weigh in to clarify what it entails for Asian American men.

Cary-Hiroyuki Tagawa, best known for his kinetically challenging martial arts performances in the *Mortal Kombat* franchise, states, "I've been criticized for playing bad guys by different people within the Asian/Asian American community because they feel that it puts us in a bad light." Indeed, the U.S. history of twentieth-century wars with Asia has made the figure of the Asian man a reliable symbol of villainy. Hollywood has gotten a lot of mileage from that past. For Tagawa, however, playing a martial arts antagonist remains preferable to the alternative, which he claims is a weak and impotent character. The actor and director Phillip Rhee similarly calls on the ability of martial arts to endow a particular type of racialized virility for Asian American men: "We have to be proud of legend Bruce Lee. He gave a lot of Asian males pride. We were able to walk down the street with our heads up." The association between Asian-originated martial arts and sexual magnetism is tenuous and arbitrary to the point of needing an explanation that the interview segment lacks. (This conflation is simply taken for granted.) Asian American male actors appeal to the physical prowess needed to deliver in these roles when explaining their favorability.

Multiple subjects speak of their disdain for portrayals of Asian American men that erase their potential as sexual agents. Tagawa elaborates on what makes the roles he has accepted empowering, despite their reliance on the predictable trope of the Asian-raced man as enemy:

> You had the choice between playing wimpy businessmen or evil bad guys. The worst thing I could do is play a bad guy, and be a wimpy bad guy, which is what I grew up with. And my intention was if I was going to choose between a wimpy businessman or playing a bad guy, I'm going to play a bad guy, because I got balls *[smiles]*. I got balls *[laughter]*, and I want kids to grow up to know that Asian men got balls.

The filmmaker Gene Cajayon reports that "mainstream America, for the most part, is uncomfortable with seeing an Asian man portrayed in a sexual light, in a powerful light." Hamamoto weighs in with more detail on his central complaint about the accumulation of one-sided portrayals: "For any group to be marginalized in terms of their power, one strategy to enact is to desexualize them, and indeed, that's the case for most Asian American males. Asian American men are desexualized." He stresses that these representations have real-world consequences: "Some [Asian American men] experience or indicate a high degree of racial self-hate. And it comes from these images of perhaps Asian American men as being powerless, impotent, and desexualized."

A chorus of agreement sounds in *The Slanted Screen* about the necessity of intervention in the representation of Asian American men in Hollywood. The actor Jason Scott Lee implores, "So there's a stereotype. Let's fight it. Let's fight to conquer it." Frank Chin concurs: "We have to challenge the stereotype. . . . We have to prove that the stereotype is false. To prove that the stereotype is false, we have to recover the history and the culture that the stereotype displaced or displaces. We have to, and that's a lot of work." The veteran actor Mako Iwamatsu (commonly known by only his first name), who died the year the documentary was released, admonishes would-be complicity. "Don't get into stereotypic image. . . . Stereotypic image is the easiest and simplest way to [get work]," he declares. "But . . . performers will not get satisfaction out of doing it. Only satisfaction may be your bank account may be a little fatter. That's about it, you know. Is that worth having that kind of a record on your soul?" Contrary to what *Yankee Dawg You Die* would have its audience assume, the interview subject from the oldest generation in Adachi's documentary—the real-life corollary to Vincent—takes the most principled and unwavering stance against accommodation, refusing even to justify the economic pressures that motivate it.

In *The Slanted Screen*, the extreme abjection that attends the figure of the effeminate Asian-raced man leaves little room for a critique of masculinities that emerge from white conventions. Paradoxically, the exhortation to resist the representations of Asian or Asian American men that have solidified in the motion picture industries can wind up replicating the very problems Hamamoto identified as germane to a stereotype: that it "constricts," "confines," and "marginalizes." The belief that Asian American male actors should push back against their connection with effeminacy by using opposing force, rather than challenge the foundations on which normative masculinity rests, *is* constraining. This is not to say that certain portrayals of people of color should be left uncontested. As Celine Parreñas Shimizu argues, "The discourse of misrepresenting a community needs to be split from the critique of asexuality/effeminacy/homosexuality as lack for Asian American men." When we insist on more capacious notions of masculine legitimacy, we see that the "representations of Asian American men as failing to achieve sexual consummation are not necessarily a psychic, material, and social castration."[19] To be sure, one interview segment with Philip Rhee raises the possibility for an alternative vision. Rhee reports that he, as a director, "tr[ies] to show the so-called Asian male in a different light. Yes, this person could be strong. Yes, this person fights for what is right. And, yes, he is sensitive and can be a real human being." At the same time, the singular and isolated nature of this qualification in *The Slanted Screen,* that we need to cherish vulnerability and multidimensionality alongside power, places the documentary in the same realm as *Yankee Dawg You Die.* Both texts display a valuing of manhood in line with white American ideals.

NEW ANSWERS
FOR OLD QUESTIONS?

In *Yankee Dawg You Die,* we see a dichotomy between "the actor" and a nebulous entity conceptualized as "the industry." A schema emerges whereby the former becomes a David making a lone stand to face his Goliath. If one were to learn about the operations of show business from only *Yankee Dawg You Die,* one might come away with a skewed idea about the extent to which actors' individualistic choices can make or break a prevailing concept about a racial minority and how solidly careers rest on individual actions. One might also assume that the industry, by nature, possesses a complete lack of regard for more just portrayals of people of color in sole pursuit of profit. Nancy Wang Yuen's book *Reel Inequality* complicates these misunderstandings, making transparent how whiteness gets institutionalized in Hollywood at every step of the way. It also explains the stakes of an entertainment industry that has transformed since the time Gotanda was writing.

Reel Inequality includes, for the uninitiated, an explication of how the various behind-the-scenes decision makers in Hollywood wield their authority. From studio executives to directors, executive producers, writers, talent agents, and casting directors, each plays a specific role in determining the racial composition and representation of a finished product. These gatekeepers, who are largely white, do not function as a monolith. However, together they work in ways that entrench whiteness in television and film. Even if those employed in these capacities do not harbor racist views or wish to circulate them, they remain risk-averse, given that television shows and motion pictures that fail commercially often do so with great financial consequences. For this reason, they tend to rely on tried-and-true formulas and are resistant to change.[20]

On the other side of this equation lie those who can turn the hand of these decision makers, an equally variegated set of stakeholders with influence. Some of the stakeholders are actors themselves. Yuen's study includes interviews with dozens of rank-and-file actors who describe their strategies, resonant with those laid out in *Yankee Dawg You Die*, for mitigating the malaise that comes with portraying demeaning characters, subverting them in subtle or not-so-subtle ways, and making sense of their participation in a flawed industry. Yet the most insightful parts of *Reel Inequality* touch on vectors of this influence that remain absent from Gotanda's play. Yuen reminds us that, for a long time, civil rights organizations have launched successful campaigns involving boycotts and legal action that have held entertainment industries accountable for their racism. The National Association for the Advancement of Colored People (NAACP), for instance, has been active in this way since its protest of D. W. Griffith's *The Birth of a Nation* (1915). Asian American activists and their allies have exerted their leverage with casting practices for *Miss Saigon* (1989) and condemned the musical's problematic portrayals. A multiracial group of civil rights organizations and independent theater companies, called the Grand Coalition, now monitors the major television networks' hiring practices to ensure they place people of color in positions of power.[21] From within the industry, formal and informal mentoring and professionalization networks exist into which actors of color can tap. Unions, guilds, and other related organizations are also part of the process of raising the profile of actors of color. Last, of course, consumers can vote with their feet by tuning in to programs that not only feature characters of color but also portray them in all their complexity. They can also speak out on social media platforms, which large entertainment companies monitor and take seriously, to express approval or displeasure.[22] Hence, the playing field is not a vastly uneven one on which the singular actor stands against an undefined but all-powerful industry. Yuen's picture of how influence works provides another dimension to our thinking about the relationship between big business and social justice.

The "browning" of the Yellow Peril in the post-9/11 era rekindled the ethical questions raised by *Yankee Dawg You Die* in the context of Arab American actors in Hollywood. The demand for actors to play two-dimensional bit parts as terrorists expanded rapidly after the attacks on the World Trade Center and Pentagon in 2001. Today, many actors of Arab descent grapple with the dilemmas faced by Gotanda's fictional Vincent and Bradley. A recent interview with a core group of Arab American men in television and film reveals that they maintain a high level of camaraderie because they need to support one another emotionally through the despair caused by playing degrading parts. One points out the lack of usual competition among actors: "Whenever it's that kind of role and we see each other at auditions, it's so comforting. We're not in this alone. We're in this together."[23] The reporter conducting the interview recounts that much of his time with the group was spent listening to them share audition advice generously with one another.

In the memoir *I'm Not a Terrorist, but I've Played One on TV*, the actor Maz Jobrani charts his trajectory from film extra to owner of his own stand-up comedy label. Jobrani grew up in an Iranian immigrant family and spent his childhood watching and being inspired by American television. His early roles as terrorists were less than satisfying and reveal the futility of attempting to change the industry from inside, as Gotanda's Bradley intends. An overwhelmingly positive reception to Jobrani's work in independent circles attests to the presence of a critical mass of "Middle Easterners and Muslims, as well as liberal-minded people who were sick of seeing us portrayed only as the bad guys and curious to see how we would do as entertainers."[24] Jobrani's memoir is a triumphant account of the rise of his comedy label, Axis of Evil, a cheeky resignification of George W. Bush's demonization of the Arab world. It has performed internationally and provided momentum for his solo career.

The kind of leverage Jobrani wields appears to be increasingly accessible for Asian American actors even on commercial television. Ken Jeong starred on the ABC family situation comedy *Dr. Ken*, which aired from 2015 to 2017 and was loosely based on his former career as a physician. In an interview, the Korean American Jeong explained how he asserted his vision for the show, stressing that its ethnic specificities needed to be "introduced organically" instead of being the program's main draw. Once, a white writer had proposed a line that Jeong described as "a very hacky Asian joke." He objected. Explaining his position, he declared, "In my life, I don't talk like that, I don't act like that."[25] Unlike the outcome Gotanda's Bradley faces when he contests a role he was to play at an audition, Jeong succeeded in his intervention because it occurred in a context in which he had the upper hand. However, it is notable that both the real and the fictional actors appealed to an assumed authenticity in their opposition to a script that was not of their own making. Echoing Jeong, the Indian American actor Aziz Ansari has claimed that he has gained the coveted autonomy that is rare for actors of color only because *Master of None*, his successful Netflix show, is his own creation. "Look, if you're a minority actor, no one would have [written] this show for you," he says. "No one would have been like, *Hey how about we get Aziz to do this ten-episode show and have [him] play this thoughtful character.*"[26] In the past, Ansari had declined a part as a call center employee for a major film, which later cast a friend. Yet he remains realistic about the limitations under which actors work and refrains from condemning anyone for making decisions that differ from his own.

Recent developments for Asian American actors in commercial entertainment may force a rethinking of the divide between autonomy and economic necessity that Gotanda lays out in *Yankee Dawg You Die*. One may conclude that Bradley's goal to intervene in entrenched institutions is not as implausible now as it may have seemed in 1988. In addition to *Dr. Ken* and *Master of None*, other television shows starring Asian American actors have arrived. *The Mindy Project* came on the scene in 2012, and *Fresh Off the Boat* premiered in 2015. Yet these successes appear to be the exceptions that prove the rule when placed in the context of other examples from recent years. Two recent controversies in the world of Asian American performance inform my thinking as I write this chapter. Both have spoken to an ongoing need for change in the commercial film industries. The first case involves the premiere of the film *Doctor Strange*, by Marvel Studios, in 2016. A white actor, Tilda Swinton, was cast in the role of a character originally conceived as Tibetan, but screenwriters had rewritten the part to change the character's ethnicity to Celtic. The second, in 2017, was the release of the filmic adaptation of a popular manga series, *The Ghost in the Shell*, by Paramount Pictures. In it, the white actor Scarlett Johansson played the role of an Asian character, and the studio attempted to justify its decision by appealing to a technologically forward sensibility, using computer-generated imagery software to render Johansson's features more phenotypically Asian.

The first example aligns with Angela C. Pao's observation that culture-making industries are simply reinscribing whiteness in narratives about Asia. When characters of color disappear altogether, it makes Asian American actors irrelevant.[27] The second recovers earlier practices of yellowface but with digital technology instead of makeup and eyelid tape. In addition, these news items came on the heels of a sustained protest about the lack of racial diversity in general at the Academy Awards in 2016, when, for the second year in a row, all the nominees for the acting prizes were white. The social media hashtag #oscarssowhite emerged to speak back to the snubbing of actors of color, despite highly acclaimed performances by Idris Elba, Will Smith, and others that had been expected to garner nominations. The debate about fair representation of people of color in the motion picture industries trended far and wide. Yet a glimmer of hope arose amid these happenings. As I write these words in July 2017, the resignation of two Asian American actors, Daniel Dae Kim and Grace Park, from the

CBS television show *Hawaii Five-O* is trending on news sources and social media. Kim and Park left the show because of unequal pay between white and Asian American actors, and the amount of attention their act of protest has received is heartening.

THE ENDURING SILENCE
ABOUT SEXUALITY

Today, as we near the third decade of the twenty-first century, an updated *Yankee Dawg You Die* might go one step further from the conclusion to which it comes. An analogous play for the present might blur the boundaries between the commercial and the independent and the racially stereotypical and the politically enabling. As with *Yankee Dawg You Die*, however, this changed terrain of entertainment for Asian American actors still shies away from an unpacking of normative gender and sexual formations. For instance, *Master of None* has been critiqued for a vision of Indian American masculinity that withholds full personhood for Indian American women. Portrayals of the protagonist, a single straight man living and dating in New York City, invariably center his experiences with white women as a way of signaling his assimilated heteromasculinity. Meanwhile, Indian American women remain only "an anonymous, unnamed, and crumpled footnote in the story . . . the punchline, the afterthought, the ad-on, or the barely explored B story. [They] will never be romanced seriously."[28] For heterosexual people of color, the dismissal of erotic and sexual connections with one's co-ethnics in favor of white partners can be a way to claim the measured amount of cultural capital that comes with this interracial pairing. For heterosexual men in particular, this validation from white women can feel akin, as Frantz Fanon has famously claimed, to becoming white: "By loving me, [the white woman] proves to me that I am worthy of a white love. I am loved like a white man." Making the leap, the conclusion to this logic becomes, "I am a white man."[29] Viewed from this perspective, the perverse queerness between Vincent and Bradley in *Yankee Dawg You Die*, even if it is not directly unacknowledged, exists in a world completely separate from that of Ansari's character.

Contemporary discussions about the barriers that actors of color face often do not provide an intersectional analysis that accounts for the significance of sexual difference. This absence echoes the oversights of *Yankee Dawg You Die* from an earlier time. One exception to this trend appears in a recent interview conducted by Tina Takemoto with the veteran gay Japanese American actor Sab Shimono. When asked about the most important concerns for LGBT Asian American actors, Shimono responds initially in a way reminiscent of *Yankee Dawg You Die*'s apoliticism: "I don't think actors go around saying they are gay. It's not discussed. You go in for the role, and if you are the actor they want, you get the part." He elaborates, "For Asians in film, it's not like there are many romantic lead parts for us," implying that, since Asian American men historically have been passed over for roles in heterosexual love stories, this sticking point is less of an issue.[30] What straight Asian American male actors lament about their exclusion turns out to be more enabling—because less psychically troubling—for their gay counterparts. However, Shimono backtracks a bit and qualifies:

> I've played romantic leads in theater, but in Hollywood film, if you were gay, it would have been a problem. When I think about Rock Hudson, if he would have been out, he probably wouldn't have gotten the roles that he did. I'm not sure how much of an issue that is now. I think it is still there, because the audience wouldn't "buy it." They would believe a straight guy playing a gay man, but I don't know about the reverse.[31]

In Shimono's depiction of what is and is not permissible and in which medium, the purportedly unmarked location of heterosexuality enjoys the benefit of universality. The particularity of LGBT film actors, conversely, restricts their opportunities.

In *Yankee Dawg You Die*, Vincent himself raises concern about the potential damage to a Hollywood actor's prospects if he is known for or suspected of being gay. Unfortunately, the play misses an opportunity to explore the differential structural locations of straight versus gay actors. In this sense, the play's narrative voice appears to align with Bradley's. Shrugging off the implications of sexual difference in a moment of discomfort, *Yankee Dawg You Die* does as Bradley does, dismissing its relevance and refusing to acknowledge that it has material consequences. In the end, Vincent's foray into the uncharted territory of independent film comes about through Bradley's sometimes bombastic but ultimately genuine advocacy for that world. Correspondingly, Bradley's equally challenging venture into a commercial production might not have happened had it not been for Vincent's wisdom about the necessity of fitting the demands of the market into one's professional aspirations. The potential for an informed and compassionate reconciliation of this intraracial divide comes from, first, an appeal to love and sexual desire between Asian American men; and second, a disidentificatory play with femininity. Ironically, the dissolution of the boundary between rebellion and compromise arises only through the suppression of non-heterosexual intimacy, which was the very precondition for its being.

4

DESIRE AND RESISTANCE

In 1877, the U.S. Senate compiled a document to assess the state of Chinese immigration. One of the experts consulted, the ship captain Thomas H. King, had an extensive track record of recruiting and transporting laborers from Hong Kong. At the time of his testimony, he had lived in China for ten years. The Senate summoned him to provide insights about Chinese customs, workers' contracts, and the day-to-day experience of transpacific travel. At one point, King reported that among his Chinese charges, the "practice on ship-board of sodomy and pollution is common."[1] Attesting in more depth, King declared:

> [Sodomy] is a habit. I would say that I have had sometimes thirty or forty Chinese boys apparently leaving Hong-Kong in good health, and on the voyage over, before arriving here, a voyage of two months, I have found them afflicted about the anus with venereal diseases. I have examined them and compelled the Chinese doctors to disclose what it was, and they admitted that it was a common practice among them. I have seen them in pollution quite frequently on ships, and often onshore in China, where it is a common practice; I have seen it.[2]

Laying aside the question of why King would take a protracted interest in the rectal cavities of his passengers, his account of homosexual activity among Chinese men implies that their behavior was situational. It arose from the conditions of assembling at docks and riding ships in close quarters exclusively with one another. In this narrative of declension, young men not yet afflicted with moral and physical "pollution" at the beginning of the voyage disembark tainted at its destination. The Senate report's accounts of Chinese men's sexual practices—which include, among other things, bestiality—situated them as heterosexuality's failed subjects. Yet it suggests that "crimes committed . . . in the absence of women" occurred only because of a lack of more appealing options—not because of the inherent depravity of Chinese men.[3] The corrupting effects of gender segregation at sea were the culprit.

Chinese workers troubled Victorian mandates of middle-class heterosexual domesticity. The rates of entry into the country of Chinese women did not match those of men. U.S. capitalists in the late nineteenth century sought male workers to perform tasks in the railroad and mining industries, which were located in regions far removed from feminized domestic spaces in the contemporaneous notion of separate spheres relegating women to the home. The gender imbalance among early Chinese settlements in the United States stemmed from the consequences of the belief, embedded in immigration policy, that Chinese women were especially prone to working as prostitutes.[4] The Page Act of 1875 barred the entry of Chinese women not already married to a man of the merchant classes bound for or residing in the United States.[5] Together, the demands of capitalist expansion and the gendered dynamics of U.S. immigration, not static Chinese patriarchal dictates preventing women's mobility, created gender imbalances in immigrant populations at the end of the nineteenth century.[6]

The preponderance of men in Chinese enclaves unsettled Anglo-Americans coping with the changes wrought by industrialization. Largely male Chinatowns lay beyond the perimeters and parameters of bourgeois heterosexual life and were thought to harbor sexual threat and opium abuse in their crowded abodes. These neighborhoods were known as "bachelor societies," despite the fact that many men living in them actually remained married to women in China. In addition, as Nayan Shah shows, a fair number of these households, in reality, contained both male and female residents. It was common for large numbers of people of both genders to live under one roof in the form of a boardinghouse. Women often reared children collectively, each member taking responsibility for caretaking, regardless of biological affiliation.[7] Together, the arrangements of Chinese homes disrupted heterosexual mores. Chinatowns purportedly put white women and girls in danger, as it was believed that their male residents, wracked with (hetero)sexual deprivation, laid in wait for unsuspecting prey.

The horror that Chinese men conjured coalesced around two high-profile cases at the end of the nineteenth century. In 1889, several thousand white men in Milwaukee incited a four-day riot to retaliate against the local

Chinese population, which they suspected of sexually trapping and trafficking white girls. The trial of two launderers that ensued involved allegations of sexual coercion and abuse from eight white girls age eight to thirteen. Victor Jew avers that this event catalyzed in small ways the redefinition of Anglo-American childhood in the 1890s.[8] The panic that surrounded Chinese men was perhaps no more intensely expressed than in the public response to an unsolved murder from 1909 that drew international attention. In New York, the body of a nineteen-year-old white woman was discovered inside the apartment of a Chinese man who disappeared, never to be apprehended. Mary Ting Yi Lui claims the ensuing fallout revealed the extent to which middle-class, Protestant Anglo-Americans had begun to fear their susceptibility to Chinese sexual infiltration. Previously, it was believed that only poor and working-class Irish immigrant women consorted with the Chinese.[9]

But what if the most upsetting possibility about Chinese men was not that they wanted to lure, abduct, drug, rape, or murder white women? What if the most prominent concerns about Chinese violation of white female bodies had been aired only because something else was more incomprehensible? What if these bachelor societies were not rife with unfulfilled erotic longing and sexual desperation? What if white women remained incidental to the libidinal investments of Chinese men? What if these men desired one another above all else?

I pose these questions not because I intend to prove, empirically, that men in Chinatowns touched one another sexually. My focus is on the realm of representation rather than that of the historical record. Instead, I propose a different way to make sense of the skewed gender ratios in turn-of-the-twentieth-century Chinatowns. Judy Tzu-Chun Wu cautions against Asian Americanist scholarship's tendency to condemn racially discriminatory immigration policies because they pervert a heterosexuality that is presumed to be natural. Instead, we might think of "the compulsory condition of 'deviance' among the early generation of Asian Americans . . . not only as an indicator of racial victimization but also as an opportunity for non-normative sexual exploration."[10] Along these lines, I wish to disrupt the aspirations to normativity that informed how Chinese men were understood by white America at the turn of the twentieth century. It is true that the economic conditions of working-class life meant that many immigrants resided in close quarters within a single domestic unit.[11] It is also true that loopholes around immigration law, such as buying paternal affiliations, gave rise to unusual and creative kinship structures, "paper families" that were every bit as involved as biologically reproductive ones.[12] Rather than assume these non-normative relationships formed only by circumstance, however, I suggest that they were actively sought after and cherished.

This chapter provides a reading of a novel by the Chinese immigrant writer H. T. Tsiang to illustrate this phenomenon. *And China Has Hands*, published in 1937, is set in New York in the 1930s. It charts a protagonist's rise from a worker with false consciousness to a martyr for the revolutionary cause. Tsiang was best known for having been a Hollywood actor from the 1940s to the 1960s. Before he began his film career, he wrote proletarian literature, garnering a following in New York for his poems, essays, novels, and plays that foregrounded pro-labor themes. He was born in China in 1899 and came to the United States in 1926 to attend graduate school at Stanford University. The Chinese Exclusion Act exempted students—as well as teachers, clergy, and merchants. Eventually, Tsiang enrolled at Columbia University, where his professors encouraged his writing. He published several texts that lent complexity to the subjectivities of Chinese men living under Anglo-America's misconceptions. In *And China Has Hands*, the forging of same-sex intimacies becomes a welcomed and absolutely necessary departure from the illusory, damaging hopes that heteronormativity and capitalist success present. By nurturing erotic desires with one another, working-class Chinese men challenge the toxic intraethnic divides wrought by a respectability politics that demands their compliance with middle-class, heterosexual mandates.

The surge of literary-critical interest in *And China Has Hands* in the recent past has been aided by the novel's reissue in 2003 after being out of print for many years. Many critics have used its deceptively simple plot to unravel the complex interrelations among race, gender, and economic relations. The story line features an initially naïve Chinese immigrant's growth from believer in the American myth of upward mobility to pro-labor revolutionary. A subplot involves the concurrent transformation of his heterosexual love interest, a biracial Chinese and African American woman. What has still been overlooked in the scholarship is the degree to which the protagonist longs for same-sex erotic and social congress with his co-ethnics. These moments of yearning erupt throughout the narrative in ways that are hard to ignore. Through *And China Has Hands*, Tsiang interceded in discourses about Chinese masculinity. The early twentieth-century popular imagination may have cast Chinese immigrants as the constitutive outside to Anglo-American gender, sexual, and class acceptability. However, Tsiang showed that what these men craved most was not an impossible replication of those normative formations. They wanted intimacy with one another. *And China Has Hands* suggests that queer bonds are central to resolving a racialized working-class population's conflicts between capitalist ideology and radical politics. Throughout the novel, internal cleavages among Chinese men arise. Business owners exploit workers. Workers fight one another. Opportunists pursue victims. However, the satisfaction from intraethnic eroticism proves to be so compelling that it quells misguided strivings for economic gain and assimilation in favor of worker solidarity.

I begin this chapter by addressing how Chinese men's non-normative affiliations trouble the foundational work in the field of gay history. Next, I address the writings of the Chicago School sociologist Paul C. P. Siu on Chinese immigrant men's intimacies with one another. I move next to a discussion of Tsiang's debunking of common misconceptions about Chinese men through a series of close readings of *And China Has Hands*. These readings demonstrate, first, a yoking of upward mobility with heteronormativity; and second, a same-sex erotics that resolves tensions between class ascent and pro-labor revolution. Toward the end of the chapter, I reintroduce Siu's work and draw parallels between the intraethnic bonds generated by his fieldwork and the queer inclinations in Tsiang's novel. Although fiction and social science writing are two different modes of knowledge production with two separate systems of legitimation, I read these texts by Tsiang and Siu together as cultural artifacts from the same period. They jointly emerge from a historical moment marked by fears about Chinese men. Finally, I conclude with a temporally queer rationale for moving the birth of Asian American activism several decades back from the years to which it is often attributed.

SOCIAL SCIENCE AND
SEXUAL NON-NORMATIVITY

Canonical gay history has duly established links between late nineteenth-century and early twentieth-century urban space and non-normative sexuality. In the well-known essay "Capitalism and Gay Identity," John D'Emilio argues that the forces of capital during this time created cultural institutions that supported same-sex erotic and sexual intimacy. Whereas the biologically reproductive family in agrarian societies may have held forth as the unit of production in previous generations, the rise of wage labor that characterized city life issued a transformation. No longer reliant on the nuclear family for economic viability, same-sex-desiring workers employed under this new system created emotionally sustaining communities of lesbians and gay men. "These patterns of living," D'Emilio claims, "could evolve because capitalism allowed individuals to survive beyond the confines of the family."[13] George Chauncey, who casts attention on the same time span as D'Emilio, mobilizes his book *Gay New York* to rethink the teleology of post-Stonewall concepts of liberation. He argues that the steady upward progress over time assumed for conditions amenable to male same-sex activity is a fiction. Lively gay subcultures that cities such as New York sustained were actually more, not less, prevalent in the early part of the twentieth century than in the mid-century.[14]

Where D'Emilio and Chauncey depart from each other is on how working-class (European) immigrants factored into their observations. D'Emilio states that within his framework for understanding the relationship between wage labor and same-sex sexuality, immigrants' options were more limited than those of their U.S.-born counterparts. For them, he writes, "Closely knit kin networks and an ethic of family solidarity placed constraints on individual autonomy that made gayness a difficult option to pursue."[15] Chauncey complicates this assertion. He notes that many Italian male migrants had a sojourner mentality. They, "mostly single men or married men unaccompanied by their families," arrived with the goal of "return[ing] to Italy after earning funds to invest there."[16] Chauncey surmises that this is why Italians participated more actively in gay life than men of other ethnicities, such as Jews, who typically arrived in the United States with wives and children. However, the described pattern of Italian migrancy here resembles that of the Chinese, who do not appear in Chauncey's very comprehensive study. This discrepancy becomes even more unsettling when we see that the temporal parameters of *Gay New York*, 1890–1940, coincide almost exactly with the period of Chinese exclusion, when Chinese immigrants found normative kin and sexual structures especially difficult to establish.

I am not taking D'Emilio or Chauncey to task for excluding Chinese men in their research. Nor am I proposing that had early twentieth-century institutions supporting same-sex attachments been more inclusive, Chinese men would have been involved and, thus, present in the archival record. What I am advancing is that Chinese men were already excluded from an abstract vision of Euro-American modernity defined by a trajectory that places urban wage employment as the endpoint from which the flight from a biologically generative, agrarian, homesteading, settler family begins. Even though a structure correlating non-normative intimacy and wage capitalism already saw itself in place during the time of Chinese exclusion, this conceptual linkage still absented Chinese men from the schema of self-fashioning and culture-making that these historians document.

Paul C. P. Siu, a sociologist, conducted extensive participant observation and interviews with Chinese immigrant men during the 1930s and 1940s. He filed his dissertation in 1953, but it was not until 1988, when John Kuo Wei Tchen decided to edit and publish the work as *The Chinese Laundryman: A Study of Social Isolation*, that it became widely available. Siu received his doctorate from the University of Chicago, the birthplace of sociology. Chicago School researchers honed their methods on local populations, and included among those they studied were Chinese immigrants. In an intellectual history about the relationship between sociology and Asian Americans, Henry Yu sheds light on the paradox of difference in the Chicago School's underlying principles. On the one hand, founders such as Robert Park and Ernest Burgess prided themselves on the budding discipline's premises, which emphasized a disinterested, objective empiricism borrowed from the natural sciences. Sociologists earned credibility by keeping their subjects at a distance. On the other hand, these English-speaking researchers remained unable to gain access to the Chinese populations they studied without the language proficiency of their Chinese American graduate student assistants. These young Chinese American sociologists found themselves in the contradictory position of being indispensable to the work of their white mentors, yet suspect because they were deemed too close to their subjects and, therefore, lacking the objectivity that whiteness takes for granted.[17]

Siu's research on Chinese male launderers challenged a commonly held assumption about urban geographies and assimilation. According to prevailing Chicago School doctrines, problems associated with immigrants—such as poverty and difficulties with post-migration adjustment—could be solved by removing them from ethnic enclaves and integrating them into Anglo-American spaces. However, Siu discovered that Chinese launderers who lived and worked outside Chinatowns did not assimilate, acculturate, or integrate. They simply remained isolated. Because of the American public's antipathy toward Chinese immigrants (combined with the U.S. state's restrictions), the pathways to structural and cultural mobility enjoyed by European Americans were off-limits to the Chinese. If migrants expressed a wish to return to China, although many were unable to afford the return trip, this sojourner mentality could be explained by their status as workers who could be tolerated as long as they did not overstep their niches in the economy.[18]

A more contemporary study, Renqiu Yu's *To Save China, To Save Ourselves*, recounts the activities of the Chinese Hand Laundry Alliance (CHLA), a New York-based leftist group founded in 1933 to combat legislation that would have put small laundries out of business. Not surprisingly, CHLA participants often forged relationships that extended beyond the realm of labor activism. Their connections were also socially and culturally sustaining.[19] Although Siu's fieldwork took place in Chicago and Boston (and therefore would not have included activists who were involved in this labor organization), *The Chinese Laundryman* makes no mention of the CHLA or any other collective action by immigrant launderers. It is difficult to discern if Siu was unaware of the organization's presence, which is unlikely given how influential it was, or if he was unable to find a way to integrate a reference to it into his research.

Siu's negative assessments of his informants' patronage of sex work might reproduce the panics about Chinese male pathology. After all, he wrote from a position where he was encouraged to internalize sociology's assumptions about sexual propriety, despite his racialized distance from the field's charmed circles. Sociology's ideas about what constituted a properly structured life remained staunchly heteropatriarchal. That Siu valued normative sexual comportment is obvious in his depictions of informants' contact with sex workers and women with whom the lines among payment, gift giving, and barter were blurred. These men's so-called vices, he claimed, stemmed from a lack of access to more favorable sexual and domestic arrangements (250–271). However, rather than read Siu's assessment at face value, I find it more productive to regard it as an uncovering, intentional or not, of the folly of seeking gratification through heterosexuality more generally. Siu's ethnographic curiosity reveals something more at stake than mere academic discovery. Throughout *The Chinese Laundryman*, Siu's exposure of the failures of normative sexuality among his co-ethnics is almost too gleeful. The Chinese American sociologist who is too close to his subjects and yet not one of them may long for the scholarly legitimacy his white mentors take for granted. He also takes pleasure in the bawdy homoerotic camaraderie of that other world he holds as an object of analysis.

RACE, SEXUALITY, CAPITAL, AND CONSUMPTION

For Chinese immigrant men living outside the boundaries of a raced and classed heterosexuality, inventive forms of intimacy readily arise. Both Siu and Tsiang document the pleasure that underlies this process, even if only inadvertently. No evidence exists to prove that the two men ever met, corresponded, or read each other's work. Yet their shared commitment to rescripting popular perceptions of Chinese immigrant masculinity put them in discursive proximity. While Siu humanizes his subjects through the patient ear of a qualitative researcher, Tsiang does something similar by crafting a fictional anti-capitalist narrative premised on same-sex intimacy. *And China Has Hands* may resonate with some of the findings in Siu's research, especially those concerning Chinese men's unsatisfying relations with women. However, the frustration from these heterosexual encounters gives way to a richer backdrop of chance meetings with male co-ethnics. These fleeting moments of intimacy provide enjoyable homosocial opportunities for Chinese men who have their (hetero)sexual affiliations tightly circumscribed by U.S. immigration law. They disrupt the aspirations to sexual and class normativity in common understandings of their erotic deprivation. Aaron S.

Lecklider argues that Tsiang "queered radicalism and radicalized sexual categories."[20] Tsiang demonstrated that anti-capitalist dissidence could not be considered apart from sexual difference, and vice versa. I would complement Lecklider's claim and say that by invoking these intertwined forms of resistance, Tsiang exposed the U.S. nation-state's reliance on Asian-raced labor at the same time it punished Chinese men for living outside sanctioned intimate configurations.

The protagonist of *And China Has Hands*, Wong Wan-Lee, immigrated to the United States with dreams of economic success. While toiling at a restaurant, he saved enough money to open his own laundry. From that place of modest, self-made ownership, he fantasizes about further gain. The scenes in the novel have an episodic quality as people come and go from the laundry.[21] We also see the protagonist going from business to leisure as he takes part in public life. There are demoralizing encounters with white women in the sex and dance hall industries and a clumsy courtship with a love interest, a biracial black-Chinese woman. In the midst of these events, a series of Wan-Lee's male co-ethnics enter and exit the plot. His interactions with them, following Lecklider, disrupt the ideology of capital and—I would add—Anglo-American assumptions about Chinese men's sexual inclinations toward white women.

Paul M. McCutcheon's insightful analysis of *And China Has Hands* claims that Tsiang decries capitalism's racially specific logic because of its distortion of a heterosexuality taken for granted.[22] Wan-Lee's dissatisfaction with his interactions across gender lines is palpable, and I agree with McCutcheon that it often arises in contexts that invoke the economic. My analysis reveals, however, that rather than regard the supposed restoration of sexual and familial arrangements dictated by heteronormativity as the goal of class revolt, Tsiang may have valued queer affiliations more highly. Wan-Lee's initial naïve wish for a charmed relationship with the nation-state accompanies his deference to heteropatriarchy. A U.S. citizen father sponsored his entry, but there is also mention of a payoff—described as "the other expense"[23]—to an immigration officer. Wan-Lee felt ashamed about the glitches in his immigration processing, and he "never talked about this matter with others" (20). In this exposition, Tsiang hints that Wan-Lee is a paper son who purchased a paternal relationship. However, the biological ontology of his connection with his sponsor matters little in a context where all immigrants fell under suspicion. Rather than understand that the United States had imposed a xenophobic immigration law, Wan-Lee internalizes the nation-state's reproductive logic of the heteronormative family. His embrace of the twinned mechanisms of capital and sexuality continues when he falls prey to a scam artist. He purchases an expensive bespoke coat on installment when the salesperson (who reappears at the end of the novel as a loan shark) convinces him that the consumer tastes it displays will impress a potential girlfriend.

Consumerism looms large in Wan-Lee's idea of upward mobility, whether or not it directly correlates with heterosexuality's mandates. Wan-Lee follows capitalism's formula of delaying immediate gratification for a more rewarding end when he saves up for the big purchase of a laundry. As he departs from his low-wage food service job, he dreams of one day becoming a high-rolling customer at the same restaurant. His fantasy of spitefully and conspicuously flaunting his success involves ordering "expensive dishes in a leisurely manner" and "two packages of cigarettes, one for himself and the other for the waiter," whom "he hated," and "buy[ing] two fine cigars: one for the cashier and the other . . . [for] the cook," whom "he hated" (21–22). Exiting the premises, he "would smile a fifty percent smile to the boss and, looking straight into his eyes, tell him to go to Heaven" (22). He imagines this scenario will be a fitting "revenge" (21) for the intraethnic tensions he endured both within and across class lines. Whereas Wan-Lee's past skirmishes with the waiter and cook speak to the highly stressful conditions of food service that cause friction among employees, these environments issue from the agents of capital—namely, the restaurant owner. This instance of failed homosocial bonding among co-ethnics sets the stage for Wan-Lee's eventual rejection of consumer capitalist fantasies for a labor movement that, while multiracial and multi-gender, mobilizes through a same-sex encounter within ethnic lines.

In the above passage, consumerism might be regarded as an end that begs a means. Wan-Lee's subsequent contacts with other Chinese men suggest, however, that opportunities for consumerism can also be a means that begets an end—that goal being homosocial intimacy. When the coat salesperson stops by during his door-to-door visits, the haggling he performs with Wan-Lee resembles that of a female sex worker who arrives immediately afterward. The similarities between the two solicitors lead the reader to wonder whether Wan-Lee's purchase of a coat he cannot afford is really motivated by the sales pitch that it will increase his heterosexual capital. It may be because of his wish to be tied, even in the form of a costly contract, to a co-ethnic because he finds the possibility of his intimate company tempting. That the sex worker remains empty-handed but the coat seller succeeds at closing his deal bears mentioning.

Another peddler, an elder selling food, provides an additional instance of intraethnic intimacy between men, but this one seems unequivocally pleasurable and not coercive. Wan-Lee invites the man into the laundry. As he presents his wares, Wan-Lee sees a mouth-watering array of vegetables, bean curd, and pork. Rather than the ambivalence and reluctance with which he interacts with the coat salesperson or the sex worker, the desire occasioned by the display of food that "when you smelled it, you said to yourself, 'I must have it'" (45) leads to intergenerational sharing. The man, having arrived as a sojourner, worked in the mining and railroad industries without intending to remain in the United States. He never saved enough money to return to China and so languished in a country that has brought him no joy. He warns Wan-Lee, "America is an evil land, and once you sink in you can never get out" (46), which is the first time an admonition against assimilation takes place. Although this meeting between Wan-Lee and the food peddler occurs over an economic transaction, the rewards far exceed what either participant had hoped. At first, the older man is simply happy to have "made a few cents" (45), but after Wan-Lee invites him to linger over tea, a gratifying conversation follows of the sort that does not get replicated in the narrative. Before the two men part, Wan-Lee buys out most of the man's remaining food. The intimacy between the older man and the younger man transcends the commercial even as a commercial transaction prompts it. Their bonding takes on a mentoring function when the former advises the latter about the dangers of normative aspirations. This homosocially pleasurable exchange sustains Wan-Lee in two ways: first, he obtains food; and second, he comes into the very beginnings of a class consciousness that will later serve as the basis for a more overt and more sexually inflected resistance to assimilation.

HETEROSEXUALITY'S DISAPPOINTMENTS

Wan-Lee's interactions with women remain invariably unsatisfying. He shows eagerness to rid his laundry of the sex worker during the adversarial haggling, noticing only later when she exits that—as someone whose surplus value goes to maintain a pimp, car, and driver—she also works under the thumb of capital. "At a dollar a piece . . . the lady would have to work with as many customers as he ironed shirts . . . [for] she had to make a livelihood for three persons, support an automobile, and leave something over for the company" (44). As much as this woman's economic subsistence is defined by exploitation, it still appears preferable to that of another, a victim of sexual trafficking who "remain[s] a slave" (100), in a Chinese-owned brothel that Wan-Lee visits. In another scene, an evening patronizing a white woman working at a dance hall yields another negative experience. Wan-Lee hopes to "talk about love" (95) with the glamorous figure, but he is only ridiculed. By laying out a series of brief scenes depicting contact with women, Tsiang shows that aspirations to heterosexuality are as flawed as those aiming for economic affluence. Thus, it becomes not a stretch to read Wan-Lee's pivotal moment of anti-capitalist conversion, which I discuss later, as a moment of same-sex erotic, if not sexual, intimacy.

Wan-Lee's string of unsatisfying encounters with women aligns with the courtship he maintains with a love interest. Pearl Chang, like Wan-Lee, also situates herself at the novel's opening as a naïve aspirant to capitalist ideas of the good life. She undergoes a parallel transformation into a pro-labor activist. Wan-Lee meets Pearl when she intervenes after witnessing a group of white youths taunting him. Her portrayal falls in line with the contemporaneous archetype of the sapphire (what today might be known as the "sassy black woman") despite initially being identified only as "Chinese" (29). She fends off Wan-Lee's attackers with verbal aggression and "hands on her hips, her head held back and her black eyes wide open" (29). Tsiang's characterization of this biracial woman offers a glimpse into the operations of the U.S. racial hierarchy. A transplant from the South, Pearl fled to New York because of the antiblack racism she faced in her hometown. However, the rationale explaining her move does not position New York as an African American utopia.[24] New York, at least initially, offered a place where Pearl could attempt to disavow her blackness because she believed that another designation, Chinese, would become more readily available to her there.

Although Tsiang depicts Wan-Lee as having a worker-based affinity with the black male dishwasher at his former job, he obliterates working-class African American womanhood. He assigns Pearl's Chinese father a name, but her mother is identified only as "a Negress" (32). In a scene where Pearl is laid off from a Chinese restaurant because she cannot hide her black ancestry, Tsiang literally kills her mother off. Despite Pearl's habits of donning a hat to cover her hair, whitening her skin with powder, and contouring her lips with makeup, she faces a series of questions from the restaurant owner:

> "Look at your hair! Curly hair! Look at your lips! Heavy lips! Are you a Chinese?"
> "I am. Otherwise, how could I speak Chinese? My father is Chang Chung-Li."
> "But your father alone did not make you. What is your mother?" demanded the owner.
> "My mother is dead!"
> "Say, your mother didn't do a good job on you. . . . We Chinese are dark enough and don't want to become any darker." (102)

The scrutiny of Pearl's corporeality resonates with the oeuvre of southern cultural production on anxieties about racial purity. It goes hand in hand with the blotting out of the black mother, who is further reduced to a "what" as opposed to a "who." Tsiang's erasure of the black female body takes place on two different levels: first, when Pearl attempts to pass as nonblack; and second, when her mother's death is revealed. It also occurs alongside a vociferous claim to Chinese authenticity premised, first, on language proficiency; and second, on paternity. The fervor with which Pearl attempts to legitimize herself as her father's daughter echoes the interrogations that prospective Chinese immigrants underwent to determine their eligibility at the time of exclusion. The restaurant owner's refusal to take Pearl's paternity at face value shows that he, worried about his own racial difference, eagerly plays along as questioner. His doubts about her parentage replicate the U.S. state's surveillance and the heteropatriarchal standards to which prospective Chinese immigrants were held. What Pearl and Wan-Lee fear in common is that their paternity, whether of biology or paper, will not be good enough.

Pearl and Wan-Lee are two castaways from heteronormativity's fold even apart from any sexual activity in which they partake or any libidinal inclinations they possess. Their one attempt at sexual consummation fails. In the scene, Wan-Lee recounts the history of China to Pearl. Interrupting him, Pearl initiates physical intimacy. Nervously, he rebuffs her advances, and after she tries a second time, she shames him for not responding favorably:

> "I think you Chinese should eat more beefsteak and lamb chops, instead of Chop Suey and Chow Mein," advised Pearl Chang. "Vegetables weaken the Chinese race, and meat makes a man brutal and able to kill! China has lost her territory to Westerners, China has been victimized by the Japanese. Vegetables were the reason, believe me!" (74)

To the pointed statement, Wan-Lee protests, "We Chinese eat no Chop Suey. We Chinese eat no Chow Mein. We eat genuine Chinese food" (74). The disagreement over Wan-Lee's inability to meet a masculinity defined by military force, physical strength, and heterosexual mastery plays out through a food metaphor: meat versus vegetables and chop suey and chow mein versus so-called authentic Chinese food.

By setting up a dichotomy between the masculine valor that meat purportedly bestows and the feminized weakness that vegetables effect, Pearl upholds but also reappropriates the figurative language that Samuel Gompers, president of the American Federation of Laborers, deployed in 1902 in *Meat versus Rice: American Manhood against Asiatic Coolieism*, which supported the renewal of the Chinese Exclusion Act. The treatise mounted an argument for the continued exclusion of the Chinese, cautioning that their status as single men, without the regulating forces that heterosexual domesticity would provide, damaged the white workforce. Gompers reasoned that without wives and children living with them, Chinese men remained poor consumers. They did not recirculate their earnings, which already undercut white wages, back into the economy but remitted them to China. The "rice" in Gompers's metaphor represents the meager subsistence on which Chinese men were able and willing to survive, as opposed to the substantive "meat" that white men with proper gender and sexual comportment would need to maintain their households: "You cannot work a man who must have beef and bread alongside a man who can live on rice."[25] Pearl's accusation of Chinese men's forgoing of meat, however, references another context: that of Japanese imperialism. She speaks the language of decolonialization, but the gendered expectations of manhood present in Gompers's rhetoric remain intact. By resignifying Gompers's words and putting them in the mouth of his female lead character, Tsiang calls attention to white labor unions' intertwining of racism and sexual normativity. The version of pro-labor and decolonial politics Tsiang espouses, which is multiracial and cross-gender, therefore looks more egalitarian by comparison.[26]

In addition, Pearl's reference to Chinese American food such as chop suey and chow mein requires unpacking. The contested status of Asian American fare, as Robert Ji-Song Ku argues, serves as a vehicle through which Asian American people are "construed as human analogs of inauthentic cultural products."[27] Efforts to tame the messiness of syncretic genealogies often focalize at the level of food. The iconic dishes from hybridized Chinese American foodscapes, which Pearl cites in her scolding of Wan-Lee, highlight the fictive status of any claim to an unsullied and pure past. Instead of contesting Pearl's oversight in his own compensatory claim to authenticity, Wan-Lee attempts to meet its terms. He upholds the expectations of heteromasculinity she demands.

What follows Pearl's taunting is a bout of foreplay in which Wan-Lee worries about his ability to perform sexually. The narration states, "He was afraid that Pearl Chang might laugh at him for being a vegetarian" (75–76), five times over the course of two pages—the repetition highlighting Wan-Lee's discomfort as he reluctantly follows along, at least initially. When Wan-Lee becomes bolder, "no more a vegetarian but a meat eater" (77), the action abruptly ends when Pearl exclaims that he handles her breasts too roughly. She accuses him of transgressing the boundaries of gentlemanly, "Confuci[an]" propriety and acting like "white brat[s]" from the "South" (78). With that, she exits the laundry and ends any hope for sexual consummation. In the awkward scene, the references to vegetarianism versus meat eating as metaphors for failed versus potent masculinity hark back to Wan-Lee's earlier encounter with the grocery peddler. Tsiang seems to have forgotten about his protagonist's previous purchase of both vegetables and meat.[28] In the interim, nothing had allowed us to anticipate a change in Wan-Lee's omnivorous habits. The relaxed homosocial pleasure from that earlier interaction stands in stark contrast to this highly anticipated, but thwarted, heterosexual contact.

QUEER INTIMACY AND
PROLETARIAN REBELLION

The Chinese grocer produces a same-sex awakening in Wan-Lee that is eventually consummated, albeit figuratively, in the critical moment that inspires his revolutionary politics. Wan-Lee's unplanned intimacy with this elder foreshadows a more explicitly illustrated account later, which involves the novelist, Tsiang, himself appearing as a character in his own fictional text. He is never named and is identified only by revealing that he is the author of his two previous novels, *China Red* and *The Hanging on Union Square*. Wan-Lee had met the fictionalized author on the street while the author was selling books and again at a community forum on proletarian literature. The book Wan-Lee bought from the man is in English, which Wan-Lee cannot read. When Wan-Lee asks a cousin with more language proficiency to translate, he is warned that the man's "actions . . . spoiled the reputation of the Chinese. He was a bum!" (84). The cousin's disavowal of a co-ethnic reveals the presence of a divide among Chinese immigrants. Those with class aspirations denigrate others who challenge the nation-state's capitalist premises. The cousin, disdainful about a Chinese man behaving in ways that might interfere with his own upward climb, regulates the unruly subject, the "bum," from within.

Keeping in mind that Tsiang was not a laborer barred by Chinese exclusion but a member of the exempted classes who entered the United States as a student, his dissidence needs to be considered in the context of his relative privilege. This turn away from a more stable position in favor of an ideological and sexual alliance with those less advantaged can open him to disapprobation from co-ethnics. His contrarian stance on capitalist success goes hand in hand with his fictionalized character's queer desire for his protagonist. In the scene above, the unnamed author is expelled from the community forum for voicing an unspecified but unpopular opinion. Feeling sympathy for him, Wan-Lee invites him to the laundry and he cooks a meal for them to eat together. The man, appreciative of the food, offers to do some washing in return, to which Wan-Lee protests, but he acquiesces after the man insists.

Unlike the painfully long and awkward depiction of Wan-Lee and Pearl's failed attempt at sex, which runs for five pages in a novel in which the prose remains otherwise sparse, the lead-up to the figurative sexual encounter between Wan-Lee and the unnamed writer is much shorter, at four sentences:

> Wong Wan-Lee looked around, and he noticed that the socks remained unwashed.
> Since in this fellow's book, the word "workers" was repeated so often, Wong Wan-Lee let the fellow work.
> The fellow smelled something he didn't like, and he looked at Wong Wan-Lee.
> Wong Wan-Lee looked at the fellow and then looked somewhere else. (85)

The exchanges of eye contact leading up to washing a load of socks are coy or slightly uncomfortable and accompanied by nervous averting. The unnamed author, chagrined by the result of his insistence to reciprocate Wan-Lee's generosity, finds himself approaching a load of garments more malodorous than he had expected. However, the moment that passes between Wan-Lee's request and the author's washing may also indicate another type of interaction. The nonverbal exchange evokes the glances between new partners, engaged in cruising, leading up to sex. Out of all the tasks associated with running a laundry, the washing of socks is what the author Tsiang wrote into the plot for the fictionalized version of himself to do. The tube-like shape of a sock, which stretches to accommodate and hug an inserted hand and wrist, resembles a rectum. After the author overcomes the initial deterrent of odor—also associated with the anus—which somewhat embarrasses his partner, he performs a metaphorical act of fisting as he washes the socks. Meanwhile, Wan-Lee, who is penetrated, looks away. The sexually suggestive action, though fleeting, is portrayed much more favorably than the sustained, but clumsy, courtship between Wan-Lee and Pearl.

Like the brief sexual encounter in *The Book of Salt*, which I examine in Chapter 2, the sex in this scene, however metaphorical, remains unrepresented. Monique Truong's prose cuts from confirming the couple's intentions to visit a secluded park to their parting of ways afterward. Similarly, Tsiang's words omit any depiction of the socks being washed, taking up the narration again only after the lovemaking concludes. This adds yet another layer to the evasion of portrayal in *The Book of Salt*. There are two deferrals in *And China Has Hands*: first, in the sexual activity's figurative rendering; and second, in its absence from the prose. As with my reading of the same-sex encounter in Truong's novel, I do not interpret these omissions through the contemporary lens of closeting. Tsiang himself was not averse to portraying literal—as opposed to only figurative—sex between men. Two scenes from an earlier novel, *The Hanging on Union Square*, show instances of hospitality similar to the one depicted here. A man is invited into strangers' homes. Unlike what transpires in *And China Has Hands*, however, the protagonist does not reciprocate his hosts' sexual interest. He stops the foreplay and rejects his solicitors' advances. Hua Hsu explains the lack of sexual consummation in this earlier novel by ascribing it to Tsiang's disillusionment with "the transactional nature of modern life . . . [and an] expression of how dehumanizing exposure to such a system could be, as these two characters ache for the touch of another person, even a random man walking the streets."[29] According to this interpretation, the sexual snubbing and the isolation it causes—not the queer desire itself—become the symptoms of a world gone awry. Because we cannot attribute the dodging of homosexual representation, albeit figurative, in *And China Has Hands* merely to authorial phobia, I claim that a likelier reason for this evasion parallels that in *The Book of Salt*. Like Truong's novel, *And China Has Hands* concludes with unfinished business pertaining to intraethnic reconciliation; to have the sex narrated explicitly in the loving conversion from capitalist aspiration to proletarian rebellion would suggest a closure that is not.

The scene conveying anal fisting through the vehicle of sock washing lends additional meaning to the title of the novel. *And China Has Hands* directly indexes the synecdochic meaning of "hands"—that is, the parts of a worker that stand for the entirety of his or her whole. The title references Wan-Lee's co-ethnics who occupy the most precarious sectors of the economy. Calling workers "hands" can relegate them to their manual tasks in a way that objectifies and fragments. Indeed, Wan-Lee's fantasy of self-possessed freedom deflates once he comes to the realization that even when he owns his own business, his "hand was not a machine, but he had to move his hand as fast as a machine" (27). The flesh and the metal, the organic and the inorganic, the living and the nonliving merge under capitalism's forces, despite the former's propensity for pain and fatigue not suffered by the latter. Instead of the autonomy about which Wan-Lee had fantasized while employed in food service, the pressures of managing the laundry create conditions of mechanization that resemble wage labor. However, the word "hand" also invokes a class-specific pride the proletariat takes in corporeal tools that elevate them from dehumanization.

In *Dialectics of Nature*, a text published only three years before *And China Has Hands*, Friedrich Engels located the line between humans and their nonhuman primate cousins in the inextricable bond between the hand and labor. Humans' upright posture and manual dexterity led to a behavioral shift away from activity spurred by subsistence to that motivated by the transformation of the natural environment. In turn, these habits evolved human anatomy into the hand with which we are familiar today: "Thus the hand is not only the organ of labour[;] *it is also the product of labour.*"[30] According to Engels, this hand-labor connection laid the foundation that made possible the faculties of reason and free will so prized by modernity. Capitalism's abuses lay in the distortion of this hallowed relationship. Engels's valorizing of the distinction between human and nonhuman animals may be regressive in light of the posthuman turn in Asian American studies. Critics have cautioned against the temptation for social minorities to empower themselves within existing hierarchies of life by maintaining their distance from forms of nonhuman being.[31] I concur with this caveat, but I also want to add that for subjects who have not yet attained full human status within liberal humanist standards—people of color, indigenous people, the working classes, queers, and disabled people—the casting away of this validation is more fraught than for those whose humanity remains unquestioned. (Ironically, but not surprisingly, ableist and colonialist language peppers Engels's book.) When the fictionalized Tsiang fists Wan-Lee, if only figuratively, the celebrated hand transforms itself into an instrument that humanizes, accomplishes work, and produces sexual pleasure. Although the labor generated by the hand under capitalism may be alienated, the sexual intimacy it effects recuperates the worker from that loss. The intraethnic bonding between the unnamed author and his protagonist expresses anti-capitalist politics through a sexual formation that is also fiercely anti-heteronormative.

The transformative potential of this sexual encounter becomes obvious in what happens next. Once the author finishes washing the socks, he composes and recites a poem on the spot in the copulation's afterglow. The first four lines of it read as follows:

> *To the masses*
> *I blow the horn*
> *To the crooks*
> *I nail the thorn.* (86)

The improvised verse is not payment in return for a meal but a spontaneous gift. It exists beyond either capitalist or barter economies and expresses joy shared by two co-ethnics in the spirit of social critique. Some of the words in the poem, such as "nail" and "thorn," contain Judeo-Christian overtones. When taking the poem's content into consideration, however, it remains clear that the recipients of the chance allusions to crucifixion, the "crooks," do not prove themselves worthy of martyrdom. Acts of "blow[ing]" and "nail[ing]" can be phallic—or, potentially, penile—references. They might signify the giving of oral pleasure to one's political allies or the masculinist retaliation against exploiters of labor. The intimacy between the author and the laundry worker in their brief time together enacts a pro-labor politics and a critique of common misconceptions about Chinese men's heterosexual deprivation. Instead of being failed heterosexual subjects, as the previous scene with Pearl might suggest, Chinese men become agentially queer.

The sock-washing scene is not the first time Tsiang's fictionalized character appears. Earlier, Pearl meets the unnamed author at an art school where she models, and the two go for a walk in a park. With some pleading on Pearl's part, the author writes a poem for her, but unlike the scene later when he does the unsolicited same for Wan-Lee, the gesture misses the mark:

> Slowly they walked through the park.
> It was not light and it was not dark.
> Slowly they walked through the dark,
> It was not light and it was a park. (35)

Pearl, whom Tsiang characterizes as vain, wants words that praise "her eyes" or "her lips." She becomes "furious" (35) about this unsatisfactory alternative. The poem portrays an interaction in line with conventions of Anglo-American, middle-class, chaste heterosociality. Its rejection by its recipient reveals Tsiang's attempt to satirize these sentiments. However, the poem also contains the seeds for the author's vision of leftist cross-racial organizing. According to Lynette Cintrón, the statement "It was not light and it was not dark" might describe most readily the time of day when this twilight stroll occurs, but it also writes into existence a labor movement that transcends racial categories—black, white, and other. Later, as protesters walk the picket line at the novel's climactic scene, the gathering is neither "light" nor "dark" but racially integrated to counter the capitalist strategy of pitting workers against one another.[32]

INTRARACIAL VIOLENCE AND HETEROSEXUALITY'S RETURN

And China Has Hands ends on a note of pro-labor solidarity comprising workers who are "white," "yellow," "black," and everything in "between" (124), but it also reminds us that this utopian ideal exists concurrently with intraethnic and intraracial strife. Right after Wan-Lee's sexual respite with the fictionalized Tsiang, the coat seller pays a return visit to the laundry, but he now works as a loan shark. Possibly because Wan-Lee is still postcoitally content, his resistance is subdued, and he signs for the loan. This instigates a chain of events, including a night spent at a Chinese-owned gambling house, that causes him to lose his laundry. The narrative also reports on other occurrences that establish a thematic through-line of intraracial competition, such as the murder-suicide of an employer and employee at a neighboring Chinese laundry and an armed robbery by Filipino perpetrators at another laundry that leaves one worker dead. The final scene finds Wan-Lee shot and martyred while he pickets the Chinese cafeteria where he and Pearl worked after their loss of employment, in Pearl's case, and property, in Wan-Lee's case. The rationale provided for the murder, however, remains unrelated to the labor dispute at hand. The shooter turns out to be a pro-imperialist Japanese sympathizer who retaliates against Wan-Lee for protesting Japan's invasion of China a few days prior to this incident, which the reader learns of only at this moment.

Tsiang's depiction of Wan-Lee's death references the phenotypic similarities between Chinese and Japanese people. It eerily portends the climate only a few years later during World War II when the general American public became concerned about distinguishing between "dangerous" and "benign" Asians.[33] When Pearl initially witnesses the shooting, she describes having seen a "Chinese running away" (125). Later, it would come to light that "the [Japanese] agent . . . thought the real killer could never be discovered, as Japanese looked just like the Chinese and the picketing [of the cafeteria] was a fight between Chinese" (126). The incongruity between Wan-Lee's immediate actions and his murder is meant to work in favor of the killer, who leaves the scene of a crime that could reasonably be assumed to take place intraethnically.

The conclusion of *And China Has Hands* restores the heterosociality between Wan-Lee and Pearl that, until then, had been a failure. In the triumphant finale, Wan-Lee dies in Pearl's arms, and she becomes the romanticized "angel" (125) that recurs in his dreams, forgiving and forgetting the repeated tensions that accompanied their relationship. The end recapitulates heterosexuality's oft-invoked power to establish narrative closure, but many literary critics have pointed out that it seems forced and unsatisfying. They tend to note the abruptness with which Wan-Lee's anti-imperialist activism appears.[34] Although it is true that the critique of Japanese empire seems like an imperfect appendix to Wan-Lee's pro-labor activities, what makes the conclusion even more jarring is the restoration of an unconvincing heterosexual dyad and the erasure of intimacies among men. The previous same-sex connections get pushed to the background once Wan-Lee achieves martyrdom in accordance with the schematic plot of the proletarian novel.

If *And China Has Hands* possesses a failing, it lies not in its stylistic imperfections, as some would claim. The flaw is the ultimate decoupling of pro-labor and queer inclinations that spurred Wan-Lee's escape from false consciousness. The brief meeting and conversation with the grocery peddler becomes a distant memory when the narrative concludes. The author's own decision to turn himself into an object of desire and sexual partner for his protagonist, if only figuratively, is forgotten. These homosocial and homo-erotic relationships, which previously had been linked with anti-assimila-tionist critique, do not factor into the novel's vision of heroism. Wan-Lee's death is a deus ex machina that paradoxically relies on the heteromasculinity that earlier stood at odds with cross-racial, anti-capitalist radicalism.

I assert, however, that despite the conclusion's attempt to impose a nor-mative social or sexual formation, the queer tendencies of the novel prevail, not so much within the plot as at the level of the author's own libidinal in-vestment in his protagonist. The figurative fisting between Wan-Lee and the fictionalized Tsiang in the laundry may be portrayed as an act of com-forting intimacy between co-ethnic partners, but the author Tsiang's desire for his protagonist is not always benign. Tsiang's extravagant portrayals of Wan-Lee's failures at heterosexuality are conspicuous because his prose is otherwise economical. These incidents drip with schadenfreude. I make this claim about authorial subjectivity only because Tsiang has written himself into his own story to be paired with his protagonist. Like Wan-Lee, he ex-periences a heterosexual rebuffing from Pearl when she refuses the ode to companionate solidarity during their date, wanting instead an homage to her physical features.

Pearl does receive in due course the blazon she wanted, but it does not come from the fictionalized Tsiang. Rather, the author Tsiang grants it to her, somewhat antagonistically, during the foiled attempt at sex with Wan-Lee. This literary gesture appears in prose rather than the verse traditional for the genre. Pearl's "nose" is described as an "almond seed," her "eyes" like an "autumn stream," her face a "watermelon seed," her breasts as "two tennis balls," and her nipples "Lee Chee nuts" (77–78).[35] The ungenerous and bizarre description of Pearl's physical appearance mirrors the ungainly fumbling with which Wan-Lee tries to meet her sexual demands. Aggression emanates from Tsiang's language as he functions as both author of and third-person narrator-voyeur to Wan-Lee's humiliation at a woman's hands. It is not far-fetched to speculate that he might set Wan-Lee up for a heterosexual letdown of colossal proportions (which is painful for the reader, too, to endure) so he can make his grand entrance as his rightful partner once Pearl has been eliminated as sexual competition.

THE INTRAETHNIC SOCIOLOGICAL GAZE

At first glance, it may seem arbitrary to pair H. T. Tsiang, a fiction writer, with Paul Siu, a sociologist, as participants in a conversation about masculinity among early twentieth-century Chinese immigrants. Imaginative literature and sociological writing are two distinct genres. Given sociology's fervent pursuit of the legitimacy that comes with the objectivity and empiricism of the natural sciences, one could even say they remain diametrically opposed. However, sociological knowledge production and fiction can be placed in proximity as historical artifact alike. Moreover, Roderick A. Ferguson makes a convincing case for the mutual relevance of creative writing and sociological knowledge production in "struggles and confrontations over the meaning of gendered and sexual diversity," especially those associated with the racially marginalized.[36] His study shows how these intellectual and cultural productions converged in their debates over the nature of capital, queerness, race, and social heterogeneity. Cynthia H. Tolentino reveals that some writers of color used sociology as a mode of validation. Given that sociological scholarship had become the ascendant discourse about racial difference in the mid-twentieth century, intellectuals of color found it imperative to engage with its force. On the one hand, people of color were perceived by social scientists as racial problems, "objects of study and interpellated figures of canonical sociology." On the other hand, they were able to effect "a range of disidentifications that enabled them to position their lives in relation to broader, systemic frameworks and hierarchies, shaping their literary practices of self-representation."[37] I do not imply that Siu consciously spoke in concert with Tsiang, because no direct evidence exists that he did so. Nevertheless, the queer pleasure in the midst of assimilative heterosexuality's pressures in Tsiang's novel resonates in Siu's sociological writing, which comes directly on its heels.

The Chinese Laundryman situates itself in early twentieth-century sociological mores about proper kinship and sexual organization even as it reveals Siu's enjoyment of transgressing those norms. If Tsiang's preoccupation with his protagonist's unsatisfying relationships with women stems from wishing them gone so he can have him all to himself, might Siu have had a corresponding interest in the portrayal of his informants' sexual behavior? As with Tsiang's passages that describe Wan-Lee and Pearl's strained courtship, depictions of launderers' experiences with women in *The Chinese Laundryman* are extensive and produce a similar discomfort for the reader. In a universe that collapses the fictional with the historical, Siu may have crossed paths with Tsiang's protagonist, not literally but in a realm of social theorizing. We might imagine the researcher establishing his ethnographic contacts by soliciting door to door in the manner of salespeople or sex workers who stop by Wan-Lee's laundry. What do we make of the libidinal motivations that, as in Tsiang's novel, inform Siu's relationships with his co-ethnics?

In Chapter 1, I referenced an oft-overlooked scene in John Okada's *No-No Boy* in which a minor character, a draft resister, brags about his sexual escapades with a married woman. The disgust-laden narration does not elicit identification. However, Siu concludes that out of all the sexual options available to Chinese immigrant launderers, this arrangement was valued most highly. "The love life idealized by the married bachelor is not with the call-flat girl, in the 'hotel room,' or with the streetwalker. He dreams of real romance with a housewife" (262).[38] What follows is extensive dialogue with one launderer who maintains a relationship like this with a woman whose husband leaves their residence during the day. When Siu's prose shifts from the citation of this interview back to analysis, he expresses disbelief about the content of the man's noticeable bravado. "To what extent this story is true is another question" (262), he writes. This gesture resembles a response to an earlier conversation he recounts among four informants. Over the course of the dialogue about the men's sexual experiences, Siu interjects with expressions of disbelief three times. I agree with Siu when he claims that it matters little whether these stories are fact or fiction, but unlike Siu, I am not interested in the cultural truths they reveal about Chinese immigrant men's fantasies. Rather, I find Siu's repeated tendency to dismiss his subjects' reports of heterosexual gratification notable itself. It mirrors Tsiang's wish to downplay and dismiss the sexual component of his protagonist's heterosocial relationship with Pearl. Might the reason be that, like Tsiang, he wanted to imagine a place for himself in these collectives rich with homoerotic energy? I venture to answer "yes."

Siu's paradoxical mix of dogged interest in and incredulity about his informants' heterosexual activities reveals his insider-outsider status in ways that play with and against the claims in Henry Yu's research. As I mentioned earlier, Yu found that Chinese American graduate students in sociology at the University of Chicago existed at the contradictory juncture of racialized delegitimation and ethnic-specific linguistic competence. As bilingual children of Chinese immigrants, these students could gain access to informants for their white mentors to study. However, because early twentieth-century sociology regarded them as too close to their subjects, and therefore not objective enough, they held second-class citizen status in a profession dominated by white men. Siu recognizes and effects a performance of compliance with these discourses when he discusses his positionality as a researcher: "The worker [meaning himself] speaks the dialect spoken by most of the Chinese laundrymen. He knows the cultural background well enough to comprehend the personal problems of the laundryman. This, however, may be an advantage or it may be a disadvantage. The disadvantage is bias" (6). In this exposition about method, Siu is upfront about his possible "bias" while remaining silent on the biases held by white sociologists with more access to professional capital. As a novice working at the margins of his field, Siu could have distanced himself from his subjects in compensatory ways to emulate privilege. Instead, he found a more amenable and erotically attractive companionship among his working-class co-ethnics.

It remains unclear, when Siu enters a laundry during a typical day and in the middle of a spirited conversation about women, whether his intentions behind requesting a sex worker are related to his research. One of the workers asks him, "Have you a girl for us?" (141). Siu volleys that query back at him, "I was thinking that you might get me a girl instead. I understand that some prostitutes come to laundry shops, soliciting business. Any of them come to your place?" (141). Since Siu included this part of the dialogue in his dissertation, it could reasonably be assumed that he wanted to interview workers in the sex industry as part of his investigation into the lives of the Chinese launderers who patronize them. When the conversation persists, Siu's involvement in the bawdy cheer of his informants blurs the lines between participant and observer. In a key moment, the physical intimacy of sharing a pipe while one worker speaks about its appeal to women dissolves this distinction altogether:

> Ming-lung: Some of the girls prefer a pipe smoker for a sweetheart.
> So I began to smoke a pipe. I still keep some of my old tobacco.
> Here, do you want to try it? It is good tobacco, expensive.
> Observer: How many times did you pick up girls in the West Side?
> [smoking]. (143)

The pipe—which operates as an analogue for phallic power, a leisure commodity, and an instrument of homoerotic bonding—passes from its owner to the guest, cementing the connection between them through oral pleasure. In the male-only space of the laundry, the pipe's supposed role in enhancing one's desirability to women becomes moot. Siu accepts Ming-lung's offer to try his tobacco in what seems like a choice to indulge his inclinations with another man. However, the dialogue's turn back to heterosexuality, as he asks about Ming-lung's encounters with women, shows that the two entities do not stand at odds. Here, same-sex and heterosexual attachments rely on each other for their conditions of possibility.

The co-constitution of same-sex bonding and heterosexual activity intensifies when Siu describes the practice of seeking services from female sex workers among his informants. Although he reports that a Chinese launderer can and does seek paid sex from women on his own, "He would prefer to go with company; in company he has more fun and is less self-conscious, perhaps" (254). A lengthy excerpt from an interview follows in which the subject describes in detail one evening with friends as they travel from place to place looking for a sex worker. Just when it seems that the search might turn up empty, it ends in an anticlimactic conclusion at a brothel. The good-natured teasing and joking among the men throughout the journey convey an easy familiarity. These accounts of camaraderie with friends are much more compelling than the depiction of the heterosexual economic transaction at the close of the night. In this story, the professed wish for heterosexual sex is not the end but the means. Siu and I remain in agreement when we observe that the almost hyperbolic search for heterosexual sex is the vehicle through which the men bond with one another, but he and I differ in our conjectures about this connection's appeal. Siu claims that "a laundryman takes part in an adventure to the brothels or call-flats without feeling passionate or even desirous of sexual satisfaction. He goes along because he has nothing to do" (256). However, I do not relegate this enjoyment simply to an avoidance of boredom. The homosocial and homoerotic energy here and elsewhere shows that the intimacies launderers forged with one another, which exist under the radar of Siu's gaze even as he was drawn into them, were the most highly cherished among all their human contacts. This hierarchy of value contests popular assumptions about Chinese men's grudging acceptance of heterosexuality's consolation prizes in the absence of cohabiting wedded options.

POWER DIFFERENTIALS
IN ETHNOGRAPHY

Lest we too quickly celebrate Siu's queer desire for his working-class subjects as a defiance of sociology's mandates, we need to remember that he remained part of the institution his implied libidinal urges seemed to oppose. The Chicago School was considered revolutionary for its time because it identified problems such as poverty and crime not in the inherent inferiority of aggrieved populations but in an entity called "social disorganization." In other words, Chicago sociologists blamed flaws in the social structure for problems experienced by the disenfranchised. However, these sociologists held very particular ideas about what constituted proper, healthy social comportment and valorized the atomized family, defined as a two-parent, biologically procreative household.[39] Because this was untenable for most Chinese immigrants subjected to exclusion laws, the men in these bachelor societies were denigrated by the discourses of early twentieth-century social science. Siu could witness and engage in the spirited conversations that unfolded in that largely male world. He could banter lightheartedly with his informants about women and share a moment of sexualized oral enjoyment by smoking a pipe offered by another man. One wonders whether he felt a twinge of wistfulness listening to accounts of trips to brothels for his wish to be part of a group that stood defiantly outside the boundaries of respectability. However, because of his privilege relative to the launderers under his observation, his sexual fascination with them amounted to a sort of slumming. The middle-class Siu, who may have found the solitary spaces of the academy dull and lacking, as well as racially marginalizing, lived vicariously through his working-class informants.

Neither Siu nor his informants were U.S. citizens at the time of his dissertation research because of race-based naturalization laws. The restrictions on naturalization for people of Asian descent would not be lifted until 1952 with the passing of the McCarran-Walter Act. However, despite this congruence in their relationship with the U.S. state, Siu remained more advantageously positioned than his informants due to the conditions of his immigration. His father's story resembled that of many of Siu's launderer-subjects. Upon his arrival from China, he toiled long hours in a laundry while sending remittances home, and these resources allowed the teenage Siu to receive a Western education at a missionary school in China. The father eventually saved enough money to bring Siu to the United States. After he arrived, he enrolled at Macalester College in St. Paul, Minnesota. One of Siu's contacts from the missionary school introduced him to Ernest Burgess at the University of Chicago, and the esteemed sociologist recruited Siu into his program. Siu met his wife, a Chinese American student in social work, and they had one child.[40] Cultural and structural differences stood between the researcher and his informants along lines of English-language proficiency, access to higher education, and the option of assuming heterosexual family structures. Whatever doubts sociology may have held about the competence of researchers such as Siu, he and the immigrant population under study were far from being one and the same.

The power imbalances between Siu and the launderers created ethnographically uncomfortable moments that went unacknowledged in his analyses. One passage stands out for its similarities to Tsiang's narration of his protagonist's heterosexual humiliation.[41] During participant observation, Siu sees a woman enter the laundry. She pleads with one worker for money and ignores the catcalls of the other. The man being solicited expresses angry exasperation, asking first for intercourse and next for fellatio. This interchange follows:

> Dotty: Oh! You bad boy! What do you think I am. I'm not that kind of girl. I'm no street walker. . . .
> Lum: No money. You search my pocket if you don't believe me. [*Dotty put one hand into one of his pockets and he embraced her. He hugs her closer while she flirts with a look and says*]:
> Dotty: Will you give your baby some money to buy something to wear? I got to buy some stockings. I have nothing to wear. (268)

After much persuasion, Lum acquiesces, and Dotty leaves the laundry with five dollars. (Prior to this scene, we learn that Lum's weekly pay is only ten dollars.) A co-worker expresses consternation that this woman asks for money constantly. Upon her return with her purchases, Dotty "put the box down on the table, and Lum, taking her hand, led her inside [the sleeping area]. They were alone about half an hour" (270). In the dialogue between Lum and Dotty, the two recognize and disavow sex work in the process of its actualization. Dotty's dismissal of the economic component of their relationship contrasts with his blunt acknowledgment of it.

Yet what remains notable is not so much Dotty's sexual power over Lum as sociology's power over the both of them together. The knowledge issuing from the academy pathologizes this interchange and exerts discursive control over those whom it studies. From his position of relative privilege, Siu can experience vicariously the homoerotic energy of his informants while safely ensconced in his wedded, child-rearing heterosexuality and affiliation with one of the most elite universities in the world. One can imagine the researcher gazing licentiously at his subjects under the purported objectivity of early twentieth-century social science. He even measures how long their sexual encounters last. Much of Siu's fieldwork took place before the advent of voluntary participation and informed consent in human subjects research marshaled by the Nuremberg Code in 1947. He himself reports that during interviews, the "persons who took part in the conversation did not know that the interviewer was making a study or gathering information" (5). I am not using anachronistic logic to condemn Siu personally, or even the discipline of sociology more generally, for a breach of ethical standards that did not yet exist. It simply bears pointing out the irony that the exchange of sex for money between Dotty and Lum is consensual (even as Siu strongly suggests that the former exploits the latter's loneliness and susceptibility to coercion), but the ethnographic relationship that produces knowledge about this scene is not.

SPONTANEITY, TRANSIENCE, AND ASIAN AMERICAN ACTIVIST HISTORIOGRAPHY

What stands out while reading *And China Has Hands* and *The Chinese Laundryman* are the brief and episodic moments of unsanctioned pleasure in both texts. Tsiang proposes metaphorical sexual contact among men in rejection of capitalism's deceitful promises. The fleeting intimacies, especially between the author's fictionalized self and his protagonist, disrupt aspirations to upward mobility that keep working-class Chinese men invested in the existing economic and sexual order. Siu takes respite in his place of marginal indispensability within the Chicago School by nursing an eroticized identification with his informants, an attachment that can be read as an implicit rejection of sociology's premises. However, he still maintains, from his perch of class and heterosexual privilege, the aggressive authority of the ethnographic gaze, which resembles the spiteful pleasure that laces Tsiang's depictions of his protagonist's attempts at heterosexuality.

It is with this queer, but not utopian, spirit of cherishing the spontaneous, the brief, the temporary, the unplanned, the stalled, the fragmented, and the transient that I propose a rewriting of Asian American activist historiography. Social historians locate the late 1960s and 1970s as the moment in which a recognizable anti-racist and anti-imperialist politics coalesced around the emergence of an identity called "Asian American." These movements valued the panethnic and the cross-racial, organizing within and across racial categories. They contested the U.S. wars in Southeast Asia, residential segregation and gentrification, the wealth gap, police violence, the prison system, and public institutions' imbrication in these forces. Events such as the San Francisco State University strike of 1968 to establish an ethnic studies curriculum and the decade-long but unsuccessful campaign to preserve the International Hotel (the I-Hotel), a building inhabited mostly by working-class Filipinos, galvanized the coalitional efforts of student and community activists. Meanwhile, in the realm of the arts, a literary movement thematized these political commitments and provided cultural visibility for them.

William Wei's seminal work on the genesis of a large-scale, sustained Asian American movement locates its beginnings squarely in this period. His master narrative centers the efforts of second- and third-generation East Asian Americans' aforementioned priorities—qualifying that other instances of activism, such as those of U.S. Filipinos against the Marcos regime, fall beyond its scope. His rationale for excluding these other initiatives stems from their focus on what he calls "homeland" issues, which, as is implied, come from a pre-assimilation attachment. As time passes, he suggests, immigrants will "produce a second generation" that will dissolve these commitments.[42] Wei's parameters overlook, for instance, the fact that the Filipino American activists he references actually challenged the United States' collusion with Ferdinand Marcos and its neocolonial relationship with its former territory. This critique does align with Asian Americanist thought. Also, some participants in that movement were, in fact, second-generation Americans.

Daryl J. Maeda's revisiting of the convergences between anti-imperialist and anti-racist activism also foregrounds the oft-referenced events of the 1960s and 1970s. In addition, he provides a comprehensive historiographical account of earlier leftist organizing that includes labor actions throughout the late nineteenth and early twentieth centuries and socialism in the 1920s and 1930s. About the plausibility of declaring a transmission between these earlier instances and the period under discussion, Maeda remains hesitant. He declares it "tenuous," because the bulk of activists from the 1960s and 1970s actually rebelled against their parents' Cold War compliance.[43] The difficulty of "draw[ing] a solid, continuous line from the Asian American old left to the Asian American new left" is compounded by the lack of "institutional continuity" prevented by McCarthyism in the period between.[44]

Recently, Chris Eng made a case for a queer genealogy of Asian American studies. He steers the conversation in the field about parental origins into new territory by calling attention to "the complex and porous ways that queerness and the transnational are configured . . . [such that] entrapping Asian American studies within familial logics of intergenerational conflict forecloses the possible work it can do by presupposing and struggling over the content of the field."[45] To be sure, Wei and Maeda have done indispensable work charting and interpreting the pivotal occasions of the anti–Vietnam War, civil rights, and cultural nationalist movements.[46] Whereas Eng's intervention could be mobilized to call attention to the underpinnings of Wei's and Maeda's verbal and conceptual language, I want to take these claims in another direction. I probe further the possibility of assigning a greater Asian Americanist legibility to early twentieth-century activism.

The 1960s and 1970s did catalyze a larger movement that has sustained itself over time. However—following recent queer theory's work on the relationship between time and sexuality—I caution that upholding scale, longevity, and endurance over the short and ephemeral reproduces a temponormative criterion that replicates the discourses of heterosexuality. The brief and fleeting get equated with the childlike regression akin to nineteenth-century sexology's invention and medicalization of the homosexual. Meanwhile, normative subjects under a schema that dictates teleological maturation are accorded full adulthood in line with liberal humanism. Wei and Maeda invoke biologically reproductive logic in their references to the progression of generations. It buttresses their temporally laced claims, revealing the connections between time and sex most clearly. Conversely, queer theorists have deftly unpacked the links among hegemonic chronicity, normative sexuality, and capital. Elizabeth Freeman calls the naturalization of these forces "chrononormativity," or "the use of time to organize individual human bodies toward maximum productivity."[47] Dana Luciano coins the term "chronobiopolitics" to describe "the sexual arrangement of the time of life."[48] E. L. McCallum and Mikko Tuhkanen press for a critical practice that queries how "lineage can become nonlinear or nonfiliative" and asks how we can "become uninvested in lineage as a temporal paradigm" altogether.[49]

Extending the framework set by queer theory a bit further, I bolster the claim for an Asian Americanist legitimacy for activism in times predating the birth of the term "Asian American."[50] The work in sexuality studies contesting the tyranny of historicity can open up other origin narratives. Our reluctance to recognize earlier forms of activism as Asian American echoes corresponding declarations about the supposed impossibility of research on same-sex relations prior to the late nineteenth-century medical invention of the homosexual. Eve Kosofsky Sedgwick most emphatically made the case for a historically unfaithful look backward, arguing that the dismissal of the significance of same-sex activity before medical science's creation of a category pathologizing it insidiously silences its examination.[51] Rigid appeals to historicism—which overlook the fact that all analysis is presentist, as Valerie Rohy points out—discourages in subtle ways an examination of sexuality altogether. All told, the policing of temporal adherence resembles the regulatory regimes of compulsory heterosexuality.[52]

Folding these factors back into the narratives crafted by H. T. Tsiang and Paul Siu, we see that the most disruptive challenges to capital and institutional authority occur during episodes that are both temporally and sexually non-normative—short-lived, disjointed, fleeting, and queer. Why not treasure the moments in Asian American activist history that are likewise? The discursive appearance of the Asian American would only occur three decades after the era under Tsiang's and Siu's investigation. Why can we not interrupt strict historicism and legitimize Asian Americanist coalitions in times before that? Eventually, Tsiang retreats from his fortuitous sexual encounter with his protagonist and casts Wan-Lee in the direction of literary narrative's demands for heterosexual closure. Siu leaves his informants behind after fieldwork to assume his place as husband, father, and academician—joining the Department of Sociology at the Detroit Institute of Technology. However, I suspect that there may have been something more to their same-sex bonds, despite the brevity of their non-normative spells. These queer moments mark in historically flexible ways the beginnings of Asian America.

5

INTRASETTLER CONFLICT

No text in the history of Asian American arts and culture has generated as much or as heated a debate as Lois-Ann Yamanaka's *Blu's Hanging* (1997). Yamanaka, a fiction writer and poet of Japanese descent living in Hawai'i, received numerous accolades in the mainstream press after publishing this second novel. In 1998, it won the Association for Asian American Studies (AAAS) fiction award, a prestigious prize given annually by a committee of experts in Asian American literary arts. Controversy followed this event. At the heart of the contentious debate lay Yamanaka's depiction of a Filipino character as a rapist and child molester, an artistic choice that drew on a long history in Hawai'i of vilifying Filipino men for their alleged sexual deviance. The outcry against the award became so large that the membership of AAAS voted to rescind it. Afterward, the entire board of the organization, save for its graduate student member, resigned for fear of a lawsuit.

Two camps existed in the debates about *Blu's Hanging*. One organized itself around questions of social justice that called attention to the long fetch of cultural and material injuries sustained by Filipinos in Hawai'i. The other appealed to classical notions of authorship and creative license. These conflicts took place in a context of relative economic and political comfort attained by East Asians in Hawai'i since the mid-twentieth century while Filipinos, Native Hawaiians, and other Pacific Islanders continue to be socioeconomically disadvantaged. The nineteenth-century colonial-capitalist plantation economy created a multiethnic and multiracial workforce rife with internal competition. The effects of these differentials have become even more pronounced today. In addition, Native Hawaiians are completely absent from *Blu's Hanging* as characters, and their interests as stakeholders also disappeared in the controversy about the novel. The Yamanaka incident was provocative because it called attention to the deeply entrenched conflicts within Asian American groups, but it was also not provocative enough for its erasure of indigenous sovereignty.

Those who condemned the portrayal of Filipino masculinity and those who supported Yamanaka's artistic license did not fall neatly into identitarian lines. Many allies of East Asian descent opposed the characterizations in *Blu's Hanging*, and the supporters who accepted the award on Yamanaka's behalf were three of her former students, all Filipina women.[1] Because of the magnitude of this controversy in Asian American studies, it remains difficult to refocus the interpretive lenses through which the novel has been read in its wake. Discussions about it will always justifiably foreground East Asian privilege and its devastating consequences for Filipinos. However, I do not intend to "cleanse" the novel of its hermeneutic baggage and redirect attention elsewhere—far from it. I show how the uneven access to economic and cultural capital within Asian settler groups enables some to have their non-normative sexualities upheld while others remain under suspicion. Any illusion of sexual transgression depends on the ethnic hierarchy in Hawai'i. In turn, queer sexualities and kinship formations neutralize through appeals to homonormativity or are abjected through intraracial violence.

The workings of sexual regulation rest on an ongoing investment in gender and sexual comportments imposed by colonialism. Asian settler propriety appeals to values that originate from European and North American occupying forces. As Chris Finley points out, these heteropatriarchal conventions have subjugated indigenous populations through the mutually constitutive logic of imperialism and normative sexuality.[2] The novel's seemingly progressive queer politics, as shown in the positive portrayal of two Japanese women who tend to read as lesbian, rests on and reinforces East Asian ascendancy in Hawai'i. It naturalizes hegemonic kinship and sexual relations under the banner of female same-sex erotics without interrogating the settler colonial underpinnings therein.

The celebrated polycultural dynamics in Hawai'i stem from the legacy of the plantation economy, established in 1835. A racially, ethnically, and linguistically diverse workforce emerged from the rise of agricultural capital, legislated subduing of the Hawaiian kingdom, and a multiplicity of colonialisms in Korea and the Philippines. Migrants from Portugal, Japan, China, Korea, the Philippines, and other Asian and European countries settled in the islands to fulfill labor needs on land seized from Native Hawaiians and turned into sugarcane fields. Formal policy mandated the stratification of the workforce according to position and pay. Most workers in unskilled positions were East Asian or Filipino and were supervised largely by Portuguese overseers. Even when workers of multiple national origins performed the same tasks, they received differential wages, with East Asians earning more than Filipinos, to generate resentment among ethnic groups that would discourage labor solidarity. Despite these tactics, some cross-ethnic organizing did occur.[3]

These ethnic-specific class stratifications relied on imperatives regulating gendered sexual practices. Heterosexual privileges, whether offered as rewards or withheld as detriments, historically have controlled the behavior of Asian immigrants. During the time of Chinese exclusion, merchants living on the U.S. mainland were permitted to bring wives while laborers were not. This discrepancy facilitated middle-class propriety while discouraging the working classes from establishing more permanent homes.[4] Yet as I argue in Chapter 4, we need to reimagine Asian-raced men not as failed heterosexual subjects but as queer agents who challenged capitalism and heteronormativity. In Hawai'i, plantation capitalists encouraged the immigration of entire family units among the Japanese because it was believed that heterosexual domesticity, even more so than police monitoring, could tame a largely male, racialized workforce of its perceived chaotic tendencies.[5] When the contract labor system ended in 1900, workers no longer remained legally bound to specified terms of service. Plantation owners reaffirmed the desirability of having women mixed in among the men. They perceived marriage and child-rearing as incentives for male workers to cultivate stability so they would stay in their positions rather than seek employment elsewhere.[6]

Despite the active recruitment of married men over single men across all ethnic groups, a disparity still existed between males and females, with Filipinos overall having the greatest percentage of men in the population.[7] Because of wage differentials, the question of who could and could not afford to finance a spouse's migration and support a biologically reproductive household became ethnic-specific. The ratio of Filipino men to Filipino women actually *increased* between the nineteenth century and the early twentieth century.[8] Much like perceptions of working-class Chinese men on the mainland, the myth of the Filipino man as sexual threat materialized because of gender ratios that favored East Asians within the logic of heteronormative reward and deprivation. The conditions of plantation life facilitated the creation of wedded, child-rearing households among Japanese men but relegated Filipino men to a maligned social sphere of bachelor societies. Yet as the events of the Massie case in 1931–1932 showed, which I address later, Japanese men did not altogether escape scrutiny and policing. White settlers in Hawai'i painted all nonwhite men, indigenous men included, with the same brush connoting sexual danger. The figure of the Filipino rapist in *Blu's Hanging* remains one of multiple layers in a palimpsest of cultural histories about sexual aggression in post-contact Hawai'i. In contrast to the way H. T. Tsiang recovers Asian immigrant men in homosocial spaces from the stigma of deviance by mobilizing sexual difference into resistant queerness, as I argue in Chapter 4, Yamanaka keeps them firmly in their representational place.

In this chapter, I tie up the series of examples in *Sticky Rice* from canonical Asian American literature that expose most poignantly the relationship between white-supremacist perceptions of sexual deviance and the liberatory non-normativity of populations of color. A U.S. nation-state that endorsed white, middle-class heterosexuality may have attempted to surveil and punish Asian-raced subjects for their purportedly pathological inability to conform. However, these Asian Americans found affinities, relationalities, and pleasures that signaled other desires. The texts I analyze in the preceding chapters create opportunities for perversely delightful enjoyments that are anti-racist, anti-imperialist, and anti-capitalist. The queer resistance of these characters, even if not overtly acknowledged, transforms into the vehicle through which possibilities beyond uncritical assimilation could be imagined and divisions within racial and ethnic groups could be resolved. In *Blu's Hanging*, however, a same-sex dyad of middle-class East Asian women replicates structures of power. By comparison, the figure of the Filipino rapist becomes even more pronounced in its abuse of an East Asian child. Here, a portrayal of racialized male sexual deviance negates any revolutionary potential of the women's same-sex attachments.

This book ends by issuing a firm caveat about intraracial intimacy among Asian American men. As we have seen, the reason this figuration of same-sex contact remains alluring is precisely because the halves of these dyads are *not* equal even as they seem to be. They possess different levels of access to structural power. They have asymmetrical amounts of cultural capital. The terms on which they can afford to accept or reject normative values are uneven. However, the semblance of equality or sameness makes this configuration seductive as a polemic about reconciliation. Far from being an oversight, the opacity of disparities becomes purposeful. In *Blu's Hanging*, two occasions of intraracial same-sex contact solidify political hierarchies: one because it valorizes above all else East Asian middle-class domestic respectability and the other because it replicates the myth of the Filipino rapist. The first part of this chapter unpacks these two entities, an instance of coded lesbianism and an assault perpetrated by a man, to show how the former's idealization remains central to latter's demonization. This leads me to interrogate the novel's overall sex negativity more broadly. Any polymorphously pleasurable or queer transgression, however, elides the displacement of Native Hawaiians, who remain absent in a narrative that naturalizes the dominance of East Asians. I conclude with a discussion of the gendered and sexualized masking of settler colonialism.

ELITE QUEERNESS IN
THE LOCAL JAPANESE FAMILY

Blu's Hanging follows the stock plot of the bildungsroman, a triumphal rise from the hardship or humble origins with which the narration opens. The story unfolds in the late 1960s or early 1970s. The thirteen-year-old protagonist, Ivah Ogata, a working-class local Japanese girl in Kaunakakai, assumes a parental role over her younger brother, Presley (nicknamed "Blu"), and her younger sister, Maisie, after the death of their mother. The children's father, Bertram Ogata, a custodian who began working two jobs to make up for the lost income of his late wife, Eleanor, remains largely absent. His profession places him at the lowest rungs of the economic ladder, and lack of money generates tension in the family. The Ogata children's Japanese ethnicity makes them vulnerable to racial discrimination from white teachers, but it also puts them above Filipinos in the hierarchy established by the planation economy.[9] The Reyeses, the sexually pathologized Filipino family next door, serve as a foil for the functional household the Ogatas try to maintain after Eleanor's death.[10] One adult, an uncle named Paolo, minds the children, and he repeatedly molests them. The unremarkable way the narration presents this abuse foreshadows Blu's rape at Paolo's hands right before Ivah leaves home for boarding school. The novel finds its uneasy resolution in anticipation of a further shifting of household relationships that will certainly follow after the elder sister's departure.

Unlike the Reyeses, the Ogatas have an extended family beyond their household from whom to draw emotional and material support. Faith Ann (nicknamed "Big Sis"), an older cousin, happily extends herself as a parental figure. She begins student teaching at the local school and moves into the teachers' cottages close to the Ogatas. Her housemate, Sandi Ito, is Maisie's teacher, another of the story's few sympathetic characters. Understandably, it brings comfort to see two characters who are maligned for a number of reasons fashion a stable family to help the Ogatas recover from mourning. Given that the other families in the story, all heterosexual, contain varying degrees and types of dysfunction, Big Sis and Sandi's home remains a respite from the brutality in other domestic spaces. Kandice Chuh astutely points out that it "functions as the mechanism for potential salvation [whereby] the novel interrogates the presumptive vale of normatively wrought conceptions of family and home as the places and spaces of safety and innocence."[11] The warmth emanating from Big Sis and Sandi's household is unmistakable and laudable. However, its ethnic configuration—both women are Japanese—becomes salient in how Hawai'i's ethnic hierarchy is solidified at the novel's conclusion.

Yamanaka's most forceful indictments against the non- or questionably consensual heterosexualities throughout the story line arises not in conjunction with Uncle Paolo's molestation of his nieces but in Big Sis's portrayal as the only sympathetic character in the family headed by Aunt Betty. The two female siblings in that household fight constantly. As her sister Lila Beth's opposite, Big Sis possesses a gender nonconformity that creates conflict. Lila Beth initiates verbal spats by calling Big Sis "Dyke" and "Butchie," to which Big Sis retaliates with "Bitch and "[S]lut."[12] Appeals for parental mediation remain unsuccessful when Big Sis asks, "Betta butch than slut, how you figga, Dad?" (76). Aunt Betty counters, "Big Sis, wouldn't hurt for you to be a little more feminine, you know. You so god-damn otemba with that short, short hair, and T-shirt every place you go" (76–77). Uncle Myron's powerlessness as a peacemaker and Aunt Betty's escalation of Lila Beth's gender policing show that this family, though consisting of a biological two-parent household, is inadequate. When the Ogatas' Thanksgiving visit to Aunt Betty's house concludes with the assault of Lila Beth by an ex-boyfriend, Aunt Betty's pride in her daughter's heterosexual success sours, and she compounds the attack on her daughter by beating her.

Even though this depiction of Aunt Betty's household condemns the codes that govern the genetic conjugal family, Big Sis also relies on the language of biology when she intervenes in the Ogata sibling rivalries. She uses herself as a negative example when she implores Blu to treat Ivah with more respect: "One day you going wake up and you going be talking to Ivah just like how Lila Beth talk to me. . . . Fuck, man, thass no way to be with your own blood. . . . [B]e nice to your sista, you hear me, Presley? You guys is blood" (81, 86). The novel contests biology as the primary factor in kinship, but it does not foreclose its significance. The parental unit, consisting of Big Sis and Sandi, contains two adults: one who is and the other who is not biologically related to the Ogatas. Big Sis shares with them a genetic link, while Sandi defines her relationship with the children in the form of a close teacher-student bond. The two women host overnight gatherings for the Ogatas regularly, with some grateful resistance from their father, who stresses, "You no need do this, you know. Even my own family wouldn't take these three for sleep-ova" (126). Acknowledging the inadequacy of relying solely on biological kin, Bertram supports the surrogacy even if it calls his parenting into question and reminds him of Eleanor's absence.

Big Sis and Sandi's relationship carries the hermeneutic coding of lesbianism understood in late twentieth-century discourses of politicized sexual difference. My goal is not to prove that they, in their cozy domesticity, are a lesbian couple. They may or may not be, but the question remains beside the point when considering how they are portrayed more favorably than the men who are irredeemably deviant. The two characters tap into a language of non-normative gender and sexual possibilities for women that historically (especially in the 1970s, when the story is set) have been associated with the rejection of heterosexuality. When Ivah considers the aptness of this perfectly matched butch-femme pair, she notes that even though Big Sis's masculinity makes her vulnerable to verbal attack from her sister and mother, her cousin's physical appearance pleases her. Ivah describes her as "handsome, with her short hair, smooth skin, and strong cheekbones" (81). Ivah admires Sandi's traditional feminine beauty in an even more elaborate depiction:

She's the cutest teacher at Kaunakakai School.... And for a Japanese, she would also win "Best Smile," I think, because of her pink frost lipstick and bright blue eyeshadow. The only thing I might suggest is that she wear false eyelashes, but she seems to be the natural type.

She's the only teacher who wears culottes and Dr. Scholl's to school every day. The only one who doesn't look like she's sweating in her dress as if her slip is stuck to her thighs or wedged up her buttocks. The other teachers wear hot nylons and heels. (120)

The femininity described conforms to a white aesthetic, and Ivah even qualifies Sandi's beauty with the words "for a Japanese." At the same time, she concedes that the white teachers compare unfavorably in their imperfect maintenance of that standard.

The joking and teasing in the diametrically gendered Big Sis-Sandi couple provide the only moment of safe erotic interchange in the novel:

"Sandi get the whole island, all the young guys checking her out still yet. But lucky thing she sharing the cottage with me, so I run those horny buggas outta our yard, yeah, Sandi?"

"*Faith Ann*," she says, like she's pretending to run out of patience, "you're asking for a dirty lickens when we get home."

"Ooohh, I scared. I shakin'," says Big Sis, laughing. (199)

Chuh rightly notes that in a narrative punctuated with violence, this scene offers a rare glimpse of intimacy, the "dirty lickens" and the "shakin" rising not out of abuse but out of pleasure. She posits the two women's cohabitation as evidence of the novel's anti-heteronormative possibilities that disrupt an ingrained link between the domestic space of the home with the domestic space of the nation.[13] At the same time, Big Sis and Sandi's pairing replicates both heterosexual and East Asian privilege through the idealized domesticity they present. Their cohabitation becomes possible through a history that has granted them more freedom from the sexually inflected surveillance doled out on Filipinos.[14] Their alterity also masks itself in a way that slips into invisibility, given that it is customary for single teachers to share cottages with each other. Their elite lesbianism contributes to the abjection of masculinities that surround them. In this sense, Big Sis and Sandi's place in *Blu's Hanging* parallels Gertrude Stein and Alice B. Toklas's in *The Book of Salt*, which I cover in Chapter 2.

On Maisie's birthday, the children bake a cake from a Betty Crocker mix at Big Sis and Sandi's house, participating in a domestic ritual associated with middle-class, brand-name consumerism. Erin Suzuki observes that in *Blu's Hanging*, scenes of food and eating always take place alongside attempts to fill the void of Eleanor's absence. Moreover, the foods Blu craves allude to a "mainland-based capitalist system that is so closely implicated in Hawai'i's own history of colonization and disenfranchisement."[15] However, Yamanaka's description of the birthday party departs from her other references to Blu's gargantuan appetite, since it marks one of the few times he plays the role of emotional provider to another family member rather than the recipient of Ivah's care. Baking the cake becomes not only a bonding activity for the children but also speech therapy for Maisie. She had become mute after her mother died, and Sandi is the only teacher at school able to draw out her words in the aftermath. At the cottage, Sandi engages the entire family to encourage Maisie to speak again:

> "Help us read the directions, Maisie," Miss Ito says easily, no pressure.
> "We just need your help. All of us."
> "C'mon Maisie," Blu says. I hold my breath.
> "Mix . . . three . . . eggs . . . with two sticks of . . . butter." The voice is raspy and low. . . .
> "Good talking voice, Maisie. Mix in one and a half cups of milk. Then three hundred strokes. Can we all help her count this high? Maisie can you read the instructions for us?" . . .
> I push Blu toward the paper chart. He wipes his face with both

hands. Miss Ito continues reading the directions. Then, with some hesitance at first, Maisie repeats each line as Blu points to the words, mouthing them as Maisie speaks them. (130)

The counting of the strokes of the batter suggests a teleology where the finished product, be it cake or upward mobility, will be the purposeful accumulation of work and self-actualization. As the Ogatas rise "this high" economically, they will have their voices coaxed and validated by the cultural visibility enjoyed by local Japanese ethnics. Although this pivotal moment hints at an optimistic future in which all of the children will eventually find their voice, so to speak, it also suggests that this empowerment will take place through regimented guidelines. Instead of making a cake from scratch with a recipe that can be modified according to the whim of its bakers, the characters actualize a pre-packaged domesticity that requires lock-step adherence, not improvisation. This scene, while recuperative, shows that the novel's non-normative subjects will find sweetness, solace, and agency through assimilating normative class values.

Big Sis and Sandi's attention makes the Ogatas' class advancement possible. By parenting and mentoring, the two women facilitate Ivah's transfer to an elite college preparatory school. Candace Fujikane warns against reading Ivah's admission to the school solely as a function of her meritocratic scholastic achievements. After all, her ethnic identity elicits sustained advising from Japanese teachers that the Reyes sisters find harder to access because of anti-Filipino prejudice.[16] Chuh similarly tempers her recognition of any liberatory, anti-heteronormative possibility Big Sis and Sandi present, given that their "privileged status manifests . . . the erasures of indigenous peoples and the effacement of anti-Filipino racism from the novel's scene of representation. . . . Non-heteronormativity neither trumps nor excuses these representational problematics."[17] I would even argue not only that this departure from heteronormativity does not override Big Sis and Sandi's ethnic privilege but also that the very *fact* of their ethnic and settler identity (and the cultural and economic capital that accompanies it) allows them to exercise their refusal of heterosexual pairings with men. My reading of Big Sis and Sandi's relationship remains only measuredly enthusiastic, for the logic of Yamanaka's novel indicates that it must be within the maintenance of a diametrically gendered, child-rearing household that these women mitigate their coding as a queer couple and counteract the Ogatas' class oppression.[18]

Both male and female characters in *Blu's Hanging* exhibit substandard child-rearing skills, but the language of parental competence tends to be gendered female, regardless of the caretaker. When Ivah experiences menarche, Blu offers her the support usually provided by a girl's mother at this moment in her adolescence. After hearing that Ivah was teased at school about having her period, Blu gives her a present of menstrual products, gift-wrapped and accompanied by a card that reads, "Since us got no mommy to buy it, I went to Friendly Market and look for sanaterry belt and pads. . . . I not shame and I no care 'cause you got no mommy. . . . And I will buy for you again if you want me to" (101). His insistence that he takes the place of their mother is key to the gendering of his care, but it also implicitly calls attention to their father's lack of involvement. Blu's actions, surprisingly unanticipated, show unscripted spontaneity not seen in the cake-baking scene. His care of Ivah foreshadows the claim she makes at the novel's conclusion—"Us can all be Mama" (259)—as she reminds Blu and Maisie to look after Bertram before she leaves for boarding school.

If the creative refashioning of the family rests on each member's taking a turn at "be[ing] Mama," then the novel levels yet another condemnation of biological mothers who fall short. Mrs. Nishimoto, a white woman married to a local Japanese man, is an unsympathetic and even cruel teacher at the elementary school. Like Aunt Betty, who heads an emotionally barren household, Mrs. Nishimoto barely manages to mother her six biracial children. She hires Ivah, Blu, and Maisie to help with ironing, and the Ogatas shift from that to childcare seamlessly while she weeps in frustration. As much as the novel lauds the feminization of competent caretakers, regardless of gender, it also suggests that the lack of this initiative from adult men is simply a matter of course. That Bertram distances himself from his children; that Uncle Paolo is much more of a threat than a parent to his nieces; that the biological fathers of neither the Reyes nor the Nishimoto children can be found together reveal the novel's gendering of parental absence or abuse.

On the power-laden avenues through which difference is recuperated, Emily Russell asserts that members of stigmatized groups in *Blu's Hanging* attempt to rescript narratives of their marginalization through the heteronormative promise of the marriage contract and biological reproduction. In this regard, Russell looks closely at Bertram and Eleanor's status as survivors of Hansen's disease. Their wish to produce healthy offspring becomes a cure not so much for the physical illness—the sulfone medications accomplish that and eventually kill Eleanor when she overuses them out of fear of reinfection—but for the social scarring that marks them in a colonial system of public health surveillance.[19] At the same time, what I see is that parental custodianship of *nonbiological* children remains the gold standard by which characters measure their worth. Accordingly, queer non-reproducers who uphold values associated with heterosexuality incorporate themselves into this ethic of child-rearing.

FILIPINO SEXUAL DEVIANCE AND
THE SILENCING OF SOCIAL CRITIQUE

Blu's Hanging structures itself so that the rape of a local Japanese boy becomes the horrific climax of a story about maternal loss and paternal neglect, but it also functions in line with the novel's more generalized critique
of popular conceptions of Hawai'i. Far from the carefree, tropical paradise
popularized by the tourism industry, a competing image of the islands is
produced in the novel, one afflicted by quotidian traumas that accompany
life in late capital. In many ways, the novel emerges successfully in that regard. Yamanaka reminds us that the poverty, illness, unresolved grief, and
sexual abuse that are part and parcel of life in ordinary places has taken root
in Hawai'i, too. These elements not seen by tourists uphold themselves as
an arbiter of authenticity. However, as I show later, the portrayal the author
urges us to see as the unmediated Hawai'i elides Native Hawaiian displacement. It also erases the histories that privilege East Asians at the expense of
Filipinos. Bertram's class-specific parental absence and Uncle Paolo's predatory habits converge in how Blu's rape is portrayed, which makes the rape
seem like a natural occurrence precipitating from Bertram's inattention.

Blu falls prey to Uncle Paolo's sexual coercion because of his family's
precarious economic situation. He offers to wash Paolo's pickup truck in return for extra cash. When Ivah and Maisie notice Blu missing, they search
for him on their bicycles until they find Uncle Paolo's vehicle in a deserted
parking lot, with Blu and Paolo inside. Ivah quickly approaches the door and
opens it to find the "smoldering heat of bodies . . . steam on the window. My
brother's gagged mouth and tied hands, his face neon white. . . . And in that
moment, Paolo's left hand around his own penis, his right hand around Blu's,
the slapping of flesh" (247). Ivah also sees her "brother's bleeding slightly
down the legs of his pants" (248). The two sisters escape with Blu in a pan-
icked sprint, and all three hide in the night shadows, too afraid to go home,
where Paolo can find them, until Bertram returns from work.

The secondary literature on *Blu's Hanging* has pointed out the difficulty
in grappling with Blu's professed enjoyment of at least part of the rape. Ivah
overhears him praying to Eleanor afterward: "Mama, please no hate me, but
I wanna tell someone the truth. When Uncle Paolo did that to my penis, wen'
feel good 'cept for the ass part. Maybe I like do um again, but not the ass part.
Is it wrong when something feel good?" (253). Several critics have attempted to make sense of this declaration of pleasure. Whereas Crystal Parikh
speculates that Blu's admission is a melancholic response to his mother's
death, because he addresses her directly only at this moment,[20] erin Khuê

Ninh situates the comfort that Blu takes in any sexual activity, consensual or not, within larger self-soothing behaviors, which include his consumption of junk food. These coping mechanisms make him "vulnerable to all manner of exploitation—commercial, social, sexual."[21] Erin Suzuki advances a more provocative possibility insofar as she reads Blu's claim of pleasure as a rethinking of the overdetermined modes in which rape victims are understood. In the act of articulating his conflicted enjoyment, "Blu reclaims some agency in the face of such a violating act by asserting the pleasure he was able to take from an otherwise painful experience."[22] To these recuperative readings of the rape's ambivalence—the first positing it as symptom, the second as escapism, and the third as resistance—I add that Yamanaka broaches the topic of rebellious male same-sex desire only to shut it down. She writes this trope into her narrative as aggression enacted by an adult on a child rather than in the context of a more balanced exchange. When we place this instance alongside the other moments of sexual pleasure or eroticism between men examined in previous chapters, her portrayal shirks the possibility of redressing the intraracial conflicts that persist from Hawai'i's plantation economy.

A critique of the ethnic hierarchy does arise in *Blu's Hanging*, but it remains ineffectual. After the children return one evening from babysitting for the Nishimotos, they attempt to slip unnoticed past their father as he buys marijuana from Uncle Paolo in the kitchen. Paolo, who has the upper hand in this exchange, admonishes Bertram for trying to get credit rather than paying up-front. Chastened, Bertram turns to scold his children for being out late. Blu then tells Paolo that his older sister has forbidden him to visit the Reyes home, triggering an outburst:

> "Why, why," Uncle Paolo says to me, and I smell the liquor on his breath, "whass wrong with my niece playing wit' yo' bradda? What? He mo' betta than her 'cause he Japanee? Fuck, Japs for think they mo' betta than everybody else, fuckas. Especially the Filipinos. Fuck, everybody, for spit on Filipinos, shit. You fuckin' snipes." . . .
> "Fuckin' haoles. They mo' worse than the Japs the way they act like we just a truckload of fuckin' brownies picking pineapples for minimum wage. Fuckas all hate us Filipinos." (207)

Uncle Paolo nails down the ethnic pecking order in his tirade—whites and East Asians at the top, with Filipinos at the bottom—and references the agricultural capital that established it. Ironically, Bertram is the one employed as a janitor at the Dole factory, presumably for minimum wage. If we look at the class disparity between the Ogatas and the Reyeses by historicizing the structural and material advantages of Japanese over Filipino residents, a more damning elision occurs.

Fujikane claims that Yamanaka's choice to make the Ogatas working class and the Reyeses middle class elides the privileges that come with being Japanese in Hawaiʻi.[23] It is not that no working-class Japanese people or no middle-class Filipino people exist; however, when these outliers in an uneven economic landscape divided by ethnicity are represented as such, the refreshing critique of the ethnic hierarchy invalidates itself. It also does not help that the condemnation of the ethnic economic order comes from a child molester. The intended reader is not meant to agree with him. Rather than stop at revealing the critique's neutralization, I want to push its utterance further. What does it mean that the most maligned character calls out East Asian privilege? Its dubious voicing begs more interrogation. It appears that in the local Japanese imagination, an attempt to redress the inequities faced by Filipinos becomes analogous to the sexual violation of vulnerable Japanese bodies. That Uncle Paolo rapes Blu shortly after this scene signifies the magnitude of the presumed injury that such a condemnation would effect. Just as the teleology of the story suggests that Ivah's departure for boarding school is a likely and predictable sum of her disposition and choices, Paolo's rape of Blu, which takes place concurrently with the arrival of Ivah's scholarship letter, is similarly portrayed as a likely and predictable conclusion of factors that have determined this outcome. Repeated evidence of Paolo's predation, the Ogatas' financial desperation, and Blu's previously expressed curiosity about male-male genital contact all seem to point in this direction. The sensational horror of rape effaces the relative social, political, and material comfort of East Asians in Hawaiʻi built through intraracial inequality and settler colonialism. If the novel regards the contestation of this history as akin to rape, then—harking to the backlash against the backlash about the novel—it is not difficult to imagine why this critique often faces so much resistance.

Offering another perspective, Elda E. Tsou reads this scene, which is the only one that recognizes anti-Filipino racism, as a moment in which Uncle Paolo is both correct and incorrect in his assessment of how power operates in the stratified legacy of the plantation economy: "The issue here is not that the novel is unable to recognize racism against Filipinos but that its representational economy cannot articulate the larger historical relationships within which racism against Filipinos forms just one moving part."[24] This critique of the complex forms of capitalist colonialism that have subjugated East Asians and Filipinos simultaneously, even if unevenly, falls short—as does an exposure of the islands' settler colonialism. In other words, Paolo's drunken outburst does not go too far in unsettling what little security the Ogatas possess because of their Japanese ethnicity. Rather, it does not go far enough.

BETTA BUTCH THAN SLUT

The overpowering sex negativity in *Blu's Hanging* cannot be ignored. Aside from the domesticated and safe eroticism between Big Sis and Sandi and the chaste crush Ivah nurses for a male classmate, just about every portrayal of sexual desire prompts anguish or disgust. Yamanaka conflates consensual and nonconsensual sex acts in that both appear in the same wrenching or admonishing prose, making the intended reader recoil. Mark Chiang speculates that the overwhelming aversion to sex in the novel has an uncertain explanation. It could stem from "the degrading incidents [Ivah] (and we) are made to witness or . . . an imaginary projection of her revulsion"[25] of the Reyes sisters. Given that the Reyeses' home is the location of Blu's early sexual explorations, of which Ivah disapproves, and the torture of pet cats, Chiang ventures that Ivah may equate these two very different things. During the Ogatas' visit to Aunt Betty's house, yet another negative depiction of sexual behavior arises. When Big Sis voices in her argument with Lila Beth that it is "betta" to be "butch than slut" (76), she asserts an asexual gender nonconformity over and above her sister's heterosexual prodigiousness. Big Sis's words appear to stand in for the narrative voice in a wholesale condemnation of sexual pleasure.

Lila Beth enjoys partaking in what she calls a "hickey contest." In this activity, two heterosexual couples put money in a pool, and the one that can land the most hickeys on the female partner wins. When Lila Beth's ex becomes enraged by visual evidence of her new boyfriend's participation in these contests, she says, "He wen' pin me down in his car right in the Hilo Shopping Center parking lot and did this." She reveals injuries on "her face and all over her cheek, stork marks, suck marks, dark and wide. She lifts the sleeve . . . and they're under her arm, too. Then she unbuttons the first few buttons . . . all over her breasts" (84). The marks do not stop there. "Lila Beth opens her mouth. All over her tongue, swollen, red and purple welts. And when she lifts it up, the small meat under her tongue is torn" (85). The description of Lila Beth's tongue frenulum severing under these conditions references intertextually a scene of loving injury in Maxine Hong Kingston's *The Woman Warrior*. The protagonist's mother had recounted that she snipped the underside of her daughter's tongue with a pair of scissors in infancy so she could speak in multiple languages. Since the protagonist has no recollection of it, the makeshift medical procedure, which may or may not have happened, haunts her in a narrative that thematizes the unreliability, yet absolute indispensability, of memory, storytelling, language, and voice. In *Blu's Hanging*, however, the act does not invoke metaphor or metacritical meditation. Its stark literalness shuts down rather than opens up potential for recuperation. The subcutaneous hemorrhages, which Lila Beth consensually and playfully accepted at an earlier time, return in a vengeful attack. The pride with which she beams about her previous achievements—"I had mine all over my ass and back. You know for how hard to make hickeys on the ass, right?" (85)—becomes pathologized by Yamanaka's amalgamation of assault and agential pleasure.

In the multiple times I have taught *Blu's Hanging*, I have never been successful in urging my students to question how the novel demonizes Lila Beth's sexual tastes. We can all agree that Yamanaka's prose depicts the hickey contest in a way that does not intend to elicit desire. Yet no one wants to see beyond the disgust-laden framing to articulate what, exactly, is wrong with the act itself. Compare it with, for instance, some of the sexual practices that the fiction writer Samuel R. Delany sympathetically describes in his oeuvre, which include piss drinking and snot and shit eating, and the hickey contest will not seem so strange. Darieck Scott calls attention to Delany's own qualification that the events recounted in his novel *The Mad Man* remain purely fictional. Instead of taking Delany's declaration at face value, Scott questions why some readers might be comforted by the claim that the non-normative sex depicted relegates itself to the imaginary, therefore evacuating it from the realm of possibility.[26] One might say that Lila Beth's hickey contest presents a practice so puzzling, unusual, or repulsive that it cannot possibly represent reality. Following Scott, I want to assert that the sexual behavior depicted *is* plausible, and the wish to disavow it reveals the overwhelming pull of normativity's respectability, especially when it involves the sexual behavior of people of color.

The difference between Yamanaka and Delany lies in their respective narrative voices' level of friendliness toward the acts they portray. Yamanaka's blurring of an important distinction between violation and agency under the same condemnatory umbrella of abjection occurs again when Ivah visits the Reyes home to find one of the sisters performing oral sex on Blu. What Ivah reports seeing—"My brother, naked, sitting on the edge of the bath tub, his legs spread" and "Blendaline kneeling between them, her mouth around my brother's penis" (161)—somewhat resembles the portions of his rape to which Ivah is privy and erases the dissimilarities between them. Rather than understand Blu's encounter with Blendaline as consensual sexual experimentation between minors, the scene insidiously foreshadows Blu's violation by an adult. The common denominator in these two very different events is the ethnicity of the other person involved. Blendaline, who is herself victimized by her uncle, and Paolo merge into a singular Filipino sexual menace.

I refuse to conflate consensual and nonconsensual acts under the umbrella of sex negativity. With this spirit, I revisit Big Sis's declaration that it is better to be "butch than slut." I interpret Lila Beth's hickey contest, which prompts this declaration, as a corollary to the cutting noted in Chapter 2 that brings Bình, the protagonist of Monique Truong's *The Book of Salt*, relief. Bình describes what he unglamorously calls his "habit" with prose that becomes increasingly lyrical and evocative of sexual pleasure as the description unfolds. I read this scene as a call for healing among factions in the Vietnamese diaspora. Bình obtains as much pleasure from seeing his self-inflicted injuries repair themselves as he does from the pain they produce. When taken in this context, the subcutaneous hemorrhages from Lila Beth's sexual encounters, a similar but different kind of injury, suggest another message about the internal divides within the settler population in Hawai'i, one in line with Yamanaka's oversights about intraracial conflict. The scene that portrays Bình's cutting is replete with spilled blood. The internal bleeding in the hickey contests, however, offers no issuing, only a bruise. The bursting of capillaries near the skin when sucked finds no external release. Bertram believes that the scolding Lila Beth received from her mother after being assaulted by her ex-boyfriend stems from how the marks on her skin resembled his own physical appearance when he was sick with Hansen's disease. His illness embarrassed and stigmatized the family. However, I interpret these marks not as repressed shame about illness but as the novel's metacritical refusal to engage with historical injury—the wound not allowed to air. These two acts of bleeding, one internal and the other external, one overtly and the other obliquely sexual, may seem unrelated. Yet these two physiological processes resonate in how they illustrate the opposing ways the novels handle intraracial strife.

While *The Book of Salt* impels the Vietnamese diaspora to lay aside its internal quarrels by exposing the injuries incurred, allowing them to heal, *Blu's Hanging* implies that actively suppressing conversation about intraracial conflict or keeping them under the surface is the solution. Yamanaka's distaste for hickeys notwithstanding, this vision of progress implies an even playing field when historical forces have structured it otherwise. When the Ogata family's local Japanese surrogate parents prepare Ivah, Blu, and Maisie for upward mobility through a reliance on the cultural capital of their ethnicity, the lesbian undertones of this kinship unit mask a conservative maintenance of the social hierarchy. Big Sis and Sandi's relationship and their parenting of the Ogata children convey non-heterosexuality without anti-heteronormativity, same-sex affiliation without erotic or sexual capaciousness, and sanctified private domesticity without material redistribution. The concluding scene shows Ivah not pulling herself up by her bootstraps but coasting along on conditions of economic and sexual advantage that have preceded her.

CONDITIONS OF SETTLER PRIVILEGE

We can say that the debates about *Blu's Hanging* in the wake of its AAAS award therapeutically lanced the skin, a common treatment for subcutaneous hemorrhaging in cases where pressure from internal bleeding causes unbearable pain or risks damage to tissues. By allowing the blood to come to the surface, activists released the accumulated tensions and revealed the past's sedimentation of anti-Filipino prejudice and economic oppression. Despite this airing of historical inequity, a failure to redress another injury remained—that being the displacement of Native Hawaiians from their land.[27] The novel contains no Native Hawaiian characters, a conspicuous absence in a setting with a prominent sovereignty movement. The controversy about the novel similarly omitted indigenous interests, relegating discussion to matters of intrasettler conflict only among Asians.

Throughout this chapter, I use the term "local" to refer to Asian populations in Hawai'i because of its spatial and temporal departures from the more easily recognizable "Asian American" on the U.S. mainland. This label is more commonly used in Hawai'i but remains fraught because of how it flattens populations that have different structural relationships to the state. At least two genealogies of the term "local" exist, giving rise to different, but not necessarily contradictory, definitions that residents of Hawai'i summon to express emplaced belonging on the islands. Each has a constitutive outside that is demographically different from the other, yet conceptually they remain similar. John P. Rosa's examination of the infamous Massie case of 1931–1932 identifies the emergence of the local in social changes wrought by the event. Thalia Massie, a white woman and wife of a U.S. Navy officer stationed in Hawai'i, claimed to have been raped by a group of nonwhite men. On the basis of scant evidence, police arrested five men—representing ethnicities that were Japanese, Native Hawaiian, and mixed—and charged them with the assault. They were tried, which resulted in a mistrial. However, before a retrial could be conducted, a band of Massie's sympathizers, which included her husband and mother, took the law into their own hands, beating one of the men and killing a second. The vigilantes were convicted, but the territorial governor of Hawai'i commuted their sentences, and they never spent a day in jail.

In Rosa's analysis of the event, a staunchly unified notion of the local coalesced that prompted Native Hawaiians and working-class Asians to position themselves against white settlers, who tended to have affiliations with the military or plantation capital.[28] The local signified a steadfast claim in Hawai'i that distinguished itself from white-supremacist settler positionality, which reared its ugly head when it refused to hold accountable violence against a heterogeneously nonwhite collective. The figure of the white woman, whose sexual sanctity warranted protection from the purported deviance of nonwhite men, catalyzed these affiliations. The trial marked the moment at which a mainland-based racial order was transposed onto the colonial possession of Hawai'i, organizing a previously messy and complicated web of social hierarchies with respect to race, ethnicity, colonial subject status, and class into a taxonomy that more neatly defined white from nonwhite.[29] Native Hawaiians and disparate Asian immigrant groups recognized their shared scripting into the United States' pathologizing of nonwhites and solidified affinities with one another.

As my previous reference to Fujikane's work attests, East Asians may have regarded Filipino men on the plantations as dangerous because of their relatively greater difficulty in meeting heterosexually inflected standards, a situation emerging out of class oppression. However, the fact that one of the men accused by Thalia Massie was Japanese and a few others had East Asian ancestry called attention to the conflation of all nonwhites for the supposed sexual danger they posed to white women. The finger pointing that East Asians on the plantations directed at Filipinos in the nineteenth century was redeployed by whites as they admonished Native Hawaiians and Asians together in the 1930s. The late twentieth-century demonization of Filipinos that *Blu's Hanging* enacts forgets the shared oppression of all nonwhites (and a coalition addressing those oppressions) in the interim between the expansion of the plantation economy and the time of the novel's publication.

Jonathan Y. Okamura offers another explanation for the emergence of local identity in Hawai'i. His narrative of local consolidation differs from Rosa's, setting it somewhat later and during the demographic shifts of the 1960s, after Hawai'i became the fiftieth state in 1959. It also complicates a unity implied by the story of local emergence that Rosa sketches. Okamura explains the distinction between "local" and "Asian American" by illustrating the differing political commitments each designation indexes. The influx of migration, both white and Asian, to the islands from the U.S. mainland and Asia—influenced by factors such as post–World War II middle-class capital, the Immigration Act of 1965, and increasing Japanese transnational investment—created a crisis of identity for the older settler population. The term "local" became salient then as a way for descendants of nineteenth-century plantation workers, which included the Portuguese and Puerto Ricans, as well as Asians, to distinguish themselves from newer transplants.[30] Although "Asian American" may have emerged on the mainland as a panethnic coalition during the same time, the panethnic labor organizing on the islands was, by then, a distant memory.[31] The more pressing concern for residents of Hawai'i during this time of rapid development was preserving an imagined authenticity tied to a pre-statehood past. Much like the model of liberal multiculturalism on the U.S. mainland, this embrace of a multiracial local in Hawai'i hampers interrogation of inequality among Asian ethnic groups and impedes critique of Asian participation in settler colonialism.

Although Rosa's and Okamura's narratives of local emergence may seem to conflict with each other, they do not, necessarily. In each case, the outsiders in the dynamic of local fashioning—whether they are white or Asian—remain newcomers on the side of capital who have not earned their place on the Hawaiian Islands through the grit of working-class labor. How Rosa and Okamura differ in their definitions of the local lies in the function of indigeneity. For Rosa, Native Hawaiians and Asians alike found themselves in the crosshairs of anxieties exported from the mainland about the sexual threat of nonwhite men, and they saw common cause with each other. Okamura asserts that indigeneity becomes the overlooked positionality in a problematic celebration of diversity. Native Hawaiians are incorrectly regarded as yet another ethnic group showcased in Hawai'i's story of multiculturalism gone right. Yet nothing prevents Rosa's and Okamura's claims from both being true at the same time. In a Hawai'i crosscut with multiple and overlapping forms of colonialism and capitalism, the solution to inequity contains more than one prong. As JoAnna Poblete-Cross argues about American Samoa, a Pacific island with histories of subjugation that are both similar to and distinct from those of Hawai'i, indigenous people and Asian immigrants are "part of the same imperial legacy," and tensions between them always "have roots in the form and structure of the U.S. colonial presence in that region."[32] Local Asians in Hawai'i, especially East Asians, can better attend to their economically and structurally more comfortable position relative to Filipinos and Native Hawaiians while still challenging the historical arc of whiteness that has governed life on the islands.

Blu's Hanging, set during the late 1960s and early 1970s, takes place during the period that defines Okamura's version of local emergence but carries with it the earlier schema of a white-nonwhite binary from the 1930s. The Ogatas express pride in their local heritage by poking fun at mainlanders throughout the story. They feel frustration with newcomers in ways that call to mind the specificities of race and class. In a reminiscence about her mother, Ivah recounts that she ridiculed mainlanders' acts of cultural appropriation. Eleanor would entertain her children by assuming the fictional persona of a new arrival, eliciting gales of laughter: "I'm just a haole who came to Kaunakakai and renamed myself with a Hawaiian name. Oh, you don't mind if I call my first boy, Jim, the Hawaiian equivalent, Kimo, do you? And my daughter Amanda, Alohanani, do you?" (39). Later, Ivah speaks derisively of "a haole from Bloomingdale teaching Hawaiian studies. If you close your ears, you won't hear her mispronounce Kamehameha and Kaunakakai wrong every time she uses it in a sentence" (63). Although the narrative takes place during the post-statehood wave of Asian migration to the islands, the admonishment of nonlocals directs itself at only whites. This incorrectly frames the clash between newcomers and longtime settlers as one that rests on the white-nonwhite binary.

In *Blu's Hanging*, the white-nonwhite binary ties itself to linguistic identity. The populations of color converse in pidgin, a creolization of the various languages used on the plantations, while mainland white transplants favor standard American English. When Sandi code switches from the hegemonic English she uses in the classroom to pidgin in her defense of the Ogatas against a white teacher who mistreats them, she impresses the children. "I've never heard her use it" (128), Ivah notes, poignant in light of the same teacher earlier shaming her for speaking pidgin. We are meant to commend Sandi for a courageous and strategic deployment of a dialect maligned by middle-class whites. That she risks damaging her professional credibility while staking a position on the ethical rightness of her stance makes it more authentic.

These two interrelated means of laying claim to Hawai'i—the first through generational inheritance of a history of plantation labor and the second through competence in a linguistic tradition associated with that past—divert attention from the geopolitics in which Asian immigrant populations historically have taken part. Eleanor and the children may entertain themselves by mocking the Hawaiian equivalent of what Philip J. Deloria calls "playing Indian" by white mainlanders.[33] However, they are settlers themselves, albeit with a social location that is different from those they ridicule. They demonstrate what Haunani-Kay Trask observes about local Asians' management of their "subjugation at the hands of *haole* racism [and] their history of deprivation and suffering on the plantations." What follows is a dogged embrace of "an identity other than settler," which is then "strengthened in response to 'Native' insurgency."[34] As these characters in *Blu's Hanging* assert a sense of entitlement to the islands, they obfuscate their own status as nonindigenous subjects in a space that has become overrun with the military and tourism. They unwittingly embrace the tendency they repudiate, via the implication that these indigenous elements remain more rightfully theirs, in lighthearted jokes that express joy in their collectivity.

This masks Hawai'i's ongoing displacement of its Native populations and occupation by U.S. capitalist interests.

The two aforementioned scenes of local claims to Hawai'i take place at moments that signal either normative kinship or a homonormativity that is very closely aligned with it. In the first instance, Ivah's mother bonds with her children through banter that establishes intimacy within the conjugal family and Asian settler colonial claims to the land. In the second, an East Asian maternal figure who functions as a surrogate for the lost biological mother protects her wards from racial discrimination enacted by a white transplant from the mainland. Both cases, which valorize familial love from two-parent households, must be understood within the context of the U.S. occupation of Hawai'i. Finley argues that the heterosexist "structure of the nuclear family needs to be thought of as a colonial system of violence."[35] Trask condemns the United States' overtaking of Hawaiian traditions regarding sex and egalitarian relations among the genders: "Christianity and organized religion have done much to damage these traditional sexual values."[36] Without discounting the genuine affection that these scenes from *Blu's Hanging* convey, we can question the regulating forces of colonialism, which have divested Native Hawaiians of not only land but also familial and other intimate structures that fall outside the scope of post-contact acceptability. The love the Ogata children receive from biological and chosen family, along with the weaponization of negativity surrounding sexual pleasure throughout the novel, produces and is produced through multiple normativities.

MORE OF THE SAME

If the future in *Blu's Hanging* is local, Japanese, lesbian, child-rearing, almost asexual, and devoid of masculinity, then that future (like the ethnic homogeneity of Big Sis and Sandi's same-sex household) simply remains more of the present. It gives us only more of the same. It creates a teleology that is not. Even the most traumatized members of the Ogata family will reap the nepotistic benefits of their kinship connections. When Big Sis convinces Bertram to allow his eldest to accept the boarding school's scholarship, she presses, "If Ivah go now, she can make things smooth for Blu when he go, and then Blu can make things smooth for Maisie when she go" (227). Despite Yamanaka's emphasizing of Blu's queer tendencies—in, for instance, the references to his pop culture fandom associated with teenage girls or the flamboyance with which he portrays the lead in the school play—this child will not "grow sideways."[37] He will grow up. The quiet persistence of the present's disparities does not prompt us to wonder how the sexual abuse the Reyes sisters suffer will affect their ability to develop into the well-adjusted adults that Ivah, Blu, and Maisie seem destined to become. Nor does it speculate on whether or not Uncle Paolo will be held accountable for his actions. Filipinos and other subaltern subjects remain outside the ethos of self-actualization that justifies East Asian ascendancy. This dominance maintains its innocence through constant reference to an embattled position vis-à-vis whiteness and post-statehood changes.

As this chapter comes to a close, I raise the original question I posed in the Introduction about how Asian American literature invokes intraracial coupling's rhetorical possibilities. The examples in this book will raise concerns about their male-specificity. The trope of same-sex desire in this archive is an overwhelmingly male domain accompanied by a dearth of analogous possibilities for women. If erotic bonds between Asian American men animate coalitional politics and, conversely, sexual or sexualized aggression among men becomes the vehicle through which power reproduces itself, how do women factor into this equation? The fictional world of *No-No Boy* treats Japanese American women as incidental to debates about military service, even though the historical record shows they were not. The one recurring Asian female character in *The Book of Salt*, the protagonist's mother, exists only in memory. Women come and go in the diegesis of *Yankee Dawg You Die*, but they do not materialize in the flesh. A sexually trafficked Chinese woman appears briefly as a symbol for bare life in *And China Has Hands*, and a biracial black-Asian woman affirms the protagonist's agency but also exposes his lack of heterosexual prowess. In *Blu's Hanging*, same-sex love between women buttresses conservative, neoliberal values that ignore, not redress, intraracial inequality. Men and women are diametrically portrayed in these texts with respect to their political and erotic world making. Future research can most certainly take up the queer coalitional potential of women in Asian American literature, and I wholeheartedly welcome the intervention of someone who might write a companion to this book.

Throughout the book, my readings of the trope of the sticky couple show that it remains far from perfect. It is not that there is the pesky matter of power differentials standing in the way of a relationship that otherwise could be democratic, uncomplicated, and utopian. It is having these hierarchies in place, no matter how hard we pretend they are not there, that makes the figure of a set of intraracially paired men so attractive as metaphor for coalition building. Whether the reconciliation needs to occur between Japanese American veterans and draft resisters, the Vietnamese state and the diaspora, accommodationist and unruly actors, assimilationist and rebellious Chinese immigrants, or East Asian and Filipino settlers, the truth remains that healing takes work. Some of the sticky pairings covered in this book communicate that better than others. Several leave conservative elements of their vision of conflict resolution in place. The last one is a missed opportunity for redressing past wrongs. All coalitions are entities in process because barriers to organizing will continue to vex an Asian America that seems to stray ever further from the principles with which its panethnic, anti-capitalist, anti-imperialist commitments were founded.

In a twenty-first century in which the divides between global North and global South, capital and labor, cosmopolitan subject and guest worker, and immigrant and refugee are increasing *within* racial categories, we should not allow the same-sex dimensions of any match to lull us into comfort about its purported progressiveness. What is gained and what is lost in any expression of intraracial desire? Whose interests are served, and whose are eclipsed? When does sameness hurt, and when does it help? Where do difference and disparity hide under pretenses of similarity? What sticks, and what falls away?

EPILOGUE

This book revisits several well-known Asian American literary texts not to make yet another addition to the attendant secondary literature, of which there has already been a large accumulation, but to propose that we see this body of work differently from this point forward. Rather than locate the origins of Asian American literature in a primordial heteropatriarchy from which resistant discourses have later rescued it, I posit that Asian American men began from a place of dissident queerness—even if their relationship to it is sometimes inadvertent, unappreciated, or anxiety-provoking. The operations of U.S. capitalism, imperialism, and militarism indelibly sculptured a social landscape in which inequalities continue to express themselves racially. Divisions within Asian America arise in the multiplicity of stances on how best to function in the midst of these forces. Does one accommodate them? Or does one oppose them? And what might accommodation or opposition look like when they are not mutually exclusive?

To effect reconciliation among internal factions, the texts I analyze in this book propose a sexual or erotic intimacy between Asian American men who are divergently positioned in intraracial conflicts. The coalitional impetus behind affiliating with one's own disrupts the assumptions heralded by the myth of the model minority: that people of Asian descent will always choose compliance with white supremacy over critique, confrontation, and revolution. However, limitations remain on how much this figure of same-sex intraracial matching enables a progressive politics. It can sometimes replicate prevailing forms of power and more deeply cleave populations.

The drive toward sameness to maintain one's position in neoliberal capitalism is nowhere better demonstrated than in a personals ad on the popular hosting site Craigslist that went viral in gay Asian American social media circles in 2013. A man in the San Francisco Bay Area identifying as Chinese American posted a listing entitled "Quality Asian for BF and Life Partner–37" with the intention of finding his soulmate. To screen potential suitors for compatibility, he devised an extensive questionnaire.[1] The ad contained an intricate point system, addressing more than twenty attributes, for which respondents would need to add or subtract numbers based on their replies.

Beginning with race, the ad proclaims that only Asian Americans will be considered. However, ethnicity matters, with East Asians valued most highly (20 points), Southeast Asians desired less (–3 to –5 points, depending on country of ancestral origin), and South Asians bringing up the rear (–10 points). Mixed-race Asian Americans take a giant hit (–20 points). The ad requests that potential dates be age-appropriate. Respondents age 30–48 earn 10 points, while those outside that range must lower their scores. Socioeconomic class, a factor that Americans tend to downplay because of our presumption of living in a classless society, makes itself explicit. The ad's author identifies a preference for college-educated parents and grandparents on both sides of a potential partner's family (but those parents better not be divorced). In addition, he prefers to date men in the "STEM" (science, technology, engineering, and medical) and legal fields, while practitioners in the arts and social sciences remain less desirable. Least of all are those identified as "non-professional." They lose 12 points. Homeownership raises one's score by 12. The quiz also tests for relationship history. If one has never had a long-term relationship with another Asian American, that is a red flag: subtract 15 points. But a brush with committed heterosexuality is alluring. Men previously married to women receive a boost. However, those marriages better not come with children in tow. Finally, although the ad's author self-identifies as a Democrat, he grants 7 points to Republicans.

Almost two decades after the video artist Nguyen Tan Hoang's call for intraracial love among Asian American men in *7 Steps to Sticky Heaven*, as I discuss in the Introduction, we see the same desire for racially congruous same-sex matching. However, this intraracial erotics is for different ends. Rather than mounting a challenge to the white normativity of mainstream gay economies of desire through sexual congress with other Asian Americans, the favoring of sameness maintains entrenched systems of status and value. Instead of opening itself to the erotic possibilities of denigrated racial embodiments, it shuts out social positionalities with less cultural and economic capital than one's own.

The ad's appeal to sexual normativity reveals an ambivalence that creates an awkward discordance, if not an impossible situation. The author's distaste for partners whose parents are divorced seems at odds with a positive appraisal of said partners' previous experience with wedded heterosexuality. Apparently, a never married, single-parent family of origin remains so inconceivable that it goes without mention. A preference for someone with political views aligned with the other major U.S. party seems like an aberration in a profile that is overwhelmingly preoccupied with similarity. However, the fact that the ideological distance between Democrats and Republicans is not that large speaks to a superficial embrace of variation that does not disrupt college-educated, upper-middle-income, dyadically coupled East Asian American elitism. A conspicuous absence here is HIV status, an identity marker that, as of 2013, still commonly appeared in ads for men seeking men, despite its increased blurriness along lines of detectability and decreased relevance with the advent of pre-exposure prophylaxis in 2012. The omission of status in an ad that otherwise displays conservative sentiments may imply an unexpected friendliness to serodiscordance, positive status on the part of the author himself, or—like the failure to consider that a prospective date may have been raised by a single parent—a wholesale refusal to imagine that HIV-positivity is even a remote likelihood in a partner thus invented. The idealized intraracial pairing longed for by the ad's author presumes an undesirable world of unpredictable dissimilarity against which its Bay Area, home-owning exclusiveness protects. Far from ushering in political transformation through same-sex love within racialized groups, this example of sticky gone bad leaves intact the familiar and the normalized. The result is not a critique of the precarity following the economic collapse of 2008 caused by U.S. capitalism (predatory mortgage lending) and imperialism (the Iraq War in 2003). It is a demand for more of the same.

As Nguyen cautions in his critical theory, the touting of nonhierarchical sameness in intraracial Asian and Asian American pairings echoes an older, since discredited idea that gay and lesbian couples are inherently more egalitarian than heterosexual ones. For certain politicized gay Asian American men, consorting with white men may be considered "retrograde," while "Asian-Asian couplings . . . are deemed up-to-date and progressive, the new 'norm.'" However, these configurations within racial categories are often complicated by power differentials across "age, class, language, education, nationality, and body size" and the reality that there are class-privileged Asians and Asian Americans who, in addition to whites, participate in sex tourism in Southeast Asia.[2] Sameness and egalitarianism remain fictitious, no matter how much one tries to obliterate or ameliorate difference.

Despite a contemporary politics of sticky among certain Asian Americans, a racially congruent combination is still almost unthinkable, even for one engrossed in a long-form project that demands its constant thinking.[3] In the spring of 2014, while happily in the thick of research for this book, I taught a lecture course required for graduation at my university. It was part of the old core curriculum that tended to be met with boredom, if not resistance, from many students. Two humanities majors in a largely science-oriented and pre-professionally-committed student body attended every class and sat right in front of the podium at full attention. Their hands were almost always the first to spring up when I posed a question. They frequently stayed after class to discuss the material further. The two were visible as culturally gay Asian American men, and I had assumed they were best friends. Not until near the end of the term did I realize that they were lovers. Although the heterosexual couples habitually entwined and whispering between themselves along the auditorium's back row were obvious to me from day one, I wondered why the lens for this literary-critical project took so long to refocus when directed at actual same-sex, intraracially paired Asian Americans before me in plain sight.

Over the years during which the writing of this book took place, I regularly conversed with fellow literary Asian Americanists about it. Some of these discussions happened during the downtime after conference panels or talks where I had presented portions of the work. Others transpired over e-mail. One occurred during my trip to Madison to see *Yankee Dawg You Die*. These interchanges were all remarkably similar to one another. My interlocutors would claim that they had read the text in question multiple times and may have even taught it. Yet they did not until now see what transpired between the male characters, and from this point on, they will never be able to unsee it. In my lecture hall, the sticky couple a mere five feet deep into my field of vision eluded detection for months, not because of active closeting on their part, but because of my own failure to read and recognize them. Clear yet unacknowledged, evident yet overlooked, those Asian American men would become the living embodiment of my analysis in this book. The queer configurations in some of the most commonly read Asian American texts were there all along for those willing or able to perceive them. Particularly in narratives where the sexual activity or eroticism remains figurative, I have marveled at how their same-sex desiring and polymorphously pleasurable elements express themselves. My repeated and almost compulsive combing of the secondary literature, thinking that someone surely must have published on this, has turned up empty time and time again. Like those two romantically paired Asian American men right before my eyes, they have eluded us for far too long.

The possibility that we, as Asian Americans, might find one another sexy is far removed from typical realms of conceivability. It is not supposed to happen. Our rejection of whiteness, heteronormativity, upward economic mobility, and other vectors of assimilation is not supposed to occur. Turning away from the pursuit of these social advantages (however limited they are for racialized subjects) can be met with ridicule, apathy, inattention, or violence. It can draw the ire of one's co-ethnics in the name of respectability. The consequences for challenging them are costly, even fatal. However, moments will arise that compel us to reach across the hostility instilled by war, displacement, labor exploitation, or cultural invisibility. With it, the urge to touch, love, and connect with one's own will overwhelm the aversion those histories have created. What then? The test of intraracial love will be to avoid making it more of the same. The wish must be for something different, for something that does not yet exist in the world.

NOTES

INTRODUCTION

1. See Daryl J. Maeda, *Chains of Babylon: The Rise of Asian America* (Minneapolis: University of Minnesota Press, 2009).

2. Nguyen Tan Hoang, dir., *7 Steps to Sticky Heaven*, Video Out, Vancouver, 1995.

3. Glen M. Mimura, *Ghostlife of Third Cinema: Asian American Film and Video* (Minneapolis: University of Minnesota Press, 2009), 144.

4. Marlon T. Riggs, dir., *Tongues Untied*, Frameline, San Francisco, 1989.

5. Frantz Fanon, *Black Skin, White Masks,* trans. Charles Lam Markmann (New York: Grove, 1967), 170.

6. Discussions of this marginalization are in Dwight McBride, *Why I Hate Abercrombie and Fitch: Essays on Race and Sexuality in America* (New York: New York University Press, 2005), 88–131; Kobena Mercer, "Skin Head Sex Thing: Racial Difference and the Homoerotic Imaginary," in *How Do I Look? Queer Film and Video,* ed. Bad Object-Choices (Seattle: Bay Press, 1991), 169–210; Robert Reid-Pharr, *Black Gay Man: Essays* (New York: New York University Press, 2001), 85–98.

7. Darieck Scott, *Extravagant Abjection: Blackness, Power, and Sexuality in the African American Literary Imagination* (New York: New York University Press, 2010), 225.

8. Samuel R. Delany, *The Mad Man* (Rutherford, N.J.: Voyant, 1994), 12.

9. Ibid., 40–41.

10. Sucheng Chan, "The Exclusion of Chinese Women, 1870, 1943" in *Entry Denied: Exclusion and the Chinese Community in America, 1882–1943*, ed. Sucheng Chan (Philadelphia: Temple University Press, 1991), 94.

11. Richard Fung, "Looking for My Penis: The Eroticized Asian in Gay Video Porn," in Bad Object-Choices, *How Do I Look?*, 155. Nguyen Tan Hoang, however, urges us to adopt "a politics of bottomhood that opposes racism and heteronormativity without scapegoating femininity": Nguyen Tan Hoang, *A View from the Bottom: Asian American Masculinity and Sexual Representation* (Durham, N.C.: Duke University Press, 2014), 14.

12. Victor Jew, "'Chinese Demons': The Violent Articulation of Chinese Otherness and Interracial Sexuality in the U.S. Midwest, 1885–1889," *Journal of Social History* 37.2 (Winter 2003): 389–410; Mary Ting Yi Lui, *The Chinatown Trunk Mystery: Murder, Miscegenation, and Other Dangerous Encounters in Turn-of-the-Century New York* (Princeton, N.J.: Princeton University Press, 2005); Nayan Shah, *Stranger Intimacy: Contesting Race, Sexuality, and the Law in the North American West* (Berkeley: University of California Press, 2011). Shah's account provides a counternarrative to a foundational study of early twentieth-century South Asian men who maintained married relationships with Mexican women, fathered biracial children, and raised bicultural families in the midst of California's antimiscegenation laws: see Karen Isaksen Leonard, *Making Ethnic Choices: California's Punjabi Mexican Americans* (Philadelphia: Temple University Press, 1994).

13. Jennifer Ting, "Bachelor Society: Deviant Heterosexuality and Asian American Historiography" in *Privileging Positions: The Sites of Asian American Studies*, ed. Gary Y. Okihiro, Marilyn Alquizola, Dorothy Fujita Rony, and K. Scott Wong (Pullman: Washington State University Press, 1995), 277.

14. David L. Eng, *Racial Castration: Managing Masculinity in Asian America* (Durham, N.C: Duke University Press, 2001), 217.

15. Judy Tzu-Chun Wu, "Asian American History and Racialized Compulsory Deviance," *Journal of Women's History* 15.3 (Autumn 2003): 58–62.

16. Jinqi Ling, "Identity Crisis and Gender Politics: Reappropriating Asian American Masculinity," in *An Interethnic Companion to Asian American Literature*, ed. King-Kok Cheung (New York: Cambridge University Press, 1997), 313.

17. Jachinson Chan, *Chinese American Masculinities: From Fu Manchu to Bruce Lee* (New York: Routledge, 2001), 13. However, Chan also points out that his goal of destabilizing normative masculinity commonly meets resistance in classrooms full of young Asian American men who tend to believe it would still be more practical in their daily lives to embrace it.

18. Celine Parreñas Shimizu, *Straitjacket Sexualities: Unbinding Asian American Manhoods in the Movies* (Stanford, Calif.: Stanford University Press, 2012), 3–4.

19. Nguyen, *A View from the Bottom*, 19.

20. Eng-Beng Lim, *Brown Boys and Rice Queens: Spellbinding Performance in the Asias* (New York: New York University Press, 2014), 9.

21. Joseph Allen Boone, *The Homoerotics of Orientalism* (New York: Columbia University Press, 2014), 54–67.

22. C. Winter Han, *Geisha of a Different Kind: Race and Sexuality in Gaysian America* (New York: New York University Press, 2015), 105.

23. Ibid., 98–109.

24. Eve Kosofsky Sedgwick, *Between Men: English Literature and Male Homosocial Desire* (New York: Columbia University Press, 1985), 5.

25. Bernice Johnson Reagon, "Coalition Politics: Turning the Century," in *Home Girls: A Black Feminist Anthology*, ed. Barbara Smith (New York: Kitchen Table, 1983), 356–368.

26. K. Scott Wong, *Americans First: Chinese Americans and the Second World War* (Cambridge, Mass.: Harvard University Press, 2005), chap. 1.

27. Josephine Nock-Hee Park, *Cold War Friendships: Korea, Vietnam, and Asian American Literature* (New York: Oxford University Press, 2016), 12.

28. Lisa Lowe, "Heterogeneity, Hybridity, Multiplicity: Marking Asian American Differences," *Diaspora* 1.1 (Spring 1991): 31.

29. Yen Le Espiritu, *Asian American Panethnicity: Bridging Institutions and Identities* (Philadelphia: Temple University Press, 1992), 168–169.

30. Among the most commonly cited articles are King-Kok Cheung, "The Woman Warrior versus the Chinaman Pacific: Must a Chinese American Critic Choose between Feminism and Heroism?," in *Conflicts in Feminism,* ed. Marianne Hirsch and Evelyn Fox Keller (New York: Routledge, 1990), 234–251; Elaine Kim, "'Such Opposite Creatures': Men and Women in Asian American Literature," *Michigan Quarterly Review* 29:1 (Winter 1990): 68–93; Sau-ling Cynthia Wong, "Autobiography as Guided Chinatown Tour? Maxine Hong Kingston's *The Woman Warrior* and the Chinese American Autobiographical Controversy," in *Multicultural Autobiography, American Lives,* ed. James Robert Payne (Knoxville: University of Tennessee Press, 1992), 248–279.

31. Arif Dirlik defines "culturalism" as the deterministic ascription of practices and beliefs associated with a minority group to inherent, static traits rather than a dynamic interchange between populations and structural forces: Arif Dirlik, "Culturalism as Hegemonic Ideology and Liberating Practice," *Cultural Critique* 6 (Spring 1987): 13–50.

32. Donald C. Goellnicht, "Blurring Boundaries: Asian American Literature as Theory," in *An Interethnic Companion to Asian American Literature,* ed. King-Kok Cheung (New York: Cambridge University Press, 1997), 340.

33. Certainly, the practice of reading literature as theory need not be limited to texts by Asian American authors. In the introduction to a special issue on surface reading, Stephen Best and Sharon Marcus state their intent to promote more generally a "literary criticism that does not involve the untenable claim that we are always more free than those who produce the texts we study": Stephen Best and Sharon Marcus, "Surface Reading: An Introduction," *Representations* 108.1 (Fall 2009): 18.

34. Stephen Hong Sohn, *Racial Asymmetries: Asian American Fictional Worlds* (New York: New York University Press, 2014), 13.

35. Min Hyoung Song, *The Children of 1965: On Writing, and Not Writing as an Asian American* (Durham, N.C.: Duke University Press, 2013), 228.

36. Viet Thanh Nguyen, "Afterword," in *Flashpoints for Asian American Studies,* ed. Cathy Schlund-Vials (New York: Fordham University Press, 2017), 305.

37. This well-known interpretive approach comes from Eve Kosofsky Sedgwick, *Epistemology of the Closet* (Berkeley: University of California Press, 1990), 48–59.

38. Daniel Y. Kim, *Writing Manhood in Black and Yellow: Ralph Ellison, Frank Chin, and the Literary Politics of Identity* (Stanford, Calif.: Stanford University Press, 2005), 166.

39. Ibid., 168.

40. These destabilizations of the storied heteromasculinities of various nationalisms are also taken up in Julie Avril Minich, *Accessible Citizenships: Disability, Nation, and the Cultural Politics of Greater Mexico* (Philadelphia: Temple University Press, 2014); Martin Joseph Ponce, *Beyond the Nation: Diasporic Filipino Literature and Queer Reading* (New York: New York University Press, 2012); Richard T. Rodríguez, *Next of Kin: The Family in Chicano/a Cultural Politics* (Durham, N.C.: Duke University Press, 2009); Scott, *Extravagant Abjection*; Kathryn Bond Stockton, *Beautiful Bottom, Beautiful Shame: Where "Black" Meets "Queer"* (Durham, N.C.: Duke University Press, 2006).

CHAPTER 1

1. Michi Weglyn, *Years of Infamy: The Untold Story of America's Concentration Camps* (New York: William Morrow, 1976).

2. Ronald T. Takaki, *Strangers from a Different Shore: A History of Asian Americans* (New York: Penguin, 1989), 222–224.

3. Evidence that the internment was motivated more by economics than perceived terroristic threat lies in the fact that people of Japanese descent in Hawai'i were not interned. Their removal would have caused the collapse of the Hawaiian economy because they constituted one-third of the population. Although there had been some discussion immediately after the attack on Pearl Harbor about interning people of Japanese descent there, Hawaiian corporate interests pressured the military's upper administration to ensure otherwise: ibid., 380–383.

4. Eric L. Muller, *Free to Die for Their Country: The Story of the Japanese American Draft Resisters in World War II* (Chicago: University of Chicago Press, 2003), 112–121.

5. I credit Paul McCutcheon with helping me articulate this point. Moreover, the positionalities of "veteran" and "resister" were not mutually exclusive. Some resisters from World War II eventually served in the Korean War, indicating that they were not opposed to military service in general: see Frank Abe, dir., *Conscience and the Constitution*, Independent Television Service, San Francisco, 2000. In addition to the no-no boys, there were "military resisters," Japanese American men who had already enlisted before the passage of Executive Order 9066 who refused combat training as a form of protesting the internment. They received punishments of hard labor and dishonorable discharge: see Shirley Castelnuovo, *Soldiers of Conscience: Japanese American Military Resisters in World War II* (Lincoln: University of Nebraska Press, 2010).

6. Jennifer C. James, *A Freedom Bought with Blood: African American War Literature from the Civil War to World War II* (Chapel Hill: University of North Carolina Press, 2007), 20.

7. Ibid., 13–15, 26–28.

8. Viet Thanh Nguyen, *Race and Resistance: Literature and Politics in Asian America* (New York: Oxford University Press, 2002), 73.

9. John Okada, *No-No Boy* (Seattle: University of Washington Press, 1976), 59. Hereafter, page numbers from this volume are cited in parentheses in the text.

10. Although a disability acquired from war and a disability acquired from illness may have differing cultural meanings, Marc Shell notes that child polio survivors were often recuperated from the stigma of disability by referring to them as "brave little soldiers." In addition, some soldiers were polio survivors themselves, as President Roosevelt was fond of reminding people. I qualify Shell's claims with the caveat that these associations of polio with militarization presume the uncritical good of the latter: Marc Shell, *Polio and Its Aftermath: The Paralysis of Culture* (Cambridge, Mass.: Harvard University Press, 2005), 139, 187.

11. David A. Gerber, ed., *Disabled Veterans in History* (Ann Arbor: University of Michigan Press, 2000), 2–24.

12. David Serlin, *Replaceable You: Engineering the Body in Postwar America* (Chicago: University of Chicago Press, 2004), 21–25.

13. Even among Asian American ethnic groups favored during World War II, a disconnect existed between military service and U.S. civic equality. Chinese Americans felt that their position in society had improved because of China's ally status with the United States. Yet the treatment of Chinese American soldiers tells a different story. Many resented being assigned to segregated units. Even when they had been discharged with honors, veterans continued to be subjected to discrimination. One man used his GI Bill benefits to earn an engineering degree, only to find that the most favorable positions in the field remained off-limits to him. Others encountered difficulty with residential segregation and

were barred from relocating beyond ethnic enclaves: see K. Scott Wong, *Americans First: Chinese Americans and the Second World War* (Cambridge, Mass.: Harvard University Press, 2005), 172, 207–209.

14. Serlin, *Replaceable You*, 33.

15. Jinqi Ling, *Narrating Nationalisms: Ideology and Form in Asian American Literature* (New York: Oxford University Press, 1998), 37.

16. Elda E. Tsou, *Unquiet Tropes: Form, Race, and Asian American Literature* (Philadelphia: Temple University Press, 2015), 36.

17. Nguyen, *Race and Resistance*, 76.

18. Bryn Gribben warns that an ahistorical reading of the mother-son relationship in *No-No Boy* should be avoided because of "the ways in which psychoanalysis itself serve[d] an exclusionary function [at the time Okada published his novel] and prohibits uncomplicated access to Western identity for the Japanese American male": Bryn Gribben, "The Mother That Won't Reflect Back: Situating Psychoanalysis and the Japanese Mother in *No-No Boy*," *MELUS* 28.2 (Summer 2003): 33. However, Kathryn Bond Stockton remains more optimistic about the potential of Western psychoanalysis to shed light on the literatures of people of color. I address the specifics of her claim shortly.

19. Tim Dean, "Stumped," in *Porn Archives*, ed. Tim Dean, Steven Ruszczycky, and David Squires (Durham, N.C.: Duke University Press, 2014), 428.

20. Nguyen argues that this passage endows Ichiro with phallic power, too: Nguyen, *Race and Resistance*, 76. Taking this dialogue in a different direction, James Kyung-Jin Lee testifies to the intersubjective healing potential of each man revealing his wounds to the other. Ichiro and Kenji do not "determine a hierarchy of pain . . . [but] confront the other's loss without qualification": James Kyung-Jin Lee, "Elegies of Social Life: The Wounded Asian American," *Journal of Race, Ethnicity, and Religion* 3.2.7 (January 2012): 37.

21. Kathryn Bond Stockton, *Beautiful Bottom, Beautiful Shame: Where "Black" Meets "Queer"* (Durham, N.C.: Duke University Press, 2006), 70–82.

22. Nguyen Tan Hoang, *A View from the Bottom: Asian American Masculinity and Sexual Representation* (Durham, N.C.: Duke University Press, 2014), 2.

23. Eve Kosofsky Sedgwick, *Between Men: English Literature and Male Homosocial Desire* (New York: Columbia University Press, 1985), 38.

24. Sara Ahmed, *The Cultural Politics of Emotion* (New York: Routledge, 2004), 131.

25. James Kyung-Jin Lee, "Warfare, Asian American Literature, and Commitment," *Amerasia Journal* 32.3 (2006): 80.

26. Brenda L. Moore, *Serving Our Country: Japanese American Women in the Military during World War II* (New Brunswick, N.J.: Rutgers University Press, 2003), chap. 4.

27. John Okada is a veteran whose choices during World War II were believed to have been motivated by factors other than idealistic patriotism. The preface to *No-No Boy*, a short vignette about a conversation between an unnamed Japanese American man and a white man serving alongside each other in the Air Force, prompts the reader to infer the pressures under which Nisei men enlisted. It is commonly read as the authorial voice breaking through the narrative proper's lack of a more overt condemnation of the United States.

28. Moore, *Serving Our Country*, 92–93.

29. Ibid., chap. 1.

30. I claim that Hisaye Yamamoto, and not John Okada, was the first Japanese American writer to challenge the military's draft of men from internment camps. Her well-known short story "Seventeen Syllables" (1949) problematizes the assumption that the respondents who answered "yes" to the twenty-seventh and twenty-eighth questions on

the loyalty oaths did so without ambivalence. I argue that this interpretation of "Seventeen Syllables" has been overlooked because of how female Asian American writers have been pigeonholed into readings that emphasize domestic themes: Cynthia Wu, "Asian American Feminism's Alliances with Men: Reading Hisaye Yamamoto's 'Seventeen Syllables' as an Antidraft Tract," *Signs* 29.2 (Winter 2014): 323–339.

31. Recent examples are Cindy I-Fen Cheng, *Citizens of Asian America: Democracy and Race during the Cold War* (New York: New York University Press, 2013); Jodi Kim, *Ends of Empire: Asian American Critique and the Cold War* (Minneapolis: University of Minnesota Press, 2010); Josephine Nock-Hee Park, *Cold War Friendships: Korea, Vietnam, and Asian American Literature* (New York: Oxford University Press, 2016).

32. David K. Johnson, *The Lavender Scare: The Cold War Persecution of Gays and Lesbians in the Federal Government* (Chicago: University of Chicago Press, 2004), 6.

33. Ibid., 16.

34. Ibid., 10.

35. Robert J. Corber, *Homosexuality in Cold War America: Resistance and the Crisis of Masculinity* (Durham, N.C.: Duke University Press, 1997), 19.

36. Ibid., 4.

37. John Howard raises the possibility that the gender-segregated spaces of internment camps may have "provided unique opportunities to sexual and gender nonconformists" and that "as characteristic of most wartime mobilizations, dense homosocial spaces provided numerous homosexual possibilities": John Howard, *Concentration Camps on the Home Front: Japanese Americans in the House of Jim Crow* (Chicago: University of Chicago Press, 2008), 119.

38. Tina Takemoto, "Looking for Jiro Onuma: A Queer Meditation on the Incarceration of Japanese Americans during World War II," *GLQ* 20.3 (2014): 259.

39. Frank Chin, Jeffery Paul Chan, Lawson Fusao Inada, Shawn Hsu Wong, et al., eds., *Aiiieeeee! An Anthology of Asian-American Writers* (Washington, D.C.: Howard University Press, 1974).

40. Min Hyoung Song, *The Children of 1965: On Writing, and Not Writing, as an Asian American* (Durham, N.C.: Duke University Press, 2013), 60.

41. Frank Chin, "Afterword," in Okada, *No-No Boy*, 257.

42. Lawson Fusao Inada, "Introduction," in Okada, *No-No Boy*, v.

43. Ibid., vi.

44. David L. Eng, *Racial Castration: Managing Masculinity in Asian America* (Durham, N.C.: Duke University Press, 2001).

45. Daniel Y. Kim, *Writing Manhood in Black and Yellow: Ralph Ellison, Frank Chin, and the Literary Politics of Identity* (Stanford, Calif.: Stanford University Press, 2005), 166.

46. Daryl J. Maeda, *Chains of Babylon: The Rise of Asian America* (Minneapolis: University of Minnesota Press, 2009), 93.

47. Ibid., 95.

48. Judith Halberstam, *The Queer Art of Failure* (Durham, N.C.: Duke University Press, 2011).

CHAPTER 2

1. Monique Truong, "Press Release: *The Book of Salt*," Houghton Mifflin, 2003, http://www.houghtonmifflinbooks.com/booksellers/press_release/truong/#questions, accessed 1 November 2015.

2. Nicola Cooper, *France in Indochina: Colonial Encounters* (New York: Berg, 2001), 14, 22.

3. The editor of an anthology of texts by writers of Truong's generation prompted contributors to respond to questions that indirectly referenced these earlier debates in Asian American literature: see Amy Ling, ed., *Yellow Light: The Flowering of Asian American Arts* (Philadelphia: Temple University Press, 2000), 5.

4. Isabelle Thuy Pelaud, *This Is All I Choose to Tell: History and Hybridity in Vietnamese American Literature* (Philadelphia: Temple University Press, 2011), 58.

5. Ibid., 59.

6. Meg Wesling, "The Erotics of a Livable Life: Colonial Power and the Affective Work of Queer Desire in Monique Truong's *The Book of Salt*," *Mosaic* 48.1 (March 2015): 134.

7. Monique Truong, *The Book of Salt* (New York: Mariner, 2003), 12–13. Hereafter, page numbers from this volume are cited in parentheses in the text.

8. Homi K. Bhabha, *The Location of Culture* (New York: Routledge, 1994), 86.

9. Yen Le Espiritu, *Body Counts: The Vietnam War and Militarized Refuge(es)* (Oakland: University of California Press, 2014), 10.

10. Mimi Thi Nguyen, *The Gift of Freedom: War, Debt, and Other Refugee Passages* (Durham, N.C.: Duke University Press, 2012), 4.

11. Ibid., 20.

12. Yen Le Espiritu approaches the phenomenon of performed gratitude from the point of view of an ethnographer in ways that complement Nguyen's cultural theory. Her second-generation Vietnamese American informants note the discrepancy with which their parents discuss the war inside versus outside of the home: Espiritu, *Body Counts*, 150.

13. Nhi T. Lieu, *The American Dream in Vietnamese* (Minneapolis: University of Minnesota Press, 2011), xv.

14. Michel Foucault, *The History of Sexuality, Volume 1: An Introduction*, trans. Robert Hurley (New York: Random House, 1978), 24.

15. Ann Laura Stoler, *Race and the Education of Desire: Foucault's History of Sexuality and the Colonial Order of Things* (Durham, N.C.: Duke University Press, 1995), 7.

16. Ibid., 7–8.

17. Kyla Wazana Tompkins, *Racial Indigestion: Eating Bodies in the 19th Century* (New York: New York University Press, 2012), chap. 2.

18. Nicola Cooper's research shows that France's intention behind establishing European-style schools in Indochina was to inculcate vocational skills. Colonial subjects who migrated to the metropole to pursue degrees in the professions were thought to overstep their station: Cooper, *France in Indochina*, 38–40.

19. Stoler, *Race and the Education of Desire*, 109.

20. Edward W. Said, *Orientalism* (New York: Vintage, 1979), 32.

21. David L. Eng, *The Feeling of Kinship: Queer Liberalism and the Racialization of Intimacy* (Durham, N.C.: Duke University Press, 2010), 59.

22. Following Linda Hutcheon, Catherine Fung suggests that Bình's illegibility prompts a reading of *The Book of Salt* as "historical metafiction," a genre that disrupts positivist conceptions of historical fact and epistemological access, as opposed to historical fiction, which presumes a stable account of history that the author embellishes in the process of fictionalizing it: Catherine Fung, "A History of Absences: The Problem of Reference in Monique Truong's *The Book of Salt*," *Novel* 45.1 (Spring 2012): 97–99.

23. Siobhan B. Somerville, *Queering the Color Line: Race and the Invention of Homosexuality in American Culture* (Durham, N.C.: Duke University Press, 2000), 5.

24. Ibid., 120.

25. Meg Wesling perceives Bình's relationship with Lattimore to be more fulfilling and enabling than I do: Wesling, "The Erotics of a Livable Life," 137–140.

26. Viet Thanh Nguyen, "Refugee Memories and Asian American Critique," *positions* 20.3 (Summer 2012): 922.

27. Viet Thanh Nguyen, *Nothing Ever Dies: Vietnam and the Memory of War* (Cambridge, Mass.: Harvard University Press, 2016), 196.

28. Thuy Vo Dang, "The Cultural Work of Anticommunism in the San Diego Vietnamese American Community," *Amerasia Journal* 31.2 (2005): 74, 76–77, 79.

29. Kieu-Linh Caroline Valverde, *Transnationalizing Viet Nam: Community, Culture, and Politics in the Diaspora* (Philadelphia: Temple University Press, 2012), 134–135, 138.

30. Lan Duong and Isabelle Thuy Pelaud, "Vietnamese American Art and Community Politics: An Engaged Feminist Perspective," *Journal of Asian American Studies* 15.3 (October 2012): 247. Protesters had objected to an image of a young woman wearing a tank top emblazoned with the flag of the Socialist Republic of Vietnam and seated at a table with a bust of Ho Chi Minh.

31. Karin Aguilar-San Juan, *Little Saigons: Staying Vietnamese in America* (Minneapolis: University of Minnesota Press, 2009), 83.

32. Truong Van Tran, the owner, had sent letters to community leaders alerting them to the provocative display, and these figures largely ignored him until an incendiary radio host began riling up his audience: Valverde, *Transnationalizing Viet Nam*, 103.

33. Lan P. Duong, *Treacherous Subjects: Gender, Culture, and Trans-Vietnamese Feminism* (Philadelphia: Temple University Press, 2012), 7.

34. Valverde, *Transnationalizing Viet Nam*, chap. 2.

35. Y-Dang Troeung has a different reading of this passage, which sees the bridge as a "pause between overlapping, but also mirroring, histories of French colonialism and American imperialism in Vietnam": Y-Dang Troeung, "'A Gift or a Theft Depends on Who Is Holding the Pen': Postcolonial Collaborative Autobiography and Monique Truong's *The Book of Salt*," *Modern Fiction Studies* 56.1 (Spring 2010): 120.

36. Cherríe Moraga, "Refugees of a World on Fire: Foreword to the Second Edition," in *This Bridge Called My Back: Writings by Radical Women of Color*, ed. Cherríe Moraga and Gloria Anzaldúa (New York: Kitchen Table, 1981), n.p.

37. Donna Kate Rushin, "The Bridge Poem," in Moraga and Anzaldúa, *This Bridge Called My Back*, xxi.

38. Ibid., xxii.

39. In another context, Rachel Lee invokes Truong's bridge metaphor to describe the methodology of her own cultural criticism. Her work "attends to an order of thinking that 'stands on a bridge,' a phrase borrowed from Monique Truong's *Book of Salt* to describe one character's as-yet-undecided cleaving to either a territorially nationalist or a deterritorialized exilic politics." Accordingly, Lee's work pays heed to the spanning of the divide between liberal humanist concepts of life and cross-species intimacies with the inorganic or toxic: Rachel C. Lee, *The Exquisite Corpse of Asian America* (New York: New York University Press, 2014), 31.

40. Robert J. Corber, *Homosexuality in Cold War America: Resistance and the Crisis of Masculinity* (Durham, N.C.: Duke University Press, 1997), 112–113.

41. Aguilar-San Juan, *Little Saigons*, 158.

42. Ibid.

43. This is one of the main premises in Duong's *Treacherous Subjects* and Valverde's *Transnationalizing Viet Nam*.

44. Long T. Bui, "The Debts of Memory: Historical Amnesia and Refugee Knowledge in *The Reeducation of Cherry Truong,*" *Journal of Asian American Studies* 18.1 (February 2015): 82.

45. Truong's second novel similarly links male same-sex desire and emplaced belonging. The narrative does so in a locale that would seem counterintuitive to most people not attuned to recent cultural and intellectual production on queer rurality. In *Bitter in the Mouth*, gay men in the small North Carolina town of Boiling Springs are the keepers of tradition and the conduits through which family ties are maintained.

46. Anita Mannur, *Culinary Fictions: Food in South Asian Diasporic Culture* (Philadelphia: Temple University Press, 2010), 21.

47. Sau-ling Cynthia Wong, *Reading Asian American Literature: From Necessity to Extravagance* (Princeton, N.J.: Princeton University Press, 1993), chap. 1.

48. Denise Cruz claims that Bình's withholding of culinary secrets from Stein and Toklas becomes a way of "exercising power over his employers . . . a method of escape from questions, explicit and implicit, about where he is from or why he is in France": Denise Cruz, "'Love Is Not a Bowl of Quinces': Food, Desire, and the Queer Asian Body in Monique Truong's *The Book of Salt,*" in *Eating Asian America: A Food Studies Reader*, ed. Robert Ji-Song Ku, Martin F. Manalansan IV, and Anita Mannur (New York: New York University Press, 2013), 359.

49. Stan Yogi, "Legacies Revealed: Uncovering Buried Plots in the Stories of Hisaye Yamamoto," *Studies in American Fiction* 17.2 (1989): 170; King-Kok Cheung, *Articulate Silences: Hisaye Yamamoto, Maxine Hong Kingston, Joy Kogawa* (Ithaca, N.Y.: Cornell University Press, 1993), 33; Traise Yamamoto, *Masking Subjects, Making Selves: Japanese American Women, Identity, and the Body* (Berkeley: University of California Press, 1999), 5.

50. Thomas M. Hawley, *The Remains of War: Bodies, Politics, and the Search for American Soldiers Unaccounted for in Southeast Asia* (Durham, N.C.: Duke University Press, 2005).

51. Susan Jeffords, *The Remasculinization of America: Gender and the Vietnam War* (Bloomington: Indiana University Press, 1989).

52. Sylvia Shin Huey Chong, *The Oriental Obscene: Violence and Racial Fantasies in the Vietnam Era* (Durham, N.C.: Duke University Press, 2011), 176–177.

53. Yen Le Espiritu, "Thirty Years AfterWARd: The Endings That Are Not Over," *Amerasia Journal* 31.2 (2005): xv.

54. Ibid., xvii; Viet Thanh Nguyen, "War, Memory, and the Future," *Asian American Literary Review* 2.1 (Winter–Spring 2011): 285.

55. Deepa Bharath, "Religious Groups Don't Want Gays in Tet Parade," *Orange County Register*, 11 February 2010, http://www.ocregister.com/articles/vietnamese-233820-groups-parade.html, accessed 7 November 2015.

56. Ibid.

57. We should not underestimate the extent to which a North American and Western European LGBT rights-based discourse has traveled globally and how states—including the Socialist Republic of Vietnam—in these other regions have begun to brandish their sexual minorities to lure neoliberal capital: see Richard Quang-Anh Tran, "An Epistemology of Gender: Historical Notes on the Homosexual Body in Contemporary Vietnam, 1986–2005," *Journal of Vietnamese Studies* 9.2 (Spring 2006): 6.

58. Deepa Bharath, "Vietnamese Gays to March in Tet Parade," *Orange County Register*, 9 February 2010, https://www.ocregister.com/2010/02/09/vietnamese-gays-to-march-in-tet-parade, accessed 5 April 2018.

59. Ibid., emphasis added.

60. Thy Vo and David Washburn, "Judge Rules against LGBT Groups Joining Tet Parade," *Voice of OC*, 8 February 2013, http://voiceofoc.org/2013/02/judge-rules-against-lgbt-groups-joining-tet-parade, accessed 7 November 2015.

61. Anh Do, "O.C. Tet Parade Won't Ban Gays, Community Decides," *Los Angeles Times*, 4 January 2014, http://www.latimes.com/local/lanow/la-me-ln-lgbt-tet-parade-20140104-story.html#axzz2pWF6BfJo, accessed 7 November 2015.

62. Matthew Hilburn, "Tet Parade Organizers Exclude LGBT Groups," *Voice of America*, 8 February 2013, http://www.voanews.com/content/vietnamese_american_lgbt_tet_parade_orange_county/1600231.html, accessed 7 November 2015.

63. Jasbir K. Puar, *Terrorist Assemblages: Homonationalism in Queer Times* (Durham, N.C.: Duke University Press, 2007).

64. Ibid., xxiv.

65. Eng, *The Feeling of Kinship*, 74.

66. Ibid., 75–76.

67. Victor Bascara, *Model-Minority Imperialism* (Minneapolis: University of Minnesota Press, 2006), xxiv–xxv.

CHAPTER 3

1. Among the best-known monographs in this tradition were King-Kok Cheung, *Articulate Silences: Hisaye Yamamoto, Maxine Hong Kingston, Joy Kogawa* (Ithaca, N.Y.: Cornell University Press, 1993); Amy Ling, *Between Worlds: Women Writers of Chinese Ancestry* (New York: Teachers College Press, 1990); Sau-ling Cynthia Wong, *Reading Asian American Literature: From Necessity to Extravagance* (Princeton, N.J.: Princeton University Press, 1993); Traise Yamamoto, *Making Selves, Making Subjects: Japanese American Women, Identity, and the Body* (Berkeley: University of California Press, 1999). A more recent study deftly takes up these older concerns with updated methodologies. See erin Khuê Ninh, *Ingratitude: The Debt-Bound Daughter in Asian American Literature* (New York: New York University Press, 2011).

2. Philip Kan Gotanda, "Yankee Dawg You Die," in *Fish Head Soup and Other Plays* (Seattle: University of Washington Press, 1991), 124. Hereafter, page numbers from this volume are cited in parentheses in the text.

3. Gwendolyn Rice, "Two Actors Struggle with Racial Stereotypes in Madison Theatre Guild's 'Yankee Dawg You Die,'" *Isthmus*, 30 September 2014, http://isthmus.com/arts/stage/two-actors-struggle-with-racial-stereotypes-in-madison-theatre-guilds-yankee-dawg-you-die, accessed 2 July 2017.

4. Mel Y. Chen, *Animacies: Biopolitics, Racial Mattering, and Queer Affect* (Durham, N.C.: Duke University Press, 2012), 95. Chen's main premise is that a revolutionary politics must claim a connection not only to the nonhuman animal world but also to inanimate objects. Bradley's comparison of Vincent's character to a chimpanzee does not invite its intended viewer to do as Chen prescribes. The condemnation relies on the unchallenged bifurcation between human and nonhuman.

5. For a discussion of how a third risk group, hemophiliacs, was discursively produced as the normative, "innocent" HIV/AIDS demographic through the figure of the heterosexual male child, see Michael Davidson, *Concerto for the Left Hand: Disability and the Defamiliar Body* (Ann Arbor: University of Michigan Press, 2008), chap. 1.

6. Jennifer Brier, *Infectious Ideas: U.S. Political Responses to the AIDS Crisis* (Chapel Hill: University of North Carolina Press, 2009), 78–79.

7. Nayan Shah, *Contagious Divides: Epidemics and Race in San Francisco's Chinatown* (Berkeley: University of California Press, 2001).

8. Richard Meyer, "Rock Hudson's Body," in *Inside/Out: Lesbian Theories, Gay Theories*, ed. Diana Fuss (New York: Routledge, 1991), 275.

9. As Ann-Marie Dunbar notes, the ending remains "unsettling" and "ambiguous" because of what it implies about the continued restrictions under which Asian American actors must work: Ann-Marie Dunbar, "From Ethnic to Mainstream Theater: Negotiating 'Asian American' in the Plays of Philip Kan Gotanda," *American Drama* 14.1 (Winter 2005): 24–25.

10. José Esteban Muñoz, *Disidentifications: Queers of Color and the Performance of Politics* (Minneapolis: University of Minnesota Press, 1999), 4.

11. Gotanda alludes through the fictional musical's title *Tea Cakes and Moon Songs* and the song that Vincent and Bradley perform from it, which they call "Charlie's Chop Suey love song" (92), to the real-life Richard Rodgers and Oscar Hammerstein's *Flower Drum Song* (1958). One of its numbers is entitled "Chop Suey."

12. Karen Shimakawa, *National Abjection: The Asian American Body Onstage* (Durham, N.C.: Duke University Press, 2002), 119.

13. Ibid., 117, 120.

14. Josephine Lee, *Performing Asian America: Race and Ethnicity on the Contemporary Stage* (Philadelphia: Temple University Press, 1997), 100.

15. James S. Moy, *Marginal Sights: Staging the Chinese in America* (Iowa City: University of Iowa Press, 1993), 124.

16. Shimakawa, *National Abjection*, 119.

17. Frank Chin, "Come All Ye Asian American Writers of the Real and the Fake," in *The Big Aiiieeeee!*, ed. Jeffrey Paul Chan, Frank Chin, Lawson Fusao Inada, and Shawn Wong (New York: Meridian, 1991), 1–92.

18. Jeff Adachi, dir., *The Slanted Screen*, Asian American Media Mafia Productions, San Francisco, 2006.

19. Celine Parreñas Shimizu, *Straightjacket Sexualities: Unbinding Asian American Manhoods in the Movies* (Stanford, Calif.: Stanford University Press, 2012), 235.

20. Nancy Wang Yuen, *Reel Inequality: Hollywood Actors and Racism* (New Brunswick, N.J.: Rutgers University Press, 2017), 31–48.

21. Ibid., 140–142.

22. Ibid., 149–159.

23. Jon Ronson, "You May Know Me from Such Roles as Terrorist #4," *GQ*, 27 July 2015, http://www.gq.com/story/muslim-american-typecasting-hollywood, accessed 9 September 2015.

24. Maz Jobrani, *I'm Not a Terrorist, but I've Played One on TV* (New York: Simon and Schuster, 2015), 100.

25. Jeff Yang, "Ken Jeong on Dr. Ken, Becoming a Leading Man, and the Early Backlash to His Show," *Slate*, 5 October 2015, http://www.slate.com/blogs/browbeat/2015/10/05/ken_jeong_interview_the_dr_ken_actor_on_the_hangover_community_diversity.html, accessed 21 November 2015.

26. Samuel Anderson, "Remember the Time Hollywood Was Racist? Aziz Ansari Does," *New York Magazine*, 25 October 2015, http://www.vulture.com/2015/10/aziz-ansari-on-hollywood-racism.html, accessed 21 November 2015.

27. Angela C. Pao, *No Safe Spaces: Re-casting Race, Ethnicity, and Nationality in American Theater* (Ann Arbor: University of Michigan Press, 2010), 61.

28. Nadya Agrawal, "The Pursuit of White Women: Brown Actors like Aziz Ansa-ri Have Reduced Brown Women to a Punchline," *Quartz India*, 29 June 2017, http://qz.com/1016554/aziz-ansari-hasan-minhaj-kumail-nanjiani-brown-actors-have-reduced-brown-women-to-a-punchline/?utm_source=qzfb, accessed 2 July 2017.

29. Frantz Fanon, *Black Skin, White Masks,* trans. Richard Philcox (New York: Grove, 2008), 45.

30. Tina Takemoto, "Interview with Sab Shimono: On Camp, Asian American Vis-ibility and Gay Bars (with Steve Alden Nelson)," *Hyphen Magazine*, 23 May 2017, http://hyphenmagazine.com/blog/2017/05/interview-sab-shimono, accessed 2 July 2017.

31. Ibid.

CHAPTER 4

1. U.S. Senate, *Report of the Joint Special Committee to Investigate Chinese Immigra-tion* (Washington, D.C.: Government Printing Office, 1877), 97.

2. Ibid., 117.

3. Ibid., 383.

4. Susan Craddock, *City of Plagues: Disease, Poverty, and Deviance in San Francisco* (Minneapolis: University of Minnesota Press, 2000), 89–94; Nayan Shah, *Contagious Divides: Epidemics and Race in San Francisco's Chinatown* (Berkeley: University of Cali-fornia Press, 2001), 85–87.

5. Eithne Luibhéid avers that no inherent difference existed between "legitimate" wives and women brought into the country for sex work. The same discourses of immi-gration cast both social locations in ways that were "profoundly racist, sexist, and classist": Eithne Luibhéid, *Entry Denied: Controlling Sexuality at the Border* (Minneapolis: Univer-sity of Minnesota Press, 2002), 38.

6. Sucheng Chan, "The Exclusion of Chinese Women, 1870–1943," in *Entry Denied: Exclusion and the Chinese Community in America, 1882–1943*, ed. Sucheng Chan (Phila-delphia: Temple University Press, 1991), 94–146.

7. Shah, *Contagious Divides*, 83–84.

8. Victor Jew, "'Chinese Demons': The Violent Articulation of Chinese Otherness and Interracial Sexuality in the U.S. Midwest, 1885–1889," *Journal of Social History* 37.2 (Winter 2003): 389–410.

9. Mary Ting Yi Lui, *The Chinatown Trunk Mystery: Murder, Miscegenation, and Other Dangerous Encounters in Turn-of-the-Century New York* (Princeton, N.J.: Princeton University Press, 2005). South Asian men were also regarded as sexually violent during this time and disproportionally arrested for alleged sex crimes against white men and women. See Nayan Shah, *Stranger Intimacy: Contesting Race, Sexuality, and the Law in the North American West* (Berkeley: University of California Press, 2012).

10. Judy Tzu-Chun Wu, "Asian American History and Racialized Compulsory Devi-ance," *Journal of Women's History* 15.3 (Autumn 2003): 60.

11. The Cubic Air Ordinance (1870) of San Francisco, which required a minimum of 500 cubic feet of air for every inhabitant of a household, specifically targeted Chinese residences, which were crowded by necessity.

12. Estelle T. Lau, *Paper Families: Identity, Immigration Administration, and Chinese Exclusion* (Durham, N.C.: Duke University Press, 2006), 7.

13. John D'Emilio, "Capitalism and Gay Identity," in *Powers of Desire: The Politics of Sexuality*, ed. Ann Snitow, Christine Stansell, and Sharon Thompson (New York: Monthly Review, 1983), 105.

14. George Chauncey, *Gay New York: Gender, Urban Culture, and the Making of the Gay Male World, 1890–1940* (New York: Basic, 1994), 9.

15. D'Emilio, "Capitalism and Gay Identity," 106.

16. Chauncey, *Gay New York*, 75.

17. Henry Yu, *Thinking Orientals: Migration, Contact, and Exoticism in Modern America* (New York: Oxford University Press, 2001), 96, 138–139.

18. Paul C. P. Siu, *The Chinese Laundryman: A Study of Social Isolation*, ed. John Kuo Wei Tchen (New York: New York University Press, 1987), 8–22. Hereafter, page numbers from this volume are cited in parentheses in the text.

19. Renqiu Yu, *To Save China, To Save Ourselves: The Chinese Hand Laundry Alliance of New York* (Philadelphia: Temple University Press, 1992).

20. Aaron S. Lecklider, "H. T. Tsiang's Proletarian Burlesque: Performance and Perversion in *The Hanging on Union Square*," *MELUS* 36.4 (Winter 2011): 88.

21. According to Chris Vials, the nonchalance with which quotidian events are narrated in *And China Has Hands* demystifies the racialized space of the laundry and diffuses fears about the violation of white women and girls therein: Chris Vials, *Realism for the Masses: Aesthetics, Popular Front Pluralism, and U.S. Culture, 1935–1947* (Jackson: University Press of Mississippi, 2009), 124–126.

22. Paul M. McCutcheon, "Commodified Desire: Negotiating Asian American Heteronormativity," *Asian American Literature: Discourses and Pedagogies* 4 (2013): 47.

23. H. T. Tsiang, *And China Has Hands*, ed. Floyd Cheung (New York: Ironweed, 2003), 20. Hereafter, page numbers from this volume are cited in parentheses in the text.

24. Farah Jasmine Griffin contests the perception that the Great Migration occurred from a place of persistent racism to one of greater freedom: Farah Jasmine Griffin, *Who Set You Flowin': The African American Migration Narrative* (New York: Oxford University Press, 1995).

25. Samuel Gompers and Herman Gutstadt, *Meat versus Rice: American Manhood against Asiatic Coolieism* (Washington, D.C.: American Federation of Labor, 1902), 22.

26. Julia H. Lee reminds us not to be too enthusiastic about Tsiang's vision of worker unity, because Wan-Lee's misogyny very often goes uninterrogated: Julia H. Lee, "The Capitalist and Imperialist Critique in H. T. Tsiang's *And China Has Hands*," in *Recovered Legacies: Authority and Identity in Early Asian American Literature*, ed. Keith Lawrence and Floyd Cheung (Philadelphia: Temple University Press, 2005), 92–93.

27. Robert Ji-Song Ku, *Dubious Gastronomy: The Cultural Politics of Eating Asian in the USA* (Honolulu: University of Hawai'i Press, 2013), 9.

28. Paul Siu goes into detail about traveling grocers who market to Chinese launderers. The transaction between a food seller and a launderer is often "a sentimental gesture rather than a commercial exchange. . . . [A traveling grocer's] persistence may . . . result even in a friendship": Siu, *The Chinese Laundryman*, 102–103.

29. Hua Hsu, *A Floating Chinaman: Fantasy and Failure across the Pacific* (Cambridge, Mass.: Harvard University Press, 2016), 125.

30. Friedrich Engels, *Dialectics of Nature*, trans. Clemens Dutt (Moscow: Progress Publishers, 1966), 172.

31. See esp. Mel Y. Chen, *Animacies: Biopolitics, Racial Mattering, and Queer Affect* (Durham, N.C.: Duke University Press, 2012); Rachel C. Lee, *The Exquisite Corpse of Asian America: Biopolitics, Biosociality, and Posthuman Ecologies* (New York: New York University Press, 2014).

32. Lynette Cintrón, "H.T. Tsiang's *And China Has Hands* and the Poetics/Politics of Relation," unpublished paper, May 2010.

33. The popular press ran articles shortly after the attack on Pearl Harbor that purported to advise readers on how to tell the difference between people of Chinese and Japanese descent: see "How to Tell Japs from the Chinese," *Life Magazine*, 22 December 1941, 81–82; "How to Tell Your Friends from the Japs," *Time Magazine*, 22 December 1941, 33.

34. Richard Jean So has the most generous interpretation of the conclusion's unexpectedness and the narrative's overall lack of coherence, claiming that these oddities are an effect of "the anarchy of social meaning underlying life under Chinese Exclusion": Richard Jean So, "Chinese Exclusion Fiction and Global Histories of Race: HT Tsiang and Theodore Dreiser, 1930," *Genre* 39 (Winter 2006): 19.

35. Richard So has a different reading of the same passage. Whereas I see its aggressive allusion to the European-descended blazon, So favorably considers the description of Pearl's body "magically transformative." It invokes "tropes and themes taken from classical Chinese literature" and the "vernacular of Chinese mysticism": So, "Chinese Exclusion Fiction and Global Histories of Race," 13–14. So's claim is in line with Floyd Cheung's observation that *And China Has Hands* blends Chinese literary traditions into Anglophone ones: Floyd Cheung, "Introduction," in Tsiang, *And China Has Hands*, 10.

36. Roderick A. Ferguson, *Aberrations in Black: Toward a Queer of Color Critique* (Minneapolis: University of Minnesota Press, 2004), 27.

37. Cynthia H. Tolentino, *America's Experts: Race and the Fictions of Sociology* (Minneapolis: University of Minnesota Press, 2009), xvii.

38. Siu recognizes the double standard that applies to married sojourners in the United States compared with their wives who remain in China, writing, "Patronizing a prostitute [is] . . . considered unavoidable or inevitable. . . . But if [a migrant's] wife commits adultery in the native village, she immediately becomes the butt of gossip in the whole community." One of his informants, to his credit, states that if his wife in China had a lover, he would not protest, because it would only be fair: Siu, *The Chinese Laundryman*, 167, 267.

39. The oft-referenced "The Negro Family: The Case for National Action," commonly known as the Moynihan Report after its author, the sociologist (and later senator) Daniel Patrick Moynihan, identified the cause of African American poverty in purported gender, sexual, and familial deviance. However, the report's premises did not materialize in 1965; these ideas were established in the field long before Moynihan was writing: see Daniel Patrick Moynihan, *The Negro Family: The Case for National Action* (Washington, D.C.: Office of Planning and Research, U.S. Department of Labor, 1965).

40. These biographical details are culled from John Kuo Wei Tchen, "Editor's Introduction," in Siu, *The Chinese Laundryman*, xxv–xxvi.

41. Coincidentally, or perhaps not, both the fictional woman in Tsiang's novel and the real-life woman in Siu's ethnography are biracially black. The sexualization of mixed-race black women by the two Chinese American authors throws a wrench into the tendency to imagine in simplistic ways these women's emasculation of Chinese men. Both Tsiang's and Siu's depictions are in line with contemporaneous discourses of the mulatta.

42. William Wei, *The Asian American Movement* (Philadelphia: Temple University Press, 1993), x.

43. Daryl J. Maeda, *Chains of Babylon: The Rise of Asian America* (Minneapolis: University of Minnesota Press, 2009), 38.

44. Ibid., 38–39.

45. Chris A. Eng, "Queer Genealogies of (Be)Longing: On the Thens and Theres of Karen Tei Yamashita's *I Hotel*," *Journal of Asian American Studies* 20.3 (October 2017): 362.

46. An additional text that focuses on the 1960s and 1970s in Asian American movements is Michael Liu, Kim Geron, and Tracy Lai, *The Snake Dance of Asian American Activism: Community, Vision, and Power* (New York: Lexington, 2008). Although Liu, Geron, and Lai assign a greater Asian Americanist legibility to social movements during the 1930s than do Wei and Maeda, they concede that panethnic organizing during this period was stymied by the "influence of homeland governments on Asian origin communities": ibid., 32.

47. Elizabeth Freeman, *Time Binds: Queer Temporalities, Queer Histories* (Durham, N.C.: Duke University Press, 2010), 3.

48. Dana Luciano, *Arranging Grief: Sacred Time and the Body in Nineteenth-Century America* (New York: New York University Press, 2007), 9.

49. E. L. McCallum and Mikko Tuhkanen, "Introduction," in *Queer Times, Queer Becomings*, ed. E. L. McCallum and Mikko Tuhkanen (Albany: State University of New York Press, 2011), 9.

50. David Palumbo-Liu makes a strong case for how *And China Has Hands* constitutes an Asian Americanist subjectivity premised on a transnational commitment to socialism and anti-imperialism: David Palumbo-Liu, *Asian/American: Historical Crossings of a Racial Frontier* (Stanford, Calif.: Stanford University Press, 1999), 51. Michael Denning includes *And China Has Hands* in his comprehensive account of cultural productions issuing from the early twentieth-century left: Michael Denning, *The Cultural Front* (New York: Verso, 1997).

51. Eve Kosofsky Sedgwick, *Epistemology of the Closet* (Berkeley: University of California Press, 1990), 53.

52. Valerie Rohy, "Ahistorical," *GLQ* 12.1 (2006): 67, 69.

CHAPTER 5

1. Conversely, Candace Fujikane, a fourth-generation local Japanese woman, supported those who called out anti-Filipino prejudice because of an awareness of how her own communities maintained dominance in Hawai'i by resisting criticism: Candace Fujikane, "Sweeping Racism under the Rug of 'Censorship': The Controversy over Lois-Ann Yamanaka's *Blu's Hanging*," *Amerasia Journal* 26.2 (2000): 163.

2. Chris Finley, "Decolonizing the Queer Native Body (and Recovering the Native Bull-Dyke): Bringing 'Sexy Back' and Out of Native Studies' Closet," in *Queer Indigenous Studies: Critical Interventions in Theory, Politics, and Literature*, ed. Qwo-Li Driskill, Chris Finley, Brian Joseph Gilley, and Scott Lauria Morgensen (Tucson: University of Arizona Press, 2011).

3. Ronald Takaki, *Pau Hana: Plantation Life and Labor in Hawaii, 1835–1920* (Honolulu: University of Hawai'i Press, 1983), 149–152; Gary Okihiro, *Cane Fires: The Anti-Japanese Movement in Hawaii, 1965–1945* (Philadelphia: Temple University Press, 1991), 55.

4. The presence of Chinese merchants in the United States allowed the Anglo-American upper and middle classes to access consumer imports while laborers' association with filth, disease, and immorality offended U.S. class sensibilities: see George Anthony Peffer, *If They Don't Bring Their Women Here: Chinese Female Immigration before Exclusion* (Champaign: University of Illinois Press, 1999).

5. Takaki, *Pau Hana*, 122.

6. Ibid., 121.

7. Ibid., 120.

8. Carey McWilliams, *Brothers under the Skin* (Boston: Little, Brown, 1943), 236.

9. For a discussion of the anti-Filipino rhetoric that pervaded Japanese labor organizing in Hawai'i, see Moon-kie Jung, *Reworking Race: The Making of Hawaii's Interracial Labor Movement* (New York: Columbia University Press, 2006), 99–105.

10. A large part of the outrage against portrayals of Filipino sexual deviance in *Blu's Hanging* stemmed from the fact that Yamanaka had faced criticism for similar characterizations in the past.

11. Kandice Chuh, *Imagine Otherwise: On Asian Americanist Critique* (Durham, N.C.: Duke University Press, 2003), 144.

12. Lois-Ann Yamanaka, *Blu's Hanging* (New York: Farrar, Straus, and Giroux, 1997), 74. All further references to the text are cited by page number.

13. Chuh, *Imagine Otherwise*, 143–144.

14. Fujikane points out that sensationalized accounts of Filipino behavior deemed threatening to heterosexual propriety have much more purchase than accounts of similar acts perpetrated by East Asians: Fujikane, "Sweeping Racism under the Rug of 'Censorship,'" 176.

15. Erin Suzuki, "Consuming Desires: Melancholia and Consumption in *Blu's Hanging*," *MELUS* 31.1 (Spring 2006): 39.

16. Fujikane, "Sweeping Racism under the Rug of 'Censorship,'" 171.

17. Chuh, *Imagine Otherwise*, 144.

18. Sue-Ellen Case claims that butch-femme pairings between women need not be a replication of heterosexual cultures' gender dichotomies and proposes that they be read as camp, a self-conscious masquerade that destabilizes and denaturalizes identities: Sue-Ellen Case, "Toward a Butch-Femme Aesthetic," *Discourse* 11.1 (Fall–Winter 1988–1989): 55–73. However, the possibility of playful irony in Big Sis and Sandi's relationship never gets explored.

19. Emily Russell, "Locating Cure: Leprosy and Lois-Ann Yamanaka's *Blu's Hanging*," *MELUS* 31.1 (Spring 2006): 67–68.

20. Crystal Parikh, "Blue Hawaii: Asian Hawaiian Cultural Production and Racial Melancholia," *Journal of Asian American Studies* 5.4 (October 2002): 204.

21. erin Khuê Ninh, "Teaching *Blu's Hanging*," *Pedagogy* 15.2 (April 2015): 243.

22. Suzuki, "Consuming Desires," 45.

23. Fujikane, "Sweeping Racism under the Rug of 'Censorship,'" 171.

24. Elda E. Tsou, *Unquiet Tropes: Form, Race, and Asian American Literature* (Philadelphia: Temple University Press, 2015), 124.

25. Mark Chiang, *The Cultural Capital of Asian American Studies: Autonomy and Representation in the University* (New York: New York University Press, 2009), 195.

26. Darieck Scott, *Extravagant Abjection: Blackness, Power, and Sexuality in the African American Literary Imagination* (New York: New York University Press, 2010), 209.

27. One exception to this silence in the literary-critical record is Fujikane, "Sweeping Racism under the Rug of 'Censorship.'"

28. John P. Rosa, *Local Story: The Massie-Kahahawai Case and the Culture of History* (Honolulu: University of Hawai'i Press, 2014), 27.

29. Ibid., 43. In addition, the old Hawaiian oligarchy may in the past have been regarded favorably by white elites, and vice versa, because of a limited set of shared interests. However, by the early twentieth century, the annexation and ongoing divestment of land to boost U.S. capital and militarism had soured these relationships. The Massie case only further disillusioned upper-class Hawaiians from identifying with their white elite coun-

terparts, and it galvanized their identification with a multiethnic, racialized, immigrant working class: ibid., 44–45.

30. Jonathan Y. Okamura, "Why There Are No Asian Americans in Hawai'i: The Continuing Significance of Local Identity," *Social Process in Hawai'i* 35 (1994): 161–178.

31. Despite plantation owners' largely successful goals of instilling mistrust among ethnic groups, coalitional work across these divides did occur, even if they were short-lived. For a study of the most sustained instance of labor organizing between Japanese and Filipino workers in Hawai'i, see Masayo Umezawa Duus, *The Japanese Conspiracy: The Oahu Sugar Strike of 1920*, trans. Beth Cary (Berkeley: University of California Press, 1999).

32. JoAnna Poblete-Cross, "Bridging Indigenous and Immigrant Struggles: A Case Study of American Sāmoa," *American Quarterly* 62.3 (September 2010): 502, 505.

33. Philip J. Deloria, *Playing Indian* (New Haven, Conn.: Yale University Press, 1999).

34. Haunani-Kay Trask, "Settlers of Color and 'Immigrant' Hegemony: 'Locals' in Hawai'i," *Amerasia Journal* 26.2 (2000): 6–7.

35. Finley, "Decolonizing the Queer Native Body," 32.

36. Haunani-Kay Trask, *From a Native Daughter: Colonialism and Sovereignty in Hawai'i* (Honolulu: University of Hawai'i Press, 1999), 143.

37. This is Kathryn Bond Stockton's term. She asserts that normative temporalities of growth and maturation are fictive teleologies imposed on young people. All children are queered by their lack of fit therein: Kathryn Bond Stockton, *The Queer Child, or Growing Sideways in the Twentieth Century* (Durham, N.C.: Duke University Press, 2009).

EPILOGUE

1. Although the original ad has long since expired on Craigslist, the blogger Phil Yu has preserved it on his website: Phil Yu, "Weird-Ass Craigslist Posting, Part 56: Seeking 'Quality Asian,'" *Angry Asian Man* (blog), 14 June 2013, http://blog.angryasianman.com/2013/06/weird-ass-craigslist-posting-part-56.html, accessed 8 July 2017.

2. Carolyn Dinshaw, Lee Edelman, Roderick A. Ferguson, Carla Freccero, Elizabeth Freeman, Judith Halberstam, Annamarie Jagose, Christopher S. Nealon, Nguyen Tan Hoang, "Theorizing Queer Temporalities: A Roundtable Discussion," *GLQ* 13.1–2 (2007): 191.

3. David Henry Hwang reports that some gay Asian American men mock this intra-racial configuration, regarding it disdainfully as akin to lesbianism: David Henry Hwang, "Afterword," in *M. Butterfly* (New York: Penguin, 1986), 98.

INDEX

gaze: colonial, 61; intraethnic sociological, 128–131; white male, 11–12
gender non-normativity. *See* sexual and gender non-normativity
Gerber, David, 31–32
Ghost in the Shell, The (film), 103
GI Bill, 3, 31, 32
gifts of freedom, 57, 69
Goellnicht, Donald C., 17
Gompers, Samuel, 119–120
Goodell, Lavinia, 82
Gotanda, Philip Kan, 4, 9, 21, 79. *See also Yankee Dawg You Die*
Grand Coalition, 101
Griffith, D. W., 101
Gross Indecency: The Three Trials of Oscar Wilde (Kaufman), 82

Halberstam, Judith, 47
Hamamoto, Darrell, 98, 99
Han, C. Winter, 12
Hanging on Union Square, The (Tsiang), 121, 123
Hansen, Liane, 51–52
"Hard Candy" (Williams), 68
Hart-Celler Act of 1965, 3
Hawai'i, 16, 22, 139–160; conditions of settler privilege in, 155–159; ethnic hierarchy in, 140, 144, 150–152; Massie case in, 141, 155–156, 184–185n29; native population of, 139, 140, 142, 149, 155, 156, 157, 159; plantation economy of, 139–142, 150–152, 156. *See also Blu's Hanging*
Hawaii Five-O (television program), 104
Hawley, Thomas M., 73
Hayakawa, Sessue, 97
hegemonic chronicity, 136
"Heterogeneity, Hybridity, and Multiplicity" (Lowe), 15
heteronormativity, 3, 167; *And China Has Hands* on, 110, 111, 119; *Blu's Hanging* on, 147; hegemonic chronicity, capital, and, 136. *See also* sexual and gender non-normativity
heteropatriarchy, 3, 11, 13, 19, 23, 163; *And China Has Hands* on, 115, 119; *Blu's Hanging* on, 140; *The Chinese Laundryman* on, 114; *No-No Boy* on, 36, 48
heterosexuality, 14, 23, 141; in *And China Has Hands,* 114, 117–121, 125–127; in *The*

Chinese Laundryman, 129–131; in *No-No Boy,* 37–41
historiography, 134–137
History of Sexuality, The (Foucault), 58
Hi-Tek Incident, 65, 68
HIV/AIDS, 14, 21, 81, 89–91, 165
Hmong Americans, 63
Ho Chi Minh, 63, 64–65; as *The Book of Salt* character, 21, 51, 60, 62, 66–67, 68, 77; at Paris Peace Conference, 56
homonationalism, 76
homophobia, 9, 19, 22, 76; *The Book of Salt* on, 54; *No-No Boy* on, 34, 46; *Yankee Dawg You Die* on, 89, 90
homosexual panic, 81, 95
How I Learned to Drive (Vogel), 82
Hsu, Hua, 123
Hudson, Rock, 89, 105
Hwang, David Henry, 52, 80

I-Hotel (International Hotel), 134
immigration. *See* Asian immigration
Immigration Act of 1924, 27
Immigration Act of 1965, 156
Immigration and Nationality Act of 1952, 2–3
I'm Not a Terrorist, but I've Played One on TV (Jobrani), 102
imperialism, 3, 76, 77, 163, 165; *Blu's Hanging* on, 140; *The Book of Salt* on, 50, 54–55, 72; Japanese, 15, 120, 126. *See also* colonialism
Inada, Lawson, 20, 44–45, 48
Indian Americans, 9, 102–103, 104
Indochina Migration and Refugee Assistance Act of 1975, 50
Inouye, Christian, 83
International Hotel (I-Hotel), 134
Iraq War, 73, 76, 165
Islamophobia, 76
Issei, 28
Italian immigrants, 112
Iwamatsu, Mako, 99

JACL (Japanese American Citizens League), 28
James, Jennifer C., 30
Japan: imperialism of, 15, 120, 126; Pearl Harbor attack by, 15, 25, 27
Japanese American Citizens League (JACL), 28

CYNTHIA WU is an Associate Professor of Gender Studies at Indiana University. She is the author of *Chang and Eng Reconnected: The Original Siamese Twins in American Culture* (Temple).

Deepika Bahri and Mary Vasudeva, eds., *Between the Lines: South Asians and Postcoloniality*

E. San Juan Jr., *The Philippine Temptation: Dialectics of Philippines–U.S. Literary Relations*

Carlos Bulosan and E. San Juan Jr., eds., *The Cry and the Dedication*

Carlos Bulosan and E. San Juan Jr., eds., *On Becoming Filipino: Selected Writings of Carlos Bulosan*

Vicente L. Rafael, ed., *Discrepant Histories: Translocal Essays on Filipino Cultures*

Yen Le Espiritu, *Filipino American Lives*

Paul Ong, Edna Bonacich, and Lucie Cheng, eds., *The New Asian Immigration in Los Angeles and Global Restructuring*

Chris Friday, *Organizing Asian American Labor: The Pacific Coast Canned-Salmon Industry, 1870–1942*

Sucheng Chan, ed., *Hmong Means Free: Life in Laos and America*

Timothy P. Fong, *The First Suburban Chinatown: The Remaking of Monterey Park, California*

William Wei, *The Asian American Movement*

Yen Le Espiritu, *Asian American Panethnicity*

Velina Hasu Houston, ed., *The Politics of Life*

Renqiu Yu, *To Save China, To Save Ourselves: The Chinese Hand Laundry Alliance of New York*

Shirley Geok-lin Lim and Amy Ling, eds., *Reading the Literatures of Asian America*

Karen Isaksen Leonard, *Making Ethnic Choices: California's Punjabi Mexican Americans*

Gary Y. Okihiro, *Cane Fires: The Anti-Japanese Movement in Hawaii, 1865–1945*

Sucheng Chan, *Entry Denied: Exclusion and the Chinese Community in America, 1882–1943*